UNDEFEATED

The Life and Times of Jimmy Johnstone

UNDEFEATED
The Life and Times of Jimmy Johnstone

Archie Macpherson

First published in Great Britain in 2010 by Celtic FC Limited.
Designed and produced by Grange Communications Ltd., Edinburgh.

Cover design by Alice Lake-Hammond

Photographs supplied by: The Johnstone Family,
Scottish News & Sport (SNS), Offside Sports Photography, Eric McCowat,
Ian Henderson, Hugh J. Birt, Celtic View
Cover image by Jim Scullion
Back cover photographs: The Johnstone Family,
Scottish News & Sport (SNS), Hugh J. Birt

ISBN 978 1 907104 88 6

'Wee man, you'll never walk alone.'
  Billy McNeill, from his eulogy at Jimmy Johnstone's funeral.
  March 2006.

'A life-time's achievement is not marked by an absence of faults or flaws in a character. Its greatness is in having the strength of character to overcome these challenges and problems, so that the end result is magnificent; not because the life has been spotless, but because of the capacity of human endeavour to overcome the challenges.'
  Dr John Reid, Celtic Chairman. April 2010.

'The disease is like being put in prison for life, no parole, and the prison is shrinking by six inches every week. I know that at some point in the future it's going to crush me to death, but I don't know exactly when.'
  Tony Judt, historian, on Motor Neurone Disease. January 2010.

For Agnes Johnstone

Contents

Acknowledgements

I would not have been able to write a word of this book without the co-operation of Jimmy's wife, Agnes, and their son, James, both of whom talked to me both candidly and lovingly of the wee man. They were particularly keen to let the public know of his immensely moving fight against his disease, as an inspiration to others. I am deeply grateful to them for being able to talk about events which might, admittedly, appear harrowing to some, but to them was a steadfast reconciliation with his inevitable decline in a manner that reflected how Jimmy himself stood up to it – with dignity, understanding and above all with an inextinguishable sense of humour.

From his early days I am grateful to so many of his friends from around the Viewpark and Uddingston areas of North Lanarkshire, who palled with him, schooled with him, drank with him and offered me so many views of the wee boy with talented feet. I also have to thank the Lisbon Lions I talked to, and others who came later in his career, including his opponents, all of whom gave of their time to let me know how privileged they were to play alongside or against him.

I am particularly grateful to Ian Henderson, the man who admits his life was saved by Jimmy, whom I would describe as an indispensable consultant in all the matters pertaining to how the wee man coped in his final years. I have to thank Dr Roddy Macdonald, the Celtic doctor, for his advice and Dr Belinda Cupid of the Motor Neurone Research Association for her explanations. I am also grateful to many inside Celtic Park who added invaluable information to the narrative.

The list of those I consulted is, frankly, too long to include here and I can only offer my blanket gratitude to cover those who have not been mentioned personally, because of the exigencies of space. But an exception is Pat Woods, bettered by no man in his knowledge of Celtic Football Club history, who was my researcher for the sixth time, and as you will see has lasted the pace well.

Introduction

'You must have seen him playing. What was he like?'

It seemed a simple enough question, but suddenly I found myself floundering to give an adequate reply. It came from a Celtic supporter, outside the stadium on the day after Jimmy Johnstone had died. I was there to deliver a short tribute to the television camera about the wee man, amidst a reverential, spontaneous gathering of supporters, who, unlike a match-day crowd, had been muted by the sad news and were unable to compete with the unsympathetic traffic on London Road which busily reminded us that life, moving on, makes few concessions to others grieving. The lad was in his early twenties. He had approached me after I had finished with the camera, almost as if he was asking directions on how to travel back through time.

What was he like? How long have you got, I thought. But, as I surveyed this relatively young man, a couple of generations or so divorced from the era when a bristling crop of red hair atop a green and white jersey could turn leaden days to glistening gold, and whose alchemy would make bewildered opponents look like they were victims of sorcery, I felt various emotions.

The first was feeling a special privilege, in savouring that sense of superiority you enjoy when you realise that the ageing process has its compensations, and that you are still around to say that you did see him play in full spate, during an age which was replete with great Scottish players, but which may never be replicated. Although we are blessed with the fact that much of his exuberance was retained on film or tape, nothing could ever substitute for me, and others of my generation, the memory of having been there to witness a whole line of performances which greatly taxed the abilities of those charged with writing or speaking about the feats which raised him to the pantheon of the greats.

I also felt any replies to such a question about him had to evoke, not just strings of memories, but a sense of responsibility, an obligation to separate fact from myth, of placing him in the context of the liberating influence Jock Stein had on Celtic Football Club. At the same time Stein was aware that, eventually, Jimmy's lifestyle would, one day, illustrate the perils which lie in store for those who have neither the sophistication nor, too often, the inclination to accept guidance in shielding themselves from publicity and who learn, perhaps the hard way, that fame can snare you, as well as sustain you.

In 2002 Jimmy was voted Celtic's Greatest Ever Player by the supporters. In that context my reply to the young man who asked the question, 'He was great,' now seems trite. For to the succeeding generations who were deprived of the thrill of watching him in the flesh, there is a compelling need now to expand on what the simple answer I gave really meant. Time cannot dilute his achievements nor erase the memories of how enjoyable a companion he could be.

I recall a balmy evening by a poolside in Menorca just before the start of his last season with Celtic when, after serenading my wife and myself with the Charlie Rich song 'The Most Beautiful Girl,' he suddenly stripped down to his underpants, dived into the pool, swam to the other end in the frantic style of a man pursued by a crocodile, swam back, climbed out, and started to sing again, all just for the hell of it.

There was much of 'just for the hell of it' in his life. And so much more, deserving of the adulation, and the reverence, which you pay to a man who, in his final years, set an inspiring example to all of us in how to face up to the ultimate adversity.

Summer 2000

The first warning came in a public park in Viewpark, Lanarkshire, when he was training on his own. Jimmy Johnstone had wakened one morning prepared for a normal day, which meant he had gone to the local park and, as part of his dedicated routine, was doing press-ups. He had long finished with football but was transfixed by the need to retain his general fitness. His obsession with strengthening his upper body had never wavered: not just for its own sake but as a rebuttal to those who in his early days almost mocked him for his apparent frailty.

What he was then doing at the age of 56 was merely a continuation of a ritual which started when, as a kid, a physical education teacher recommended a series of exercises to strengthen the small frame which was likely to suffer physical challenges, fair or unfair, in the world of professional football, to which he was bound. The day seemed like any other. But it was not. In the middle of the sequence of push-ups, his wrists gave way, and without support he collapsed nose first into the turf.

Thinking that it was something transient that could happen in any exercise, he tried again. The wrists simply would not support him. He took the fall on his face again, stubbornly, until he realised through the pain that he just couldn't manage what, to him, had previously been a normal and easily executed drill. He sat back puzzled by this, but not unduly concerned. He rested and then tried again, but once more this sudden collapsing of the wrists occurred. He had incurred all kinds of injuries in his *time, after being tripped, pushed, kicked, hacked, and suffered the bruises with an acceptance that it came with the territory.*

But this was strange, odd. It seemed inexplicable in relation to all the pain he had experienced in the past. It was as if his hands were being cut off in a bizarre way. When he returned home, he mentioned this to his wife Agnes, but made very little of it, and it was soon put to the back of his mind. Then, later that day, driving his car, he suddenly felt pins and needles cascading up and down his arms. There and then he wondered if that had anything to do with the collapse of his wrists. It had.

ONE
Learning

When Jimmy Johnstone walked into St Columba's Primary School in Tannochside, Lanarkshire, for the first time in 1949, barely aged five, according to former teacher Margaret Wilson, he confronted the welcoming headmaster Mr Mulligan and asked him, 'When do I get into the school team?' That he was simply a fresh-faced infant, scarcely the size of an exclamation mark on a blank page, surely ranked for audacity with Oliver Twist's request for more gruel in the harsh workhouse. St Columba's was no workhouse though, but a respectable school, renowned in particular for producing football teams of great merit and with a propensity to hoarding silverware won by their boys. So this request by the tiny boy with the carroty head was met, not by Dickensian rage, but with the good-natured, pat-on-the-head tolerance of a headmaster accustomed to dealing with infants blessed with innocence and uninhibited tongues.

Mr Mulligan was never to forget that day, as, soon after, he would squint out at the playground to witness the fact that the wee boy, dribbling a ball that nobody could take off him, had not been having him on. He could recognise, right away, that the boy's self-belief, even for one so young, was not induced by fantasy, but by a pair of feet that never ceased to semaphore the simple ambition to outwit those who constantly surrounded him at play.

He was a war baby, born on the 30th September 1944, a day that included uncanny portents for the Lanarkshire new-born. For it was the very day the three-year constant bombardment of Dover by German cross-channel guns ceased, and people flocked out of their cellars and caves to its streets as a precursor to the ultimate overall surrender: the very port through which the famous 1967 *Celticade* of motors and buses would pass on their way to Lisbon, in an era when the war, to many, would have been a condition confined only to the memories of the older generation.

As he was entering the world, the figure who was to reshape his life, Jock Stein, was leaving his pithead at Bothwell that very day to go and play for Albion Rovers as part of a defence which went down heavily against the formidable Hibernian side of the day, 5-0. It was also the day that Alan Breck, a writer for Glasgow's *Evening Times*, pointed out an epochal, yet largely unheralded sporting event, when he reported that a British Services XI had beaten a French selection 5-0 in Paris, in front of 30,000 spectators, but that more importantly, the team had flown there. Thus, as Breck put it, 'The aeroplane has brought Europe to our door.'

A new age of European football travel had begun on that day, one from which countless numbers of Celtic supporters would, in the future, gain great enjoyment watching Jimmy rip defences apart in all corners of the continent. It is also worth pointing out, considering the wee man's famed phobia for flying, that the plane taking the British Forces side to Paris was almost involved in a crash with another plane which they suddenly spotted flying alongside them only 20 feet away. The new age of international travel, and of peace, would obviously bring great social advantages to society in general and to both Jock Stein and Jimmy, in different ways. They were to emerge from the mists of war and come through the succeeding age of austerity, to produce a melding of their ways that elevated the club to unquestionable greatness.

His birth also points us to the Eldorado of Scottish football. For Celtic's publicly-endorsed greatest ever player, their greatest manager, Jock Stein, and their greatest captain, Billy McNeill, were all born in that tiny industrial triangle formed by Viewpark, Bellshill and Burnbank. The talent hewn from the footballing seams formed in that North Lanarkshire enclave, no greater than eight miles in dimension, gave Scottish football its sinewy identity. If you throw in Sir Matt Busby's birth in Orbiston, near Bellshill, it is doubtful if any local parish anywhere in Europe has had such a widespread influence on a national and European game. None of these men had it easy in early life.

Jimmy was no exception. His father Matt worked in the pits and the closer you look at the environment of that time you have to wonder, who didn't work in the mines? Was that to be Jimmy's fate, as it was Stein's eventually, in his first major step in life? The tradition, after all, was handed down almost as an employment imperative. Jimmy would have learned from his father that working in the mines was not only dangerous, but also so politically contentious at the time that some of the public were too eager to forget the abominable conditions the men worked under and turned their anger on them. For even during the war there was continuing hostility between the miners and their employers.

That very week he was born, the failure of 'Operation Market Garden' in the Arnhem area caused consternation, and another kind of flak was turned on the miners by the *Hamilton Advertiser*, which castigated a mining strike in North Lanarkshire at the time, contrasting the 'steadfast courage and endurance' of the 'gallant men of Arnhem' with the selfish pitmen simply holding out for better working conditions.

So his father and his mother Sarah, bringing up their five children, and having to absorb, stoically, the tragic death of three others, faced a world in which the odds of making any kind of success in life were stacked heavily against any of their kids. They lived in the upper-flat of a squat house at 647 Old Edinburgh Road, Viewpark, which housed four separate families in the block. Jimmy had to sleep in the living-room on a bed-settee and after he went to bed, in the early school days, at about nine o'clock, his mother would move through to the scullery and could be seen sitting there dutifully looking out of her window, for the rest of the evening, so as not to disturb her son. She was never keen to watch him playing, even before he turned professional, but his father was an habitué of Celtic Park and intensely proud of his son's success.

Tom McLaughlin, who lived through the wall from the Johnstones, indicates that, although all boys in the vicinity were keen on football, Jimmy could take his passion to extremes when he was still a primary schoolboy.

'I'd be in my bed at about six o'clock in the morning, and I'd hear a knock at the window,' said Tom. 'It was Jimmy. He used to get a ladder and climb up it and persuade me to come out and have a game with him. He'd be the attacker, me the defender. Six o'clock in the morning. We'd play for about an hour and then I would climb back up and get ready for school and in all those years my mother never knew we had already been up for an hour hammering in to each other.'

It was just as well that living on top of each other's families contained a mutual understanding of the need to be tolerant of the ways of noisy brats. 'He used to keep bashing the ball against his side of the lobby wall and you could hear the constant bump, bump, bump, over and over again and my mother would end up shouting, "Jimmy, for God's sake, would you give us peace!" through the wall at him. But she never fell out with him.'

Years later, Jimmy admitted to me that his disregard for the architecture of the council house, by treating his lobby like he was playing out his fantasies of playing in a World Cup final, and constantly running up and down it, dribbling round objects he put on the floor, could have caused a sudden subsidence.

'There was an old woman lived underneath us. Mrs Watt. It must have been hell for her. Night after night I would run up and down the lobby and the noise must have been deafening at times. But do you know what, she was great. In all those years she never once complained to my mother.' And then he added, as if it was an admission of the ultimate in tolerance, 'And she was a Protestant, too.'

Jimmy's schooling was unconventional, particularly in one respect: the length of time he spent at primary level. Margaret Wilson, whose brother Sammy played for Celtic between 1957 and 1959, taught in his school and witnessed the extraordinary success of the football team principally because of Jimmy's influence. 'He was so good he was kept on until he was almost fourteen,' the former teacher said, 'Let me stress he wasn't retained because he was backward educationally. He certainly wasn't. It was because of football. Now some parents might have objected to a lad being kept on at that level for so long, because it cut back on his secondary education. But Jimmy's didn't raise any objection because they felt football was his life. And you know, in retrospect I don't think it did him any harm. Indeed, I think he benefitted from it.'

As the school leaving age had been raised to 15 in the year he had been born, you can work out that his junior secondary education was fleeting, unlike many others at that school who left primary school about the age of eleven. So why was that allowed? It is here we are introduced to one of the biggest influences in his life. He was John Crines, a class teacher with aspirations well above that of being able to explain how to perform long-division. His influence cannot be overestimated. This man was renowned in schools football throughout Lanarkshire for fielding teams which lent the impression of invincibility. They swept all before them.

John Goodwin, who was signed by Jock Stein for Celtic, as a fifteen year old, and was a close friend of Jimmy, played for Crines' teams, and speaks of him with a sense of awe, as if he were a mix of Stein and Napoleon Bonaparte.

'Mr Crines, as I still find myself calling him after all those years, was a strict disciplinarian,' said John. 'He insisted on his boys going on to the park impeccably dressed. You had to see your face shining back at you off your polished boots. You had to wash your laces, because you couldn't afford to buy them so often and you had to put them back on without a spot on them. He insisted on this whether you were playing a game or just having a practise. It didn't matter who you were. Jimmy was the star of the team at this time, but he had to toe the line as well. And it was this discipline more than anything else which brought out the best in his players.'

It emphatically did. No other teacher, devoted to football at the primary level in Lanarkshire, could come near his success: which brings us to the longevity of some of his players at the school. If you had something special to offer on the field, like Jimmy and John Goodwin, who only completed two and a half years at Our Lady's High senior secondary in Motherwell, then, as he says, 'If you were good and helped bring success and prestige to the school, he kept you back as long as he could. That's one of the reasons we had so much success. He did that for a lot of players who went on to play professionally.'

But there was another element to Crines' treatment of the boys which must certainly have been an early acclimatisation for Jimmy to the shock-and-awe atmosphere of the professional dressing-room, as Tom McLaughlin explains.

'Crines hated being beaten. You should have seen him. He would come in and punch the walls repeatedly. And he would even punch you if you got in his way. It was fierce. He especially did not like to be beaten. That made him particularly angry. This meant we had a great rivalry with the Protestant school because they hated to be beaten as well. St Columba's against Tannochside Primary, that was always a real battle.'

From listening to that, you might understand that such combat was like serving an apprenticeship for the Old Firm game. Indeed when Jimmy was thirteen and still playing for the school, in a game against the primary school in Chapelhall, a spectator ran on and kicked him blatantly. From all accounts it simply made him play better, and over and above that, he knew that the man on the touchline who did his fair share of bawling would not countenance capitulation. Crines clearly gave Jimmy the early instruction that, even at the school football level, the will to succeed and triumph superseded any Corinthian scholastic values.

These feelings might have been transmitted to parents as well, for one morning Jimmy's school team was playing in Coatbridge against St Augustine's school and found they were up against formidable opponents. Jimmy experienced the rarity of being outplayed in a match they lost 3-0, principally because of an outstanding lad who scored the three goals and who was literally head and shoulders bigger than all the other boys on the park. At the end of the game this giant of a boy was approached by three women, one of whom was an aunt of Jimmy's, who brandished umbrellas at him and almost assaulted him, making the accusation that he was over-age for that level. That was not the case. He just happened to be big for his age. He recalls that incident over 60 years later because he became a close friend and colleague of Jimmy's. He was John 'Yogi' Hughes.

Crines clung on to Jimmy as long as he could. After all, being almost fourteen before he left, he was ineligible to play in the coveted Lanarkshire Schools Cup in his last year for exceeding the age limit, yet he was still held back by Crines, almost like a butterfly collector unwilling to let a special species out of his display cabinet. Was this utterly selfish and harmful academically to a boy who needed all the schooling he could get?

In an outward sense it probably was. Crines told the *Scottish Daily Express* in November 1963 that Jimmy '...was intelligent, all right, but his thoughts were inclined to stray outside the classroom. Actually, he was a bit of a comedian in the classroom but the teachers liked him so much they rarely came down hard on him.'

What he did not admit was that Jimmy helped line Crines' pockets with honours. However, perhaps by accident more than design, Crines was in fact mapping out a future for a boy whose specially talented feet would probably be the only asset he had in making his way in life, and wanted to ensure that he matured more, physically, before being cut loose. He had an advantage over other teachers in that he had commercial interests outside the school. He helped run a couple of family pubs in the area at the same time. A publican-teacher hardly fits the mould of the traditional dominie, but it did give him a special intimacy with the roots of the local Celtic support who bolstered his pub tills and poured words into his ear about the travails of Celtic Park at that time. And Jimmy was the least surprised of individuals when he heard, in later life, that Crines' business interests were to overtake teaching eventually and he ended up buying into Hamilton Accies and, even though seen only as a board member, actually picked the team for a spell.

So the puny-looking youngster had been reared by someone with great self-belief. He was smitten by that, and always talked highly of his ex-teacher. Sadly, for all that Jimmy pocketed many medals in that time, under him, there is no personal evidence left of the harvest of success. His father, in later life, took these school medals to a local pub one night to display them proudly to many of the admirers. However, the admiration was taken a stage too far when someone stole them all. They have never been seen again, not even at a stall in the Glasgow 'Barras,' and given Jimmy's global appeal, Sotheby's would be quick on the act if ever they surfaced.

He was attracting attention in all quarters, but it was Sammy Wilson's sister Margaret, waxing lyrically about this little boy in the team, who encouraged Sammy to help make him a ball-boy at Celtic Park for a period. He was indeed enthusiastic about this until reality crept in. For it was also denying him the only thing he wanted to do in life, and that was to play: play anywhere, but just play. He told John Goodwin, 'Great. But I can't play on a Saturday with the Boys' Guild. I'm missing it. I want to play.'

Feeding the ball to others playing on the park was only frustrating for him. Although he loved the sinecure of being attached to the club he loved, it was paradoxical that it was holding him back from his first love, chasing and controlling a ball. It is a wonder he did not invade the pitch at Celtic Park during a game. So Boys' Guild football won that personal struggle in a short time.

In that respect he went back to amassing a formidable reputation around the West of Scotland for the games in which he inevitably starred, and which had put him in a limelight which was far from parochial. For that was an age when there were recurring tsunamis of scouts sweeping in from the south.

Scotland, once upon a time, was one of the breadbaskets of English club football. Jimmy was an obvious target. But it was a trip outside of Scotland which was perhaps one of the most significant in his life, and could be said to have changed his career. He was in the St John's Boys' Guild team which travelled to Salford in Lancashire in the early 1960s, to play against several sides, one of which included the two brothers who played in Herman's Hermits, the famous pop group which emerged in that decade. Indeed both men kept in touch with Jimmy and sent condolences to the family on his death, such was the impact he had made on them. As part of that trip they went on an escorted tour of Old Trafford and were met by none other than the late Sir Matt Busby. Tom McLaughlin, a member of the group, saw something interesting.

'Mr Busby, as he was then, took an interest in us and chatted to us about football, but he was all over Jimmy. There is no doubt that he knew all about him. You could tell that by the way he took him personally in hand.'

But it went further than that. One of the representatives of the Lanarkshire team had a chat with Busby in his office when the United manager made it clear that his scouts had been raving about this little boy and that he was going to pursue that. However, the man he was talking to told what might be described as an historic fib. He replied to Busby, 'Well, he's training with Celtic at the moment.'

He wasn't in fact. It was a diversionary tactic to put Busby off. As soon as the United manager heard that, he said that if that was the case he wouldn't proceed any further nor interfere with anything Celtic had in hand, having the greatest respect for the club. On the back of this, they sped back home, alerted John Higgins, the former player, who was scouting for Jimmy McGrory, the manager, and this bewildered wee boy was whisked inside Celtic Park to become a provisional signing. McGrory was one of the most civilised and agreeable men I have ever met in the game, but equally it was clear that any crucial decisions about major signings, and team selection, were made by the chairman, the late Sir Robert Kelly. But at that age level it did not really matter that they knew precious little about this fledgling, or of his attributes. United had been frozen out. He was now safely within the fold. Or so Jimmy thought at the time. He also knew that for all his obvious skills, many who watched him felt that he could not possibly survive the rough and tumble of the game, being so small.

This willingness to dramatically alter that became a life-long obsession. From then on he listened to advice: from then on, until nearly the final days, he trained hard to maintain and build up body strength: from then on, even after some of the wildest escapades off the park, he never retreated from the ritual of punishing physical exercise practically every day. The early encouragement came particularly from Tommy Cassidy, a physical education teacher in Lanarkshire, who encouraged him to take up body strengthening exercises in the hope that he could hold his own in the arm-to-arm combat that sometimes passed as Scottish senior football.

So you could say that by 1961, all the elements were in the right place. He had been born amongst a community which regarded Celtic Football Club as an extension of its own values; he had been shaped, not to say exploited, by a scholastic entrepreneur: he had tasted the acrid atmosphere of the Old Firm in its human Subbuteo form of local schools' rivalry: he had enjoyed the status of stardom at that level; he had thrown balls back to his heroes at Celtic Park: so despite all the interest from other quarters, had he not ended up at Paradise, it would have been even more astounding than discovering that Elvis was alive and kicking and, all along, had been pulling pints in one of John Crines' pubs.

Autumn 2000

The pins and needles continued. Jimmy was never, as many of his Celtic colleagues would tell you, the most careful of drivers. He would drive a car like he was finding a way through a 'catenaccio' defence, they claimed. But now there was another factor to contend with, something that he knew was there but was trying to ignore. He was not completely sure his hands were in full control of the steering wheel.

His son James recalls this element of risk beginning to develop. 'He would drive up to the Viewpark club to get my mother. But on one occasion he scraped another car, because even though he had power steering, he was beginning to sense that he could not make the car respond to his action, because the proper grip was slowly disappearing.'

It was in his nature to respond positively to this. There was nothing negative in his mind, for if he could still use his legs to do his regular running, then all was well with the world. It was obviously something which he felt he could master or that it would simply go away, like some mundane, brief medical problem. But James recalls the first time he personally wondered what was happening to his father. 'I had an electronic belt which was a muscle tenser that I used in my own weight training. You would strap it around the upper arm, to tighten the muscle. When you turned it on, it gave you a kind of shock.'

Jimmy watched this with interest as his son used it regularly. Given his unrelenting pursuit of fitness Jimmy could not possibly be a bystander to all of this. He wanted to try the contraption as well. James attached it to him. 'Sometimes when we used it, just for a laugh, I would turn it up to full strength. And that would make him jump. But even at the ordinary level you could see in his face that something was bothering him.'

It was the pins and needles, but it was worse than usual, as he also felt that his fingers were not quite connected to his body. 'But he would never give up, never,' James said. 'He never complained during that exercise. All he was doing was telling you what he was experiencing. Nothing more than that, and I suppose because of that we never gave a thought to something serious developing. Honestly I can't remember a word of complaint to us, then or afterwards.'

James would not have been conscious of it at the time, but he was witnessing the start of a long courageous battle that he, the family, and friends, would witness with both despair and pride, as an invasive scourge entered all their lives.

TWO
Making the Headline

Contracts never tell the full story. Read them and they look stark and unyielding. The very formality of the terms of the following contract for Jimmy Johnstone, given to him by the man who would turn the club's fortunes around, reveals nothing of the feeling of insecurity, and indeed of despair which preceded it after having been signed provisionally in 1961. It states *'...the club shall pay to the player the sum of Thirty-Five Pounds (£35:0:0) per week from the 30th June, 1966 to the termination hereof. When playing in the first team £40 per week. £12 per week when club is in the 1ˢᵗ position in the league Div 1. Or £6 per week when club is within 4 points of the League Leaders. Plus permitted bonuses. This agreement shall expire on the Thirtieth day of June Nineteen hundred and Sixty-seven.'* It was signed, *J. Stein.*

Note the year of termination. The piece of paper looks promising, but it cloaks the reality of an inauspicious start to his connection with the club. For on October 7ᵗʰ 1961 when he came ostensibly under their wing, nobody in a senior position there had actually seen him play. He was simply 'a provisional signing,' a wee apprentice with the kind of anonymity which can make young players feel they are invisible to the surrounding established stars. As if to exemplify that, Jimmy McGrory decided to leave him with

Blantyre Celtic, because (judging by one newspaper report) 'The Wee Celts' had been hard hit by injuries that season.

However, had anybody been paying attention to the side of the pitch during one of the days when he was a ball boy at Celtic Park, they would have seen him entrancing at least some of the onlookers by playing 'keepie-uppie' with the ball for a full fifteen minutes, as one witness calculated. But it hadn't registered at the highest level. Junior football, largely considered by clubs now to be as useful to youth development as rickets, was considered then as a routine route into the big time, especially in regard to the toughening-up process which they felt came with the experience of playing on pitches which could range from the texture of pumice stone to something like low tide at Saltcoats.

There were, though, some outstanding junior clubs, with amenable pitches and admirable traditions, but there were some which were the equivalent of ending up in a cul-de-sac with no opportunity to move into reverse gear. And there were some where the crudeness of the level of the game was like asking a youth to enter manhood by playing against men who seemed to have been nurtured by orangutans. But Blantyre Celtic was a solid club with the laudable tradition of mimicking the values of their senior brothers in the East End of Glasgow.

His debut against Ashfield Juniors, for them, was notable for the fact that it almost never happened. When his friend arrived to pick him up at his home to take him to the game, Jimmy's mother was almost in tears. 'I cannae find him. I don't know where he is.' Time was short. This friend hazarded a guess that he would either be playing football somewhere or training. He went down to St Columba's School, knowing that Jimmy was prone to going through a strict training ritual. And there he was, completely alone, hitting a ball against a corrugated wall which spewed the ball back at him at erratic and unpredictable angles. He was testing to see how well he could kill the ball and move off with it, all in one movement. If he failed he would punish himself by running round the playground once and then back to the wall. He was covered in sweat having been at it for some time. After that the only remedy would seem to have been a bath, then bed, and good-bye Blantyre Celtic. But in an hour or so he was whisked off to play in the game which would see him having to complete forty-five minutes each way for the first time in his career.

Let us just say that the left back of Ashfield, a man called Lawson, a provisional Celtic signing, would regret to his dying days that Jimmy had not tired himself out on that playground because he had shown up and turned the demented man inside-out. It was not a career-enhancing night for the defender, because Celtic never called him up after that. Perhaps he can console himself by realising that, historically, he was the very first of a long line of left-backs who were to be left thinking that life would have been better had they been confronted by a sabre-toothed tiger, rather than a wee red-haired winger.

Ned Cushley, the manager of Blantyre Celtic, and father of the late John Cushley, would take special care of him after that. But Jimmy was not satisfied. It is clear from talking to his contemporaries that he felt slighted, rebuffed. He was genuinely worried that the Celtic management had unthinkingly farmed him out there, and into oblivion. You have to recall, previously, he had been a star. He was not just a run-of-the-mill youngster getting his big chance. He had been feted at school and Boys' Guild level: Matt Busby had talked about him in glowing terms: a tactic had been cunningly employed to ensure that he would land in the Celtic fold, and yet here he was playing junior football. It wasn't ego affecting him. It was undiluted ambition.

Equally, it has to be said, his general enthusiasm for playing football overcame any reservations and he turned on the style. He dazzled. He survived the bruising encounters of a level of football in which the phrase 'smash-and-grab' was a more accurate term than 'tackle.' An early indication of how he was catching the eye comes from a short article in the *Blantyre Gazette* of March 23rd 1961, 'Blantyre Celtic's clever little forward Jim Johnstone is rapidly fulfilling his promise, noted in these columns when he was a schoolboy.'

More than the locals were watching him though. He fell under the scrutiny of mainstream journalists. Laurie Cumming of the *Scottish Daily Express* was to watch him when he crossed the Irish Sea to play for Junior Scotland on St Patrick's Day, March 17th, 1962, in Newtownards, and predicted, 'Celtic's provisionally booked teenage winger Jim Johnstone of Blantyre Celtic will be a top senior personality in two years time … already 17 year-old Johnstone is out on his own as a box-office attraction. Nicknamed 'Di Stefano' by his pals, he can kill the ball with either foot and pass it with the same golden touch as the Real Madrid idol. Yet only six months ago the Blantyre player was an unknown in Boys' Guild football.'

Such hyperbole can always be suspect, unless it is validated from other sources, and it persuasively was by the *Sunday Mail* report of that game against the Northern Irish side which identified the winger as '...a personality plus outside-right, a touchline wonder.' And went on to describe how he had created two of the goals in a 4-1 victory, one of them by means of a 'lovely cross-field pass.' He was but a slip of a lad in his teens who had never been abroad on football business before, nor had he ever been in a swanky hotel, where the Scottish players were based. He was bewildered in many ways. So, confronted by a menu with a list of items that stretched to infinity, he caused amusement amongst his more experienced colleagues by selecting the only dish which made sense to him. He asked for *'Various Omelettes.'*

If anybody thinks this might sound disparaging, it should be noted that what was occurring was the phenomenon of the first steps of an innocent young, professional working-class footballer, emerging from the chrysalis of a confined social environment, by dint of talented feet, to enter a more sophisticated world where *a la carte* did not refer to the rag-and-bone man. There were others just like him. Willie Henderson, of Rangers, his famous rival who became a close friend, once sat with Jim Craig in a restaurant recalling the days when they both played with Sheffield Wednesday, and ordered asparagus soup, then confessed, 'You know, before I started playing football I had never heard of bloody asparagus soup!' It didn't necessarily cause Jimmy or Willie to disparage their origins, but they were learning that football was offering them new inducements which could stimulate or, sadly perhaps, even blight their lives.

In terms of football, on that occasion, in Northern Ireland, it was even odder to discover that the team manager had never seen him playing. That being so, it was a scene before the game which reflected on the recurring doubt about his physique, something that continually irritated him and unfortunately was dampening his spirits despite the rave reviews. It happened in the dressing room. Sir Alex Ferguson's brother Martin, who played for Kirkintilloch Rob Roy juniors at the time, was in the Scottish side, playing at right-half just behind Jimmy. He recalls how they were sitting around waiting for what might have passed as a team talk in those days.

The Scottish side was picked by a selection committee and then left to the coach, a man called Mackenzie, to take over on the day of the game. He was casting his eye round his charges when he spied this little lad sitting quietly in the corner, as if all he had turned up to do was clean the boots then read about Desperate Dan in the *Beano*. 'Hey, son,' he shouted, not knowing who the lad was 'Can you run?' It would be nice to think that that question gave birth to that delightful riposte to utterly naive questions, 'Is the Pope a Catholic?'

For Mackenzie would have been shamefaced at what he eventually witnessed, as Jimmy ran the Irish ragged. There was someone there, though, who had the kind of eye which could detect talent at a glance. Jimmy Gribben, the man responsible for reminding Celtic in 1951 about a certain centre-half with a great left leg and a pathetic right one, but with the 'auld heid' on a broad pair of shoulders. Playing for Llanelli in Welsh non-league football, he had taken the trouble to cross by ferry to see the match. He was practically frothing at the mouth in his need to get back to Celtic Park and tell them to bring this exceptionally talented, provisional signing in from the apparent cold. Just to back up his feelings about the player he watched him play two further representative games, one of which was against an Irish 'B' League at Firhill, on April 7th 1962, where, according to the *Sunday Post*, he '...stole the show,' making the first two and scoring another in the 3-2 victory.

Gribben was scout and boot-room man, but in essence he was also a Merlin at the court of the late Sir Robert Kelly. On the back of that Jimmy was called up and went into reserve team football. If some of the hierarchy were not aware of the pulling power of their winger, then they soon would find out.

Bob Kelly, as he was then, prided himself in his relationship with supporters and tried to communicate with them as often as he could. He was taking a meeting with the official Celtic supporters' executive in the centre of Glasgow, late one afternoon, in the early part of Jimmy's first full season as a reserve player (1962-63), when he was intrigued to hear one of the branch secretaries talking about the need to get away in time to take the bus to a reserve match. When he enquired about that he was told that not one, but seven buses had been booked to go to the second XI game.

Much as he respected the fervour of supporters, he couldn't

quite understand why there was such an interest in Friday night reserve football, until he was told they were all going to watch this new sensational winger, called Jimmy Johnstone, who was giving them so much entertainment. When he phoned Celtic Park to record his amazement at this information, to his horror he was told that Jimmy had not been selected for that particular match. Thinking of the seven buses heading their way, there was only one thing he could say through the phone, 'Pick him!' They snapped to it.

That endorsement might seem backhanded now, but you have to put it in the context of a chairman who was going through hell trying to stabilise a club which seemed to have reached a pinnacle of success in their 7-1 demolition of Rangers in the Scottish League Cup final of 19th October 1957, but since then had floundered. They were not to win a trophy from that autumn day until April 1965. Bob Kelly was not simply a club chairman, but a spokesman for an entire community which felt its views were under-represented in the media. He aroused respect by his mix of blunt obduracy and lucid dignity which distinguished him from a surrounding sea of waffle. It gave his club, and the community it mirrored, a distinct definition. But within these ranks there was, nevertheless, unrest. Celtic were massively underperforming on the field, and it could not go on.

So, at that time in the early 1960s, what chance did a diminutive winger have of being seen as part of a turnaround in the fortunes of the club? Precious little. Even his long-time room-mate, and indeed soul-mate, Bobby Lennox, who spent hours with him daily through their careers, had to admit to a feeling, when he saw him for the first time at Celtic Park. 'I just saw Jinky at first as a wee fella, nothing more than that. And I admit I never thought he would make it. It says something that he did.'

Bertie Auld reiterates that sentiment, in telling the story of the first time he really took notice of Jimmy. 'When I came back to the club in 1965, I hadn't paid too much attention to Jinky. I had played some matches with him but he hadn't made all that much of an impression. He was just a wee lad on the fringe. I hadn't heard much about what he was like. We had to go to Austria to play a friendly just after Celtic had won the Scottish Cup against Dunfermline. Jock Stein wasn't there with us. Sean Fallon was in charge. Now Billy McNeill had to go off on Scotland duties, so for some reason Bob Kelly decided to make me captain for the trip and I was told this lad Jimmy Johnstone was coming with us. But when he was selected for this particular game I could hardly believe what I was seeing.

'This frail wee laddie looked as if somebody had given him the wrong jersey. The shirt was too big for him, the shorts were dangling below the knees and he gave you the impression that he was like somebody in primary school with a borrowed strip. Now it was a mud heap we were playing on, in torrential rain, and I wondered how this tiny lad could cope. Cope? He was brilliant. It was astonishing what he was doing on that surface. But then during the game I felt a tug on my jersey and when I turned round there was Jinky dancing on the spot. I thought as captain it was something tactical he would be on about. "What's wrong with you, have you a problem?" "Bertie, I need the toilet. I'll be back in five minutes."

'He just turned and sprinted towards the pavilion with positive signs on his shorts that he was suffering from diarrhoea. Then he sprinted back on again and proceeded to take the mickey out of the opposition. That was the early sign that told you somehow only Jinky could do something like that. From then on I was just captivated by the wee man.'

In Jimmy's early days at Celtic Park, being faced by a successful Rangers side which agonisingly seemed to have a physical prowess which gave them the edge so often, a view was arising that they could not succeed without confronting them on the Ibrox club's own terms; of meeting might with might, whatever traditional values of flair, and attacking football were still cherished within the club. Jimmy simply did not seem to measure up to that, despite the obvious affection of those fans who saw his reserve team performances as the most exhilarating aspect of watching Celtic in those days.

They had turned up at a pre-season public trial in August 1962, in which he gave the reliable, trustworthy defender Jim Kennedy such a going over that the left back was prompted to tell the former Celtic player John McPhail, then journalist for the *Daily Record*, '...Johnstone has a bundle of guts and ability. This boy has a great future.' This encouraged McPhail to demand in the paper that, 'Jim Johnstone, a right-wing bomb, be exploded on Scotland's defences.' However, although some of Celtic's selections in those days looked as if they had consulted a spiritualist for them, they certainly did not allow a journalist, even a respected ex-Celt to pick the team for them. Indeed, perhaps, in a paradoxical way, that hardly boosted Jimmy's chances of complete acceptance.

But at the very least they knew they had an outright entertainer in their midst. Then events took over. On March 23rd 1963, Celtic beat a strong and highly respected Dundee side 4-1, who were European Cup semi-finalists at the time, but in doing so incurred a host of injuries. On the following Monday morning they ended up with no fewer than eight players on the treatment table including Jimmy with a calf-muscle problem. But he recovered to play in a game, that night, against a Scottish Professional Youth Eleven, in a trial match, before a youth tournament the following month.

Of his performance that night, the *Daily Record* match report carried the headline, 'JIMMY IS A WOW!' and the rival *Scottish Daily Express* talked of 'A GRAND DISPLAY.' The directors watching this game could not ignore that. In any case, because of the injuries, they had to make radical changes to the side to play Kilmarnock, two days later at Rugby Park, on March 27th 1963, and turned to several players to make their debuts for the first team, including John Cushley at the heart of defence, and Dick Madden in goal, but above all Jimmy, who ran out for the first time at that level in the Hoops.

To say the least, none of these Celtic players in that improvised selection would be maintaining a record of that day in their scrapbooks, as they went down 6-0 to a Kilmarnock side which admittedly was one of the strongest teams in the country at that time. If you are a winger, turned into a mere spectator as the debacle unfolds, and you cannot get a touch of the ball, you can be absolved of some blame. The performance was so hurting that, perhaps to block it out of their memories, the only thing the players talked about afterwards was the fact that their goalkeeper Madden's family had just won £10,400 in Littlewood's 'Treble Chance.' It was the only competitive game the keeper ever played for the club. Jimmy Dunbar of Glasgow's *Evening Times*, wrote that he was 'particularly disappointed in the performance of Jim Johnstone, a lad about whom we have been hearing so much.'

Jimmy went back to the reserves, and it took another injury to give him a place in the team to play Hearts five weeks later, on Monday 29th April 1963, just five days before the Scottish Cup final. Celtic were two down at half-time. Then came the passage which has been printed indelibly on the minds of Celtic supporters present, who previously had been delighted by his undoubted ability to entertain but were now seeing a slim lad looking like he could also be hugely influential. For in the space of six minutes, at the beginning of the second half, he helped lay on two goals and scored the third to put Celtic 3-2 up, although they went on to lose eventually 4-3. This must have implanted itself in the mind of Bob Kelly. He had decided he was going to gamble on this winger on the Saturday. So here we had the first Old Firm Scottish Cup final in 25 years, with all the historical baggage which goes along with such an event, being faced up to by a lad playing in only his third first-team game.

On then to Hampden on the 4th of May 1963. To see him from the height of the press-box at Hampden that day trotting out with his team-mates, was to imagine, at first glance, that a ball-boy had mischievously donned the green and white Hoops and decided to swell the ranks. He looked so incredibly small, set against friend and foe, and miniaturised even more by being surrounded by the vast multitude of 129,527 wrapped around the great bowl. Although many of the Celtic support had heard about him, this would have been the first time the vast majority of the fans had set eyes on the small figure. Early on in the game, when he seemed to possess a sense of bravura against the towering Rangers defence, he was treated almost with indifference at first.

After all, Scot Symon was not a manager who indulged in much pre-match analysis of opposing teams, so the Rangers players would have known practically nothing about him. But, when they realised he was like an escapologist who could wriggle himself out of a tight situation, they stopped the supply of the ball to him, and when he was in play they spared him no slack in the way they tackled him. By and large Celtic could be grateful to Frank Haffey in goal for having helped Celtic take the game to a replay after the 1-1 draw. This not only set in motion another confrontation of the two clubs on Wednesday, 15th May 1963, but also a debate which would rage amongst the supporters of the club for some time after, and beget some soul-searching amongst those within Celtic Park who had to make crucial decisions about players, and even among the first team themselves. It could be said that what happened over these intervening few days before the replay initiated the process which would ultimately bring Jock Stein to the East End of Glasgow as manager. It was all about the team selection for the game. Jimmy was dropped. However, the teenager had not personally let his side down.

The disappointment in Celtic's performance overshadowed the fact that Jimmy emerged as *the* personality of the first match of a dour final played under grey skies and swirling rain. Consider how Peter Wilson of the *Daily Mirror*, brought up to lend a Sassenach view, was entranced by him, writing '...the red-haired feather-weight imp,' as he described him, who 'ranged up and down the wing and cat-footed it around the penalty-box, his clown-white face a-jump with excitement, as he chased the ball in a manner reminiscent of Harpo Marx chasing blondes in his palmy days.'

Such praise for a player who had provided a splash of colour on a dreich day, made no impression on the minds of the Celtic management. But after they played against Dundee United, during the intervening eleven days before the replay, and lost 3-0, a Celtic insider told the *Scottish Daily Express*, he had been dropped, because he had lacked strength in crossing the ball, and then went on to quote them as saying, 'We expect great things of Johnstone, but had he flopped in the final [i.e. the replay] it might have set him back two years. We felt it too much to ask a youngster to go in and win the Scottish Cup for us.'

Which begs the question, why did they play him in the first game, if they thought that? What they decided to do eventually was to bring in Bobby Craig, a veteran inside-forward, signed from Blackburn Rovers earlier in the season, to play on the wing in Jimmy's stead. He had never played in that position before, and after this final was never to play again for them. The Celtic supporters had left in big numbers long before the end of a game which Rangers won 3-0. They were angered, not least because this was the fourth Scottish Cup final in a row, 1955, 1956, 1961 and 1963, in which they had been denied watching their team in a victory parade because of what they perceived as bizarre team selections.

Everywhere he went, Jimmy was the subject of discussion amongst increasingly frustrated fans as to what was happening inside Celtic Park. Not even the veterans of the institution could offer an explanation, and certainly not a perplexed little winger, who nevertheless signed on for the club the day after the replay. So he was glad to get respite from all of that, from time to time, and especially did so when a chance encounter brought into his life an influence which was to provide an anchor for him as the tide of events would pull him one way, then the other, through life. He met Agnes Doherty. She was much taller than him. As such he always called her 'Big Yin.'

Spring 2001

Despite the increasing problems with his fingers and arms, Jimmy still wanted to be the life and soul of any gathering he joined. The singing, the jokes, the banter with all of his friends, never ceased. But as a long-time friend Joe Reilly, whose son Martin became Neill Lennon's agent, recounts, he did notice something when they went out together for a pint or two.

'Jimmy was downing his pint in an odd way. Instead of lifting the glass to his mouth off the table, he was bending down to lift it gently about an inch or two, and with both hands. Every sip was the same, down and up again, almost as if he was doing an exercise. Now it's all very well me saying now that it was odd, given I knew Jimmy of old, when he could run about the place drinking. But it <u>was</u> odd. I passed it off at the time though. You feel like kicking yourself when you now know what came about. But what could you have done anyway? But then again, Jimmy never once mentioned that he was having a problem, so we just thought nothing of it.'

His son, James, did notice. 'You could see that taking a simple cup of tea was beginning to be a task, because he would practically not lift the cup at all but just bend down and sip.' He and his mother Agnes were becoming aware that Jimmy was trying to disguise this creeping disability, so as not to cause embarrassment to anybody. At that stage he was just getting by. But when he visited Celtic Park, about then, his former colleagues noticed a peculiarity which had developed.

As John Clark says, 'He would keep exercising his jaw. He would open his mouth wide, and it was as if he was chewing something big, he just kept the jaw working as if something was aggravating him. We thought it was strange because we had never seen him doing anything like that before. Maybe there was nothing sinister in it, but it was definitely strange. We never said anything to him.'

Bertie Auld noticed the same but mentioned it to nobody. 'I was in Ireland with him long before there was any mention of a disease and I noticed that he kept opening and closing his mouth as if he had lockjaw, big jaw movements like gigantic yawns, over and over again. I asked him if there was something wrong, but he just brushed it aside. So it didn't register that much with me. Now I know.'

John Hughes, the man who operated on the other side of the field from the wee man, also noticed something that seemed odd. He attended the funeral of a friend with Jimmy and noticed that he wasn't wearing a tie, but a black polo-necked jumper. He came home and remarked to his wife that it was unusual because Jimmy was always meticulous in his dress, particularly on these occasions. 'I suppose I'm like a lot of people who saw things unusual, and then, after we all heard about his condition, it struck you what they meant. He couldn't wear a tie because he couldn't use his fingers.'

In uttering those words, tears welled up in Hughes' eyes. Like many people who noticed tiny signs but carried on with barely a pause in life, it is as if they almost carry a sense of guilt about it now. There was a doctor though who quickly read the signs and decided to intervene.

THREE

A New Era

Agnes Doherty met Jimmy at St Columba's youth club when she was sixteen and he a couple of years older. It is only when you talk to her now that you realise she couldn't have coped with marriage to such a public personality, who at the height of his fame was as often in the newspapers as the weather forecast, and just as unpredictable, had she not possessed an inner calm, reminiscent of the eye of the storm. She is a woman still rooted in the ways which shaped her working-class life, and not a single molecule of her personality has changed in all that time.

She makes the WAGS of contemporary mode as authentic as shop-window mannequins. Her treasure trove of anecdotes about her husband who, to say the least, led a hectic social life and tested her patience to the limit at times, demonstrates the skill with which she organised her married life. But the most important aspect of their relationship was that she has a superbly witty tongue. In their company, the banter between the pair could have been scripted by the Monty Python team. They were skilled in hilarious insults to each other. Even towards the end, when I saw them chatting, the harmony was both comedic and touching. In that respect Jimmy was blessed by the choice of woman he married in 1966.

During their courtship, life for young working-class youths

along the Clyde Valley then was simple and logical. There was little money about so they had to make their own entertainment, helped and encouraged by the church institutions. They paid a shilling each to get into Greyfriars, a local parish church club, on the south side of the Clyde near Blantyre, and because they could not afford to pay for a band Jimmy would bring along his small record player with his own assortment of records, which always gave him the opportunity to warble the larynx as he was wont to do at the slightest encouragement. He then graduated from that to playing in a small group, and it is clear from those who heard him at that stage he could easily have headed for Tin Pan Alley.

If that is thought to be an exaggeration, then his friend since childhood, Billy Donald, would put doubts to rest. The pair were to remain close until his death, having started out their friendship as kids by going out at Halloween as one man, with Jimmy sitting on the shoulders of his friend, who remained hidden under a large coat. A Rangers man carrying the man who would be Celtic's greatest ever player promotes an image that is as enduring as their lifelong friendship actually was. Donald recollects holidaying together.

'When we were about seventeen we went on a trip to Jersey,' Donald said. 'It was big-time stuff for us then. We had heard there were singing contests on the island. We got hold of an old Morris Minor, the kind with the wood strips along the side and travelled to the three contests. Jimmy won them all. You might remember Vince Hill, who went on to be a real star and had a hit with *Eidelweiss*, well, Jimmy beat him in these as well. We thought we'd win a lot of money. In fact all we got was £50. And there was something else for us, which was of no use. We won magnums of champagne. Neither of the two of us drank then. So he spent his time going round giving everybody a drink. It's true, not a drop did we touch.'

Although Agnes knew all about that melodious singing, she knew little about what he did on a football field. This was simply due to a life-long reluctance of Jimmy to bring football talk into the home, even at the height of his fame. It could be interpreted as modesty, but was more likely to be the simple fact that the only thing he wanted in football was to play with a ball, not to talk incessantly about it. Agnes never knew when he was playing, either for the junior club or the Celtic reserves at that time, and frankly could not have cared less, but went about their courtship, little realising what was in store for her in life as Jimmy sought various jobs, with professional football still a distant dream.

He had worked firstly in a hosiery factory in Uddingston as one of the few men in the place, pushing barrows of bobbins to almost five hundred women in the mill. He admitted he really liked the attention he got. After that, in a more macho environment, he worked in Finlay's steel mill in Airdrie as an apprentice welder, and was involved in a day release system where he ended up by fighting with one of his instructors. After having been found pinning this man to the ground and been hauled off by Benny Rooney, the son of the Celtic trainer, he was shown the door. In his restless seeking for a job that would suit him, he also had a spell with Perrit and McFarlane in the Glasgow Meat Market for two or three months.

This typified the experience of the average unskilled teenager of the time: unskilled only in the sense that the marvellous ability that was in his feet was still to be unleashed on the wider public. At least he was earning some money to enhance his courting of Agnes. But they got off to a dubious start, in the sense that on their first date there was an identity crisis.

'We were going to the pictures and he came over to pick me up one day and knocked on the door,' said Agnes. 'My mother looked out of the window and thought he was the roll-boy. "You'd better go out and pay that wee boy the roll-money," she said to me. I said, "That's my boy friend, ma." "Whit?" she said. "In the name of God, he's awfy wee."'

Agnes benefitted from the fact that her six brothers did know something about football and knew a great deal about his skills on the park, but treated him only as a suitor to their sister, not a budding star. 'Because we were a big family and there were lots of grandchildren, the house was always packed on a Sunday. We'd play cards, pontoons, Scabby Queen and such and I noticed right away that he was terrible when he lost. He just couldn't take it. My brothers used to hold him down on the floor and rub his nose with the Scabby Queen if he was acting up. One night we tied him to a chair and forced him to pay out for ice cream for the lot of us or else he was going to stay there all night or get a doing.'

Their rumbustious courtship lasted three years, in which time Agnes is the first to admit that as a pair they were not exactly the Romeo and Juliet of Viewpark. She still has decided views. 'Romantic? Judge for yourself, if I tell you that often I would go up and sit with Mrs Johnstone, his mother. And what would he be doing? He'd be in the lobby, running up and down, dribbling a ball between the bottles he had laid out for himself there. And then he would take me down to Thorniewood Park. Ah, ha, you might say! But what did we do there? Well, he would climb on my shoulders and I would help him up to the rail round the park so that he could walk round it balancing himself. He thought that would help him keep his feet when he was playing. If he fell off, he would jump on my shoulders again and I would heave him up. He'd get irritated with me and shout to me to stand at peace until he was up. I just shouted back that he was a ton weight and to get on with it. I once said to him in later life, "The only reason you married me was because I was tall enough to help you up to that rail."'

At least he had developed a sense of decorum in not wearing the pit boots, those which he had used for his constant running to strengthen his legs in his Boys' Guild days. So he had a girlfriend who could match his wit, did not pester him to go to watch him in games, and could understand and tolerate his passion for fitness.

By now he was a first-team player, occasionally. If anybody had any doubts about that degree of affection which had built up for Jimmy so quickly within his first two seasons, then the passengers of the green bus from Lanarkshire which went into Glasgow via Parkhead Cross would certainly testify to that. John Clark explains. 'We had no cars in those early days so all the Lanarkshire players would pick up the bus at different stops to go into training. The drivers of the bus would halt in front of Jimmy's house in Old Edinburgh Road and just stand there and wait for him to come out. And it would stand there and stand there. I've seen passengers rising up, bawling at the driver to get on with it because they had their work to go to. But no, the drivers wouldn't budge. Despite all the howls of outrage, they would wait until Jimmy sauntered down and got in beside them. And since he was never one to leap out of bed in the morning that happened almost every day.'

So, apparently, he could not only wreck defences, but bus timetables as well. This delighted him of course. But it was only half the story. He was deeply concerned about the unfolding of his future and whether he had one – or not – at Celtic Park. The division of opinion about him was therefore clear-cut. Can you imagine the turmoil which might have gone through his mind, from time to time, at that period? Barely out of puberty he wasn't yet mature enough to assess matters correctly, rationally, and make sense of some of the chaos surrounding him, especially trying to ride out the tide of resentment which was beginning to swell within the Celtic support, some hundreds of whom gathered at the front entrance to Celtic Park after an undistinguished 1-1 draw against Queen of the South, in August 1963 to vent their fury on the board.

He would read in the newspapers about the abortive rebellion being organised by Baillie James F. Reilly, whose intention was to take over the club: a movement that was shorter than an Arctic summer. He would suffer in dismay at times as Celtic tried various right-wing permutations – Johnstone/Turner, Chalmers/Murdoch, Gallagher/Turner, Lennox/Turner – clear evidence of instability. It got to him. Recklessly, he ran all of ten yards to thump 'Tottie' Beck of Rangers in the Ne'erday match of 1965 and was sent off.

It was true he had been treated like a rag-doll for most of that match and snapped. But Celtic, with an insistence on good behaviour on the park, took a dim view of any excuse, since with ten men they would find it well-nigh impossible to pull back Rangers' 1-0 lead. The fact that it was the same referee, Tom Wharton, who had sent him off 14 months earlier, with Partick Thistle's Ian Cowan, was neither here nor there. He was dropped for the next match against Clyde because of that, and felt more intensely than ever that he was falling out of favour. This was not taken kindly by the support, who during that Clyde match were heard chanting, 'We want Johnstone!' You could hardly blame him for taking all these factors, the political battle against the club, the outrage of the supporters, the craziness of selections, for sensing that his deep love for Celtic might turn out to be unrequited.

There were factors, though, which both Jimmy and his supporters could cling on to; especially that season when Scottish football recognised his quality in being picked for his country twice, against Wales and Finland in autumn 1964. Playing for his country, however, was an experience which had its mixed blessings. There were those in the crowd who clearly did not like the club he was attached to and booed him. This upset him so much he went over the incidents with his wife Agnes, despite his normal reluctance to bring his football chat home with him.

'He really was disgusted by that,' Agnes admits. 'He was the kind that didn't bother about being slagged off in Old Firm games. That was just part of the business. But there he was playing for his country and proud of it, yet some of them hated that.' And he spelled out in detail to Agnes how, when he and Bobby Lennox were in the Scotland squad in 1968, during a training session he was asked by trainer Walter McCrae to act as a linesman rather than actually play. Lennox says his reply was abrupt and negative, with the added suggestion as to where McCrae could stick the linesman's flag. He delighted in telling her of how in a later game against Walter McCrae's Kilmarnock, he took pleasure in running riot and destroying their defence. He told Agnes that on the final whistle he passed McCrae on the touchline and remarked, 'Not bad for a linesman, eh?'

The fact is that playing for Scotland was simply a distraction from playing for his club, whose unexpected run to the semi-finals of the European Cup-Winners' Cup in season 1963/64 enhanced his growing reputation as an entertainer. They looked for a while like turning a corner, as Jimmy and John Hughes on the other wing, swept aside some excellent defences to reach the first leg of the semi-final of the cup, and at the same time produced a surge of winning form in the league, pushing the club nearer Rangers.

Peter Hendry of the Glasgow *Evening Times* wrote, 'Hughes and Johnstone, side by side, are a sort of 'Jack and the Giant' twosome, the long and short of it.' And added that against Dinamo Zagreb in the quarter-final of that competition, Jimmy had, '...produced a variety of moves which baffled the Zagreb defence.' That he was to score the first goal in the semi-final against MTK Budapest in Celtic's solid-looking home 3-0 victory moved him to an apparent peak of acceptance by the management. All that reads well, up to this point.

But then, as was almost customary with Celtic at that period, the momentum disappeared, inertia inexplicably set in, and in one of the most remarkable turnarounds in the history of the competition, MTK won 4-0 in the return leg, and progressed to the final. It is little wonder that Bobby Murdoch was quoted as admitting that the flight back was the longest journey he had ever taken. 'We all sat there on the plane with our own silent thoughts, not looking at each other.'

That might also summarise the state of Celtic Football Club in January 1965. How could anybody connected with the club accept that in the previous season Rangers had won all five of their meetings, and Celtic could only reach third place in the league behind them? Something had to give. Jimmy, still getting good reports in the press for his performances, might never have been able to survive the blasts of criticism that were directed at others, and could have perished like an orphan in the storm in the general malaise which could affect even the innocent.

He was still absolutely confident in his own abilities, adored far and wide by the public willing to pay up to see him, and yet not fully confident that he was winning over the man who called the shots. For although Bob Kelly loved the winger as well, you can tell from the team selections, and the way matters were handled through to the end of season 1964/65, that he was still unsure as to offering a long-term future to the boy from Viewpark. He was beginning to feel that his self-confidence did not match the feelings of the management, although he outwardly remained a cheery, witty presence in and around the dressing-room.

One thing was clear, as Bobby Lennox emphasises, 'Jinky was a great trainer. It doesn't matter what he might have been doing the night before, it doesn't matter if you felt in the morning he might have been down in the dumps, he trained harder than anybody else in the side. He took everything in his stride.' As John Clark, that superb Celtic defender points out, selection for the team, during the McGrory period, and even immediately after Jock Stein came to the club, was varied and unpredictable. 'You would never know from one week to the other if you were going to be picked. And honestly, we were young and just delighted to be there.'

This is echoed by Jimmy's long-term room-mate and best pal, Bobby Lennox. 'He never really complained all that much about being dropped for a game in these early days because it happened to us all. And when you think about it, that was good for us.'

Then came the decision which changed the course of events. The man who had captained the side to their famous Coronation Cup final in 1953, and their League and Scottish Cup 'double' in 1954, was brought back to the club as manager and the earth began to move under their feet. It was a time in Celtic history when you have to refer to the Richter Scale to understand the impact of one man. Jock Stein knew more about Celtic than anybody at the club, even before he arrived. He knew full well that Bob Kelly would come for him one day, and he did. So he was prepared.

Stein himself told me about that now famous encounter with Jimmy in the toilet during half-time at a reserve match before he had actually officially become manager, when he had turned up to verify what was in store for him at the club he was rejoining. There is no doubt that Stein relieved himself of more than body fluid. 'By and large I told him to get the finger out. He wasn't performing the way I thought he could,' is how Stein put it to me simply. Some have interpreted this as having cleared the air. It did not. Jimmy certainly turned in a virtuoso performance in the second half, and in most of the games he played in during the rest of that season he was never satisfied that he had done enough to have Stein finally make up his mind about him. So, he still felt his feats on the field were not clarifying his future at all, as he read conjecture in the newspapers about the growing interest in him from south of the border. The most notable evidence of Stein's uncertainty came as a shaft to the heart for him, for he was not picked to play in the Scottish Cup final against Dunfermline in April 1965. John Clark puts that into perspective.

'Although you could say he was disappointed in being dropped for that final replay in 1963, against Rangers,' said Clark, 'the worst moment for him, in all the time he was with Celtic, outside of leaving the club, was when Big Jock didn't pick him for the Scottish Cup final in 1965. He was devastated. It was the worst I ever saw him in all the time I knew him. It specially hurt him because he had played in the game before that against Partick Thistle, when we lost 2-1, and thought he had performed all right. But he and Jim Kennedy were left out of the side. He was just inconsolable. And you know what hurt him more than anything else was that he loved going down to the coast to train.

'We were at Largs for that final but he loved our regular place, the Seamill Hydro to prepare for a match. You could almost see him growing in size when he was down there, striding along the beach and saying to me, "You're lucky if you live down here in the salt air." And then of course, believing that he was right on his mettle, and assuming he was a certainty, Jock didn't pick him for the final, so he was shattered. Everybody knew Jimmy as a bubbly guy, full of life and fun, but underneath it all he was actually a worrier. Things did get to him.'

He was also learning that Stein was no sentimentalist. Celtic's greatest manager has sometimes been portrayed as something of a romantic, somebody who had lofty ideas about how to approach his job. He was nothing of the kind. He was a hard-nosed realist. His pragmatism meant he was quite ruthless in picking his sides if he felt it helped the cause. Given what had preceded him, where, you have to ask, would Celtic have been without that attitude? That is the reason he had not conclusively made up his mind about Jimmy.

In the early days of season 1965/66 Celtic showed signs of resorting to their old ways of inconsistency when they had suffered two defeats in their opening three matches, leaving them trailing in their League Cup section. The 2-0 home defeat against Dundee particularly riled the manager, who although stating publicly that he was not basically the kind of coach who made wholesale changes in a side, nevertheless, stated pointedly to the *Celtic View* of August 25th that, 'One that will be made, however, is at outside-right, where Steve Chalmers will be brought in again.'

Jimmy would have cringed when he read that. He was being clearly singled out in a reflection of the manager's dissatisfaction. That was the period when he truly began to intimate to his friends that his coat was on a 'shoogly peg,' since his next four games were in the reserves. At the same time Tottenham Hotspur, stricken by injuries, especially that to their outstanding winger Cliff Jones, and badly in need of a replacement, contacted Stein with an interest in Jimmy. This was not initially rejected. Bobby Howitt, the Motherwell manager, also made a tentative inquiry about his availability. But it was in the south where the interest was greatest. Bill Nicholson, the Spurs manager, alerted his assistant Eddie Baily to cast his eye over Johnstone. At that stage you could say Jimmy was on the brink of leaving Celtic. His friends will testify to that. Publicly, he said the right things to Ken Gallacher of the *Scottish Daily Record*, 'As far as I am concerned a move from Celtic doesn't interest me. I would never leave unless the club told me they did not want me ... and that just hasn't happened.'

But one night Jimmy sat in front of a friend in tears. 'They're going to let me go,' he told him. This was on the back of what he perceived to be an increasing indifference to him, and also obviously because of something he had been told. He sounded as if he had been jilted at the altar. He knew about the Spurs interest and also suggested to his friends that the manager was intent on selling John Hughes as well at that time. That offered him no consolation. However, he still had to report for duty and turned up for what might have appeared to be a friendly reserve match against Clydebank on September 10th, but which proved to be nothing of the sort.

He asked some of his friends to come and give him some support in a game that was to turn out to be as meaningful to a career as any he had ever played in. And that is exactly what it proved to be. He was simply his true self, uncatchable, unstoppable, bewildering. But, as he went through the whole gamut of twists and turns, which transfixed a bigger than normal crowd, since Celtic were fielding two Brazilian trialists that night, there was one man there he thought had given him up for lost – Stein himself. The manager was essentially there to see the Brazilians. However he was blinded to their capabilities as one man ran the show in Celtic's 7-1 victory.

Jimmy did not appear for the second-half. It wasn't until after the game when Jimmy came rushing out of the ground that his friends realised the significance of that. 'They're keeping me,' he shouted to them like he had just won a reprieve from the hangman. The manager had told him at the interval, 'You're going nowhere.' But Spurs were clinging on, in pursuit, because they had still not been officially rejected. So when Stein decided to play Jimmy in the League Cup quarter-final tie against Raith Rovers at Kirkcaldy on September 15th, and he ran riot in Celtic's 8-1 victory, Eddie Baily told Nicholson to put in a serious bid for him. Stein politely rejected the offer. But it had been a close-run thing: perhaps closer than many have thought since. Thus began a relationship between the two men which would make Stein feel, at times, like he was riding a bucking bronco in a rodeo, as he tried to exploit this prodigious talent but at the same time tame Jimmy's wildly careering lifestyle.

But, as Celtic's greatest manager would tell me often enough, he would not have missed it for the world. And only a few weeks after that sequence of events, when Jimmy's future had been in the melting-pot, came the game that was to turn Scottish football on its head and which caused the Celtic manager to imagine he was thrice blessed in having taken the trouble to take in a reserve football match one night to look at South American talent. For the club, desperate to break out of the historical shackles placed on them by their great rivals, was to benefit handsomely from that evening in Clydebank when Viewpark had upstaged Copacabana.

Summer 2001

Dr Roddy Macdonald, when he was appointed medical officer for Celtic under Martin O'Neill, had an ambition lurking in the background. He had always wanted to meet Jimmy. He had idolised him as a fan, and it is clear he was as devoted to Celtic as he was to the Hippocratic Oath. The problem was that Jimmy did not come around Celtic Park much at that time. The doctor saw more of the other Lisbon Lions, but eventually when he did come across Jimmy, it was brief, too brief. He really wanted enough time to chat with his favourite player.

In short, he was a hero-worshipper in a serious way. He had not noticed anything untoward in the brief occasions they met up during Jimmy's infrequent visits. Then, one day, in a quite unsolicited manner Jimmy approached him and asked for advice on a physical problem he was encountering. He talked about the collapse of the wrists, the pins and needles, the increasing feeling of lack of positive control of his hands, and the suspicion of weakness in his arms. Dr Macdonald, who thought that overall Jimmy looked bright and breezy, as usual, started to examine him.

'I noticed right away the wasting of muscles in his hands. Now as I observed this, something came to mind. I recalled something I had studied in my last year as a medical student, something I had not seen since. I just began to wonder.' What passed through the doctor's mind alarmed him. He is too modest a man to claim any special qualities in diagnosis, but he was heading in the *right direction. It was obvious that there would have to be some specialist input, so he insisted that Jimmy take some diagnostic blood and neuro-physiological tests at the Southern General Hospital in Glasgow.*

Bobby Lennox recalls that the doctor, although not wishing to cause alarm, would get slightly impatient with Jimmy in not pursuing this matter quickly enough, and failing to keep appointments at the hospital. 'The doc said to me, "Tell that wee man to get cracking and get to the hospital. He'll have to go." To be honest I think Jimmy was a bit scared about that prospect, although he wouldn't say as much.'

Eventually he did go. The tests were taken and it was a case of simply waiting as the difficulties with his hands and arms intensified but without the slightest indication that he was unduly concerned. The Celtic doctor had taken great care to be calm and measured about his examination. Equally, he was pondering that if his suspicions were confirmed, how would his great hero take it?

FOUR
Champagne Time

If you are into Big Bang theory, then you can point to the afternoon of 23ʳᵈ October 1965 as to when the new Celtic universe was created. It is true that the Scottish Cup final win against Dunfermline the previous April had been highly significant. But in Stein's mind, that was dwarfed by the events of the Scottish League Cup final against Rangers on that autumn day. It wasn't merely a cup final. It was the cure for insecurity: it was confirmation of a generational change taking place within the club. Billy McNeill frames the manager's mind perfectly as regards any Old Firm match for Stein, 'I've had a good laugh at all those people who were taken in by Jock when he used to say, po-faced, that a game against Rangers was just another game. That is a load of bloody nonsense. A game against them was THE game. It was the be-all and end-all. Outside of winning the European Cup it was the greatest thing in his life when he beat them. He lived for it.'

Celtic had simply caved in too often against Rangers in the recent past, though. A hint of what the new attitude would be, from hamper-boy through to player, came from director James Farrell, who said to Alex Cameron, then of the *Scottish Daily Mail*, 'We will meet fire with fire.' Inside the first couple of minutes Ian Young, at right-back, tackled Rangers 'Bud' Johnston in a manner that stamped Celtic's new signature on their approach to a derby match. As Billy McNeill describes it, 'Bud went down as if he wouldn't get back up again.' What effrontery, Rangers must have thought! 'Bud' Johnston was an absolutely key player for the Ibrox side. It was a tackle over which Stein berated Young afterwards, in possibly endangering the side, by risking being sent off. On the other hand he had made it obvious he wanted Johnston to be 'sorted-out' as the Celtic players recall, but perhaps not as dramatically as all that. There would be no more pussy-cat indifference to Rangers' physical prowess.

What then followed was described by Jack Harkness of the *Sunday Post*, as if he had come from a horror film. 'It was a hard, grim game and it could be there are some who like their football this way. People who chew tobacco, bite their nails, eat razor-blades and that sort of thing.'

Raymond Jacobs of the *Glasgow Herald* wrote, 'Some of the tackles were intimidating. Man went for man. Tripping, kicking, hacking and jersey-pulling were rife. How can Scottish football raise its hands piously in horror against the same gambits of continental players, when the two leading teams in the country indulge in an orgy of crudeness which made this so unpalatable a spectacle?' So where was Jimmy in this apparent blood-bath? He was the rapier amidst the bludgeoning. His piercing darts caused upset every time the ball came his way. His opponent Davie Provan, the Rangers full-back, tall, lanky, stiff-jointed by comparison with the elasticity of the little man weaving in front of him, tried everything he knew to stop him and eventually brought him down in the box for the second of John Hughes' penalty goals. The first had come from an inexplicable handling of the ball in the box by Rangers centre-half Ron McKinnon. 2-1 was the final score.

There was a furore in the press about the award of the second penalty to Celtic. Walter McCrae, in his capacity as assistant manager to the national side, tells the perfectly true story that the following weekend after that final, when he was in Rome with Stein as temporary Scotland manager, on a scouting trip for Scotland, out of interest they went to the Pope's weekly appearance in Vatican Square and when an American woman beside them asked out loud what the pontiff was saying, Stein quipped, 'He's telling them it _was_ a penalty!'

It is perhaps difficult now to appreciate the effect this had on

Celtic. Their first major cup win in eight years and not just that, they had shown a new-found grit. Above all else, this had been a physical victory, and there was something in the air, something intangible, but which those who had been accustomed to one of the verities of Scottish life, that Celtic's role in life was as gallant runners-up, were now talking as if this was not just one victory but that, just possibly, a new force was emerging in Scottish football. This new-found solidity would bring out the best in Jimmy.

Too often the great entertainer had been hailed for his efforts, but too often had ended up on the losing side in crucial games because the teams had lacked conviction. Now he had a developing power base around him, especially in the galvanising presence of Bobby Murdoch in midfield, enabling Jimmy to be seen as more than a side-show but as a full-blooded menace, an arrowhead to the bow. For from Hampden that afternoon, Celtic, with the manager gaining his first trophy in an Old Firm match, and Celtic's first League Cup final victory in eight years, the players had cast off any vestige of inferiority to their great rivals. A league title win, for the first time in twelve years, was no longer a chimera but a vivid possibility.

They had the dimension of Europe to take on as well. With it came another test of the relationship with the manager. They went to play what would appear to be a routine match against the Danish side A.G.F. Aarhus in the European Cup-Winners' Cup, which they won by a solitary goal from Joe McBride. But over that stay there were breaches of club discipline. They had spent too much time in town and broke curfew. This angered their relatively new manager, who was eager to show his players that an eruption by Etna was but nothing compared to his own lava-flow. And since he interpreted Jimmy's apparent lack of concern about it as a personal lack of respect, in a burst of temper Stein told him he would never play for the club again. Extreme you might think, but he knew that he had to get through to his player in a way that would shake him. It did. But only up to a point.

This was the start of a whole series of confrontations through the years in which there seemed to be an unequal pull in the tug o' war between a giant of a man with supreme authority and a wee man at the other end who had the apparent ability to perform the Indian rope-trick and disappear out of harm's way.

But, that incident apart, his colleagues could see that he

flourished in Europe. Jim Craig could see the difference. 'It's not that he made any special effort abroad. It was because he got a little bit more freedom in Europe and the Scottish game was definitely much more demanding physically. There was a lot of tough tackling in those days. But there was another factor that he became steadily aware of. His reputation was spreading. People around Europe began to sit up and take notice. He was aware of that. And in general he was good for the big occasion. He was at his best when he knew a large public was watching him.'

Not too many of the public on the continent saw all that much when Celtic flew to Tblisi in Georgia in January 1966. They were to play Dinamo Kiev in a climate more amenable to the human frame than sub-zero Kiev where the game ought to have been played. Travel in that part of the world had certainly improved since the days of Marco Polo, although Celtic would not have thought so. There were so many delays, and so much rerouting in the round-trip that Stein joked that the dolls they had bought for their kids in the former USSR would be useless as the kids would have grown up by the time they all got back home! At that time it was not the dicey flights which bothered Jimmy all that much, it was simply the tedium of travel.

Their return journey might have scared the wits out of him when they had to stay overnight in Stockholm, and the following day, when they tried to take-off it was aborted, after which Bob Kelly refused to let the players back on the same plane again. But Jimmy was not then the scared wee boy on a plane which, eventually, he certainly became. So he was part of an exhausted team which eventually flew back to play at Tynecastle on the following Saturday, only after arriving in Glasgow on the Friday evening, and heading straight for Celtic Park for a nocturnal training session. They lost to Hearts the following day. This wasn't just football. It seemed more like commando training, but in the rigours of balancing domestic and European football, Jimmy was maturing.

Not that it guaranteed selection for any game. In the semi-final of the Cup-Winners' Cup against Liverpool, in mid-April 1966, he played in the first leg and was dropped for the second at Anfield, when Celtic went down 2-0, although they would have gone through to the final on the away goals rule on the back of their 1-0 lead from the first leg if the referee had allowed to stand what appeared to be a legitimate last-minute goal from Bobby Lennox. It begs the question, would Jimmy have made the difference on that wet and windy night, when his ability to wrong-foot opponents in slippery conditions was self-evident?

Hindsight is of little relevance in the record books. And in any case, at the back of Stein's mind was the niggling thought that if his winger didn't listen to advice and instructions he would squander this amazing talent. So what we are witnessing from then on is a mutually admiring relationship, but one which had its recurring tensions and could hardly be described as relaxed, even in moments of triumph. Stein had felt from early on he could never lower his guard while watching over this unique player.

There was plenty evidence of that as Celtic, with remarkable consistency, kept just ahead of Rangers in the battle to wrest the title from them. At the end of April 1966, they had arrived at a situation in which every league game was like a cup-tie, so narrowly were they ahead of their rivals. There was therefore consternation when Jimmy fouled Morton's Alan McGraw at Cappielow to concede a penalty, a moment more than matched by extreme relief when Neilsen blasted the ball over the bar. When that sort of incident imperils the side then those with uncanny ability can sometimes, quickly, make amends. Jimmy did, when he scored with a slightly deflected shot just before half-time. It was Celtic's first goal in almost seven hours of football, including not only the defeat at Liverpool but also the loss of the Scottish Cup involving two matches (final plus replay) against Rangers. And to further his case for natural selection Jimmy provided a superb cross for his room-mate Bobby Lennox to score with a header in the last minute to ensure the victory. He had helped Celtic keep on track.

When eventually they arrived at Motherwell on 7th May 1966, such was their advantage in goal average, that it seemed only an astonishing collapse would deprive them of the title. Jimmy had scored their decisive goal against Dunfermline Athletic at Celtic Park on 4th May to win maximum points, 2-1, after Alex Ferguson, now Sir Alex, had opened the scoring for the visitors. So his manager was now deeply indebted to a player who had sorely tested him throughout the season, for taking them to the brink of success. He simply could not have kept him out of the side for the last game, no matter what tactical considerations would apply. Whether it was to unnerve Celtic or not, on the morning after that Dunfermline match, a telegram arrived at Celtic Park which read, 'The chase is over. This proves that the Old Firm are not infirm. Congratulations on winning the Scottish League. Best of luck in Europe next year.'

It was signed by Rangers' vice-chairman John F. Wilson. Was it going to be such a formality at Fir Park? Rangers having completed their programme, Celtic just needed to avoid a 4-0 defeat in order to clinch the title. Their aspirations were higher than that though. Jock Stein was demanding the title be won by a clear points margin. It was evident to the players around him that that Jimmy was typically on edge. There was nothing surprising in that, since they knew that an explosion of effort from him would surface on that very basis. You could not have expected anybody to have been relaxed about this situation, and they required more than their customary trips to the toilet.

Looking down, as I did, from the press-box at Fir Park, which at the best of times induces a feeling of claustrophobia, you had to wonder at how so many people could crowd into such a relatively small space. Bertie Auld could hardly believe it. 'Twenty thousand? When we ran out on to that park that huge big terracing on the right-hand side began to sway and roll with everybody looking as if they would fall on to the pitch. We could see people climbing up on trees outside the ground to try to get a view. They were standing on a wall at the back of the terracing. They were on each other's shoulders. It was an amazing sight.'

In such circumstances this was never going to be a free-flowing game of football. I don't know where the phrase, 'playing ugly' originated, but you could make an argument that it was defined on that very afternoon, as Celtic, too conscious of the epochal significance of the occasion, were far from their best, but still good enough not to be in any danger of a defeat. Jimmy was hardly subdued, but against a very respectable Motherwell side he was making no serious impact. The goal came in the very last minute of this last game of the season. Technically speaking it was undistinguished, but it was the one which effectively started one of the most illustrious sequences of league title victories in the history of the game. Lennox scored it, Craig made it.

'I joked with Bobby about the goal,' Craig recalls. 'I told him my pass to him was so perfect all that he needed to do was to knock it in with his shins. But it made a perfect ending. We just relaxed and celebrated.'

Bobby Lennox points to the fact that a picture of him with

Jimmy, both holding large bottles of champagne, after the game, did not tell the full story. 'You might have thought that we all got steaming. Jimmy and I didn't. That champagne was purely for the press. He and I didn't touch a drop of that stuff. If we drank at all, during that time, you might have called it social drinking, very moderate amounts.'

It does indicate that his colleagues have a time scale of when these circumstances changed because of the reputation for hard drinking that was eventually attached to Jimmy so widely in his later life. This was the relative age of innocence. But what certainly was beginning to shape well, domestically, was that he now had thoughts of settling down, although that conventional concept would never fully apply to a man with such a restless personality. Marriage was on the horizon, the date set for 11th June 1966 in St John's Church, Uddingston. There was one slight hurdle to clear. Celtic were bound for the States in the preceding weeks that summer. Immediately after the final whistle at Fir Park, all the players had received injections for the trip.

Jimmy had actually been asked by Stein to delay the wedding in order to take in the whole tour of the States and Canada which would stretch from the Atlantic to the Pacific, but he wholly rejected that. And we should note that, at this stage, he was looking forward to the flight across the Atlantic, without realising of course that his view on that was about to change abruptly.

What followed was the five-and-a-half-week period when Celtic turned a close-season, outwardly innocuous, leisure trip into a character-building, player-bonding experience that simply came out of mixing the social events with the rigours of training, and playing against sides of the level of Tottenham Hotspur, who were part of the tour circuit. What they did was to stand in awe of the sights of America, intermixed with days in which they worked as hard on the pitch as they would mid-season. They did go out and occasionally carouse, but for Jimmy it was a totally non-alcoholic relaxation. Bobby Lennox, who roomed with Jimmy in every trip they made with the club, stressed that nobody stepped out of line.

'Because of what happened in later life, people think Jimmy was drinking heavily all the time he was with Celtic. That's just not the case. We would drink nothing other than cokes, nothing added. I know when teams go abroad in the close-season they can let their hair down and step out of line. There was just a different kind of atmosphere about this trip. And remember we were young players then, Jimmy was about to turn twenty-two. We were just not into booze. There was even a prominent photo of me and Jimmy with sombreros on, in the plane returning from the European Cup final in Lisbon. We have two huge bottles of champagne in our hands. But looking round at us from the seat in front is big Jock. If anybody thinks we were drinking the stuff in front of him then they must be crazy. But in any case we just didn't think about it. That wasn't when the drinking started.'

So during that summer, under the eagle eye of the manager, and with everybody conscious of how this man was changing direction for the club, they would have been risking peremptory end of career had they stepped out of line. The point is though that the self-discipline engendered lessened Stein's need for that sort of Stalinist clampdown. But it existed as a possibility, and that was enough. Unity of purpose was being established. That, however, did not prevent Jimmy from looking forward to cutting the tour short and marching down the aisle back home. Little did he realise what was in store for him. Bobby Lennox recalls Jimmy's last game of the tour in Vancouver, in which he made his mark in a controversial way.

'We were playing Spurs. We had already beaten them on the trip so they were up for revenge. We were in the lead 1-0 when they got a corner. In it came and there was a bit of pushing and shoving in the box and the ball ended up in the net. We all protested that there had been a foul on the goalkeeper but the referee allowed the goal. Jimmy went spare. He just roared at the referee right into his face. Then he turned away and would you believe, came back and gave the referee another mouthful. He was ordered off. But, at that, down the field came that great Spurs player Dave Mackay who insisted that Jimmy be kept on, since there were only about five minutes left and people had paid to see him anyway. Astonishingly, the referee changed his mind and allowed him back on. After that we never saw him as he headed for the airport.'

It was during that return passage that he suffered a trauma from which he never fully recovered. He was travelling with Ian Young, the full-back, who was also on his way home to march down the aisle, and in mid-Atlantic the aircraft hit an air-pocket. It dropped like a stone. They were serving dinner at the time, so meals were being spilled all over people. Hand luggage was flying from the racks, articles were spinning around the cabin like they were under a malevolent hand and Jimmy's inside had turned several somersaults. He claimed thereafter that it fell for two minutes. Perhaps terror might have exaggerated the time it took. But it only needs a plane to do that for only a few seconds, for anybody to arrive at a loathing for what the Wright brothers added to civilisation. Those who do not suffer this crippling fear of flying, which the specialists call 'aviophobia,' cannot begin to understand how defying the law of gravity seems, to some, like an offence against nature.

That, in a nutshell, is how Jimmy put it to me when he talked about his fears through the years. He was utterly convinced that it was all unnatural, and that disaster was lying in store for him. Even when he was forced by Agnes to fly with the family to Spain, in a future year, he could not hide his anxieties from them all, and had to endure a slam-dunk landing once when they were returning to Glasgow through thick fog, with his wife having to warn him, 'Don't let the weans see you panicking!'

But they did fly to their honeymoon in Magaluf in Spain, in that June week in 1966, where on two occasions George Best, hearing he was there, came around to swap tales with him, both of them resisting the inducements of the hotel staff to play with the waiters on the sands. Then came an invite from a certain colourful ex-Celt, Tommy Docherty, manager of Chelsea at that time, for dinner with the pair of them, during which the Doc joked that he might come seeking Jimmy as a player for the coming season. It was not taken seriously. A second proposal, from another source, was initially serious, as Agnes and he thought. The manager of their hotel, who spoke impeccable English, told him he was connected with Barcelona, who had been interested in his performances, and he had been asked to pass on a message to say that Barca would be interested in signing him.

On such occasions when a Celtic player was approached clandestinely by anyone, they knew, even if an overture was pointless, that if Jock got wind of it he would go for the predator and the player, like a hornet out of its nest. Jimmy, appreciating by now the biblical wrath which the manager could summon up in a trice, which could part the waters of the Firth of Clyde, preferred to say nothing, even jocularly, about it within Celtic Park. But you can tell from that, long before his marvellous month of May in Iberia in 1967, when he sent Spanish and Portuguese heads spinning, that he was well enough known by people around the continent who sought talent constantly.

They flew back from their honeymoon with Jimmy still in a high state of tension about being up there amidst the clouds. It might seem a curious contradiction to twin this fear of hearing the phrase, 'Fasten your safety belts,' with the fact that he had a life-long fascination with the global reports of the sighting of UFOs. Right to the end he took the reports seriously. He would watch endless television programmes and read countless articles through the years on the subject. Once he almost persuaded John Clark to go sit with him on the hills at night, overlooking Cumbernauld, and peruse the skies, for it had been reported somewhere that there had been prolific sightings of curious lights in that area. When John said to him, 'Can you see the pair of us being seen sitting there together in the middle of the night looking up at the skies?' After a moment's reflection they collapsed laughing.

His feet safely on terra firma again, he was about to embark on the greatest season of all.

Autumn 2001

The battery of test results came back to Professor Bone, at the Southern General Hospital in Glasgow. He alerted Roddy Macdonald and arranged an appointment with Jimmy. Knowing that his initial suspicion was about to be verified, and that Jimmy might need some moral support, the doctor decided to accompany him to his appointment. He took John Clark with him, as someone whose calm, well-grounded personality had been obvious to supporters on the field when he played, and even more so to his colleagues around and about Celtic Park, including, above all, Jimmy. The very man you would want with you when facing traumatic moments in life. But Roddy Macdonald was not surprised that Jimmy was simply himself, prior to the visit, brimming over with jollity, and, at least on the surface, quite unconcerned, even though he must have guessed that this was hardly a routine visit. The professor then spelled out calmly what had been diagnosed. It was a form of Motor Neurone Disease.

There was on the one hand the technical jargon which would have been above anybody's head. Then there was the stark and brutal explanation of the consequences of his condition that he would have to face up to. There was no known cure. There would be a gradual wasting away of power in all his limbs. There was no way of telling how long this erosion would last. He could possibly end up in a wheelchair in a matter of months. It was, by any standards, like the pronouncement of a death sentence. Dr Macdonald was aware that it took some time for the implication of this to sink in to the wee man by his side. There was no panic, no dramatics, no outburst of any kind. There was only the impassive, numbed look on his face.

The doctor and Clark decided that it would be better to inform Willie Haughey, the former Celtic director and highly successful Glasgow businessman, who was a great admirer of the former player, and someone who, in helping him out when he was experiencing some financial difficulties, had become close to him. They called in at Haughey's office after having taken Jimmy home, and spelled out the bad news to him. It is not likely he would forget that. 'I had to sit for a minute, maybe it was even longer than that, but just sit and think. Roddy was superb,' said Haughey. 'He wanted to tell me as Jimmy's friend, but he didn't spare the details and what the outcome would almost certainly be. He was great in having seen what was coming. The average GP might just have sent Jimmy home with a sore hand on that first consultation. And I thought, is there anything we can do about this, anything under the sun?'

He went immediately to the Johnstone house thinking that he would come across a deeply depressing scene. But the hollow look had gone. He was Jimmy again. Agnes, even now, feels guilty at not having accompanied him to the hospital that day. But there had been nothing in Jimmy's demeanour beforehand to suggest that he was deeply anxious about his symptoms. Nevertheless she felt devastated. Haughey, though, recognised that Jimmy was already battling against the notion of inevitability. 'He was confused. There was nothing morbid about him. One minute he would be babbling on about how it might not be as bad as the doctors were saying. Next minute he would look at you as if some deeper thought had just struck him. But not for long. He would be back chirping away again at you, talking about the future and what he was going to do: all kinds of things other than the horrors that might have gone through his mind. Not once could I say that I was sitting there watching a man in despair.'

Jimmy even phoned his close friend Billy Donald, who recounts how the conversation went. 'He told me that he had been at the

hospital and he couldn't remember the name of the illness, so I
heard him shouting to Aggie, "What was that they said I had?"
And I could hear Aggie shouting in the background, "Motor
Neurone." "Imagine that," Jimmy said, as if all he had been told
was that he had the mumps. Honestly, there wasn't a worrying
note in his voice.'

Bertie Auld admits that he knew little about what the ominous
phrase meant as well. 'Jimmy told me he had been diagnosed
when we were driving to the funeral of Jim Craig's father. He
just turned to me in the car and said, "The tests are back. I've got
Motor Neurone." I tried to crack a joke and said, "Motor Neurone?
I thought you only drove Mercedes!" How ignorant you can be on
these occasions. I didn't know any better.' Bertie need have felt
no guilt about that because humour was to be woven into the
fabric of resistance in the Johnstone household thereafter.

'I'm gonnae beat this,' he then told Bertie, with a sound of quiet
determination in his voice which seemed to reflect the great
self-belief that his colleague had always recognised, in his desire
to become one of the best players of all time. He said to Agnes
defiantly and with stark indignation, 'Would you believe that
bugger in the hospital said I would be in a wheelchair in the next
few months? Not on your life!' For the day after he had been told
he had one of the cruellest, most crippling of terminal diseases,
Jimmy demonstrated that spirit by donning his track-suit and
embarking on another long run, his arms, now merely useless
appendages, dangling helplessly at his side.

FIVE
The Rising Star

'The best laid schemes o' mice and men gang aft agley,' as Burns said, but not for Celtic under the sway of Stein now. Between the summer of 1965 and the day they stood in the sun of Lisbon on the 25th May 1967, there had been two years of a rebooting of their heritage, of allowing an esprit de corps to develop which owed more to man-management by Stein than simply mastery of tactics. And above all they were resilient and consistent, both elusive qualities of a past Celtic generation. The proof was there for all to see. By the end of October 1966 Celtic had won twenty-one games in all competitions to date that season. They were a juggernaut where only a couple of seasons previously they had been a three-wheeled wagon. Jimmy had unquestionably played his part.

I recall the innumerable games I commented on when he turned defence into attack with superb bursts. It was like watching a quick-change artist at work. First, Celtic would be on the back-foot (although not all that often) then suddenly they would be at the other end of the park, when the ball was at his feet. From time to time he was also continuing to test his manager's patience.

In early November 1966 Jimmy was dropped from the first team following the club's first setback when they had to settle for a 1-1 home league draw with St. Mirren. Not playing him in the next game, the Glasgow Cup final, nor against Falkirk five days later was explained in the next edition of the *Celtic View* when Stein went public with his misgivings. 'Some of our forwards' play against St. Mirren was just plain stupid.' He added that some players had '...persisted in going their own way, not doing as they were told in pre-match planning.' He then went on to add a rider that steps were going to be taken '...to ensure that Celtic came first and individuals second.'

It requires little effort of thought to work out to whom he was referring. Now when the manager had gone across to Italy to study the methods of Helenio Herrera, three years previously, in late 1963, he did not return with his head stuffed with new tactical ideas, as some wrongly concluded. Stein knew as much about modern football as the Italian guru. After all, he had employed a 'sweeper' in Willie Cunningham, his captain at Dunfermline, when they played in Europe, before anybody else in British football had known about that tactic. But what he did learn simply confirmed his own basic views, that success at the highest level was based on discipline, a rigorous acceptance of preparation and planning. But he was up against a free spirit in Jimmy. Jim Craig could see what you might describe as the artistic conflict between the two men.

'Jinky saw himself, essentially, as a soloist. I would say if you are as good on the ball as he was, as Ronaldo is, as Maradona was, then it's hard to think of the other players around about you. If you are of lesser talent then you need these players more. Remember he was a star, and sometimes that might suggest he developed a kind of prima donna attitude, but, in the best sense, for he was truly wonderful. There were certainly periods when he gave you the impression he was going through a prima donna phase. Counter that with the memories of that wonderful season, when we couldn't have done without the sheer brilliance he displayed. He could do so, because at times you felt he was oblivious to everything around him when he had the ball. He just wanted it at his feet. That was where he came alive. He was never really interested in team-talks. When Jock was speaking you would see him picking his finger nails at times.

'Jinky would sometimes beat a player and then go back and do it again just to show that it wasn't an accident. Occasionally I would try to give him support, and go up alongside him and wait for the ball to be played to me, but he would lose possession and since I was upfield beside him by then, we were stranded for the counter-attack and I would carry the can for that with the manager for having been caught out of position. And I was only trying to help out the wee man.'

David Hay, the outstanding Celtic midfielder of the 1970s, endorses Craig's verdict, speaking of another later stage of Jimmy's development. 'Jinky played like a prima donna, but didn't act like one.'

You can read into that a degree of tolerance from someone who could understand the licence you extend when you are watching command performances. However, although publicly Stein might have appeared to be handing out warnings and punishments in a despotic way, he was much more human than that. In a practical sense he soon learned he simply could not do without Jimmy, but cared for him in ways which might not at first have seemed obvious.

Examine some of the occasions when Jimmy wasn't selected for games in that season and, as Jim Craig points out, consider too the names of the left-backs with fearsome reputations he would have been playing against. 'We all knew certain full-backs would give Jimmy a rough time. Some of them would show him no mercy. He would be chopped. There were some thugs around in those days. So if you have an asset like that and you think you can get away without him, why take a chance of likely injury? He was looking after his health.'

It is also incontestable that Jimmy did not shirk any tackle, which is perhaps ironically the strongest reason for the kind of selective protection Stein provided. For a brave player like that could get himself hurt so easily. But a pattern had been set. Here we have a manager irked by a continuing disregard for the template of discipline and team-talks, but also willing to cosset him and use his exceptional abilities, and which he could not ignore when the crunches came. This was perfectly illustrated towards the end of season 1966/67. In the early stages the searing pace of Bobby Lennox and the unerring ability of Joe McBride to be in the right place at the right time to capitalise on his side's dominance in possession, was bolstered by Willie Wallace when he joined the club from Hearts in the middle of the season, all of which led to a crop of goals that gave Celtic the head of steam to keep them marginally in front of Rangers.

By the beginning of March 1967, they were two points ahead at the top of the league. It was from about then that Jimmy's influence was as distinct as a bugler sounding reveille. Not that he played sequentially in all that time. On March 11th, he was involved, five minutes from the end of Celtic's home Scottish Cup victory against Queen's Park, in an incident with inside-forward Miller Hay. He was only booked. But if you have a manager standing on the touchline waiting to grab you at the final whistle, as Stein was, then you cannot underestimate the implications of the booking. Hay was himself a colourful character who had been asked to funnel back in support of his full-back, who was being tormented by Jimmy. In doing so, he indulged in a fair amount of jersey-pulling which angered the winger. Eventually the referee awarded a free-kick against the Queen's Park player for one more offence, at which Jimmy retaliated by pulling at Hay's arms to get free. Thus the booking. You could only have seen that as a very minor offence. But Niall Hopper, the Queen's Park midfielder who scored a couple of goals in that game, recalls something vividly after the game.

'I can remember when we were making our way to the bus after that game we were astonished to hear Jock Stein screaming at Jinky. We could hear him saying something to the effect that Celtic had a reputation for good conduct on the field and he was letting them down.'

It went further than that though. For the manager had told Jimmy to stay on after his mates had gone to hear the outcome of a board meeting which was held at the instigation of the chairman Bob Kelly, who, it must be emphasised, was a stickler for on field discipline, and it was announced that Jimmy would be suspended for seven days as a result of 'misconduct,' a decision which forced his withdrawal from the Scottish League team to play their English counterparts the following Wednesday. It does suggest that Stein was perhaps looking for a kind of showdown. The incident on the field was of no great note, but seemed to be regarded as the perfect opportunity to draw a line in the sand.

So the club, by acting in that way, was not only looking for some form of contrition from their occasionally errant player, but performances which would transcend the ordinary. He obliged. It should be recalled that the Queen's Park cup-tie came on the Saturday after Celtic's amazing last minute victory over Vojvodina in the European Cup, which might explain why they looked drained at times, and had conceded an own-goal through Tommy Gemmell inside 15 seconds, and only came through the Scottish Cup tie 5-3.

For they were now performing on two stages, and the crowds were in raptures about their performances in which Jimmy was prime instigator in the best sense of the word. In their European Cup second leg game against Nantes at Celtic Park, on December 7th 1966, he scored the first and impeccably laid on the second and third in the 3-1 victory which ensured their place in the quarter-finals. In doing so he was also cementing his reputation on the continent. The nicknames were beginning to emerge. His pals had dubbed him 'The Flying Flea,' long before the famous 'Jinky' surfaced and took hold. A DC Thomson publication previewing Celtic's imminent European campaign first publicised the nickname.

This nickname was picked up by a writer for *France Football* who described him as 'The Flying Flea' but translated it into 'La Puce Volante' which made Jimmy look as if he was a gigolo on the Cote D'Azur. But the name had actually stemmed from our own domestic observations of him. However, that was to be scrubbed like a piece of graffiti from a wall, to be replaced by 'Jinky. Jinky Johnstone.' This summed him up as the figure in a green and white shirt, but it also reflected something of his basic personality. It had that alliterative lilt to it which suggested buoyancy and good nature: an image which suggested a little bit of the impishness of Puck, combined with the sprightly timelessness of Peter Pan, with a dash of the Artful Dodger round the edges. The latter quality was a necessity as he was now a marked man, a pest to every defence he faced up to. And after his seven-day suspension came not one, but several command performances on the field.

It was he who had won the corner in the last minute of the game against Vojvodina, on 8th March, with a typical surge, from which came the most famous of all the headers Billy McNeill ever scored in his career, a victory which took them through to the semi-finals 2-1 on aggregate, after having lost in Yugoslavia. A goal coming after Jock Stein had just turned to Sean Fallon in the dug-out, before that Johnstone run, and muttered to him, 'Looks like bloody Rotterdam!' where a play-off had been designated. His unpredictable winger had rerouted them to Prague instead, and the army side Dukla.

This occasioned one of the most interesting interviews I ever had with Jimmy. In writing my biography of Jock Stein I wanted to know something about the return leg of the Dukla tie, on April 25th, on the back of Celtic having won the first-leg at Celtic Park 3-1, Jimmy having scored the first and Willie Wallace the other two. I was intrigued by the game in Prague which was goalless and achieved the distinction, if that is the correct word, of being the most defensive game ever played by Celtic under Stein. Jimmy was in the throes of his illness when I met him, but his memory was as sharp as ever. I recorded what he told me.

'Nobody told me to lie deep. Bobby (Lennox) and I just couldn't get the ball. Dukla were great. I was bloody mad because I was chasing back looking to get into the play. Honestly, I was never asked to be defensive in that game. I don't think anybody was asked to do anything different. We were just outplayed for a lot of the game and big Billy (McNeill) and the rest of the defenders saved us.'

Others, including his closest colleague Bobby Lennox, echoed these thoughts. Lennox told me very succinctly, 'If the Big Man (Stein) set out a defensive pattern for us, then I must have missed the team talk.' Whatever interpretation Stein quickly imposed on the events of the game for the benefit of the press, the incontrovertible fact was, that after a goalless semi-final second-leg game, in which Ronnie Simpson had only one decent save to make, they were utterly deserving of being the first British team to have reached the final. And on top of that, praise was heaped on Johnstone by foreigners, obviously surprised that a player could exhibit skills normally associated with South America.

Robert Vergne of *France Football*, the newspaper whose poll of journalists voted Jimmy into third place in the *'Ballon D'Or'* awards, at the end of 1967, could not take his eyes off the winger whom he ranked with the great Garrincha of the Brazilian side in his 'irresistible dribbling,' and watching him in the first-leg against Dukla Prague, compared Jimmy's low centre of gravity as he bobbed and weaved past opponents as akin to 'clinging to the ground like a rock in the Clyde estuary.'

One of Vergne's colleagues described Jimmy as '...Le Joyeux Fantasiste' which, translated into Viewpark lingo would be 'A Wee Stoater.' And some forty years later, one of the finest players I have ever watched, the great midfielder Josef Masopust, captain of Dukla Prague, talked of Jimmy with an almost respectful regret that he had been the one who had done the most damage to the Czech's last chance of reaching the final, '...the Flying Flea Johnstone. He was amazing. We occasionally played man-to-man marking and we tried it against him. It didn't work. He did things no-one expected.' He should have paid attention to Nantes midfielder Jean-Claude Suaudeau, who had found the experience of marking Johnstone in that earlier round as, '...like trying to pin a wave to the sand.'

Such praise might insulate you against the possibility of a manager falling out with you again, and in a way I suppose, Jimmy and everybody else in the side knew that his ability, his growing reputation would mean that Stein would call on all his managerial powers to keep this incredible individual momentum to the maximum advantage. At that stage it is clear that Jimmy himself could appreciate like anybody else that they were verging on unprecedented glory. They had won the Scottish League Cup, beating Rangers 1-0 in the final back in October through a goal by Bobby Lennox in the 19th minute and now they were homing in on an unprecedented quintet of trophies [League, League Cup, Scottish Cup, Glasgow Cup, European Cup] they could not have anticipated back in August. As if to add to the growing significance of the players around him, Simpson, Gemmell, Lennox and Wallace were in the Scotland team which beat England 3-2 at Wembley on April 15th, a match Jimmy missed through injury. Then came the merry month of May.

They went to Ibrox needing a single point to win the championship for the second consecutive time. May 6th 1967 in Glasgow was a surly day. The dark skies offered only unrelenting rain. The weather was not assisting those persistent advocates of summer football. Just before going into the stadium we were offered the spectacle of Helenio Herrera walking through throngs of supporters after having been dropped off at the end of Edmiston Drive, and in his drab raincoat and unsmiling appearance he did not seem like the *eminence grise*, the innovator of effective negativity, but merely the insurance-man coming to knock upon your door for the dues.

Coming through the hordes of Celtic supporters at that end, he was lucky to a certain extent that most people knew him only by reputation. But press-photographers gave the game away in virtually surrounding him after which, as he made progress, he was given a good-natured preview of what the Lisbon support would be like in three weeks time. Inside Ibrox you could see from on high that the pitch looked like it would eventually resemble the 'glaur' of Passchendaele battle field. The whole setting seemed so reminiscent of that Scottish Cup final back in 1963 at Hampden, when Jimmy had looked so diminutive and initially insignificant, like it was no place for boys. But this was different. He was a much hardened character now. He had reached the peak of physical condition, standing only 5 feet 4 inches but weighing nine-and-a-half stones, with a broad pair of shoulders which had been fortified by his constant exercising, the buttresses against the occasional mauling he would take. By now defenders in the league, not least Rangers', knew he could not be intimidated.

This game has hardly been ignored by football historians in their overall assessment of Celtic's season. It clinched the league title, it equipped Celtic with a winning mentality prior to heading for Lisbon, it confirmed their status, long held by Rangers, as the premier club in the country and in miserable conditions it showed that Celtic's vibrancy of play could not be affected by Mother Nature herself. However, except for one particular moment, it is not a game that Jimmy mulled over all that much within the family home, where he did, occasionally, when prompted by his friends, talk about his fondest memories. Other games, one in particular, which we will come to later, stoked his reveries more. But I would submit that what we saw that day from him stamped his imprimatur on football as one of the greatest talents of his time, anywhere in the world.

Even supposing Lisbon had not turned out the way it did, and the subsequent benefits of that had not accrued, the ninety minutes at Ibrox that day would have confirmed his status. You have to understand that it was never easy for Celtic to go to Ibrox even against sub-standard Rangers teams, of which, in those times, there were hardly any. And they were up against a formidable and well-organised Rangers defence, whom you might have thought would have benefitted greatly from the increasingly marshy conditions. What we witnessed was a game turned on its head, and conditions mastered by sheer audacity. For Jimmy to have scored an equaliser within a minute of Sandy Jardine opening the scoring for Rangers, five minutes from half-time, is the kind of response which can produce trauma with its suddenness. This instant reply transformed Rangers from gradual dominance to a side which, lacking the flair of their opponents, looked vulnerably unsure of themselves in the second-half. Jimmy had tilted the game Celtic's way.

There was no sign in his play of the admission he made to the *Evening Times* in 1999 when he told them, 'I could never sleep the night before a game against Rangers. I used to wake up in a cold sweat.' He had obviously rid himself of that feeling by breakfast time, for his second goal could have been copyrighted as his best ever. On such a demanding, heavy surface, you might have imagined his legs would have been sapped as players ploughed over the unforgiving surface. Then you take into account the countless miles he had run, privately, around the banks of the Clyde, and the balancing techniques he had been obsessed by in his courting days, to come to realise that one day this would pay off. This was that day. Willie Henderson on Rangers' right-wing could hardly fail to be impressed. 'Our full-back Davie Provan got the biggest run-around of his life that day. He was a big, tall lanky man, and he just couldn't pin Jinky down.'

A Celtic fan and poet, one Owen M. Ferguson, more McGonagall than Wordsworth, but aptly catching the sense of the demolition, wrote an ode to Jimmy which contained this verse,

'One day we played the Rangers, with Jinky on the wing,
The Wee Man played a blinder, the crowd his praise did sing.
He punished this defender, Dave Provan was his name,
If Jinky beats him one more time he gets to take him hame.'

Jimmy was sure-footed and tireless. Now he was to produce the end product. In the 74th minute, from the press-box, I watched him pick up a ball way down below from where we were watching, near the touchline, feinting, first to the outside, then swivelling and cutting inside. On the other side of the pitch Bobby Lennox was providing an inner commentary to this movement. 'I remember feeling as if I should shout, 'Don't shoot! Don't shoot!' because I felt it was the kind of diagonal run across the field that when you get near goal you tend to get underneath the ball and it flies up and over. I just wanted Jinky to pass the ball. I definitely wanted it to be laid off. Of course he didn't.'

To prove there was no telepathic connection between himself and Lennox, Jimmy chose to do what had been in his mind all along. He let fly with his left foot and, from the surface which was giving him no real support, astonishingly he summoned up such a strength of shot that even the net seemed reluctant to get in the way as the ball ended high up there like a swirling, captive bee. Even though the game was to end in a draw, because of a late Roger Hynd equaliser, Jimmy's goal was of such significance that memory imprints it as a winner. The league was won, and up there in the stand the Argentine master of defensive football could have written an analysis of the winger, in his ever-present notebook, of epic length and depth, about the influence this wee man could have on a game of football.

Given what we knew of the meticulous preparation Herrera indulged in, paradoxically what he was noting in his book was partly to lead to Inter's downfall.

Jimmy was now a celebrated figure, although you would not have guessed that, had you seen him amongst his ain folk in Viewpark. He was simply the lad he always had been. In his first couple of years with the club, and beginning to be accepted as a regular, he could not resist the temptation to play in the public park with his mates. Sometimes there would be about 15-a-side in matches which one would guess would be lacking the subtle guiles of the sport, a public park which lamentably reflects the changes of mores in our sporting society, for no football is seen on it now.

A friend had to go and drag him away from these games for fear of doing damage to himself. His natural instinct to want to be involved wherever a ball was present conflicted with his professional obligations. He could not help himself. But in the weeks prior to Lisbon there had to be constraint. He was about to become a father for the first time, after all. Moreover he had been warned that he would face a personal opponent in the Portuguese capital who had the attributes of a dogged bounty-hunter. But, as a reflection of how little he was concerned, he told me years later, with a glint in his eye, 'When I heard that name Burgnich for the first time I thought it was something you ate.'

Winter 2001

Right from the outset he was up for the fight. The daily running was a cry of defiance. His legs were still powerful. He could run for an hour without feeling any strain. He was at it every day after the diagnosis of the disease, particularly after news of the illness broke in late November 2001. People in the vicinity became accustomed to the small figure pounding the streets as he made his way to the park. Agnes, though, was to learn that this was not as straightforward as Jimmy himself thought. Increasingly his arms were unable to maintain the synchronous running action. They were now, sadly, rag-doll arms. Or, as the specialists would call the state of them, 'the flailing arms syndrome.'

He never suffered the slightest embarrassment about this in public, and his neighbours became accustomed to his unquenchable desire to keep going despite the balancing difficulty. And that is where the trouble began. Agnes would sometimes take him to the park to save him running through the neighbourhood, and then go back for him after about twenty minutes. One day she arrived and saw a huge twig-like thorn sticking from the back of his head, with blood pouring down it. She adopted the light-hearted approach as they both did on so many occasions. 'Is that a television aerial you've got on your heid?' she asked him. It was more like a stiletto dagger though.

He had fallen into the bushes at the side of the park and it had taken him all his time to get back up because of the impotence of his arms, and, of course, since his arms were now virtually *useless he couldn't pull this large thorn out of his head. She had to prise it out for him. They both saw the funny side of that, as they often did, facing their problems. She was angry with him, though, for taking this risk. Not that this deterred him. Soon after that incident she went to collect him again, at the same park, but there was no sign of him this time. Agnes had been accustomed through the years to Jimmy dropping into the local pub for a pint or two, or more. And at first she imagined that is where he would be, because he was nowhere to be seen.*

Just as she was about to give up she heard his voice. She walked forward. There was a depression in the ground which had been difficult to detect from where she had been standing. He was on his back, unable to pick himself up because the arms would not function properly. He had been lying there unseen for about half-an-hour and quite incapable of gaining any kind of leverage to raise himself. There had been nobody in the park to come to his aid and in a way he would have been mortified if that had been the outcome. He looked utterly helpless. It was Agnes who was perturbed. She ranted at him and told him that he would have to stop the running. But she knew she would have been as well talking to the trees. Nothing could stop him. There seemed to be no safe area for him now though. Shortly after that, out in the garden patio one day, he stumbled, and his head slammed against the French window handle, knocking him out, and again without the use of his arms it was his cut and bloodied face which showed the evidence of the monstrous disability.

This seemed again to be more harrowing to Agnes than to Jimmy who, figuratively speaking, would simply bounce back up again, as he had when he was a player. But if this sounds traumatic and alarming, as it certainly was, there were moments when the pair of them made light of the preposterousness of some events coming out of his disability. He came back one day from his run and sheepishly announced to Agnes that to help his breathing he had spat out his false teeth in the park and obviously, without the use of his hands, he couldn't lift them back again. She tried hard not to laugh, but couldn't help herself. When she started, he couldn't help himself either. Leaving false teeth in a public park was to be put down as another exceptional Jimmy achievement. When they had recovered and wiped the tears from their eyes, she admits she slunk up to the park, hoping nobody would see her and that kids would not have found the teeth and were playing fancy-dress games with them. She scoured the park and there they were, lying there inoffensively, waiting for their owner.

Laugh though they both did after that experience it was also a chilling reminder, to her and perhaps to the world in general, that the norms most of us live by, in the most mundane ways, the simple tasks that we take for granted, become mountainous obstacles for those blighted by infirmity. It was not going to get any easier.

SIX
Fulfilling Dreams

His son James heard the name, Burgnich, mentioned often in the following years, not with any great affection, but with respect. There was another tale, though, which he heard more often. It is the one Jimmy would savour with his friends as well, over and over again, as if it marked some historic milestone in his personal career. It was not what people might have thought it would be. Of course there was the triumph of that remarkable day in Lisbon when Celtic became the first British club to win the European Cup.

The 25th of May 1967 stands out as the day on which the sun has never set for the global Celtic community. If there is such a thing as time standing still, then at the mere mention of the Portuguese capital, the mind leaps into its time capsule and you would think that Dr Salazar is still running the country, Mateus Rose is still a little-known exotic drink, Jock Stein is still limping around the field before the final whistle, the turf from the pitch is still being transferred to pockets and bags, Tommy Gemmell is still having his arms almost pulled out of their sockets by admirers, Billy McNeill is still slipping across the ground out of sight of the crowd to get to the podium for the presentation, and Helenio Herrera, the Inter coach, is still walking back to the dressing-room at the end, like a wee man who had turned up at the wrong wedding.

For the global Celtic community, Groundhog Day was invented in 1967. Nothing of that went out of Jimmy's mind, and hardly could. But there was a special niche there, in which was lodged something precious he would more often share with his family and friends. It was of a night in Madrid.

You would have thought that it would take a considerable degree of self-denial to have any other memory upstage Celtic's greatest triumph, but Jimmy paired if off with another. Those few weeks in the Iberian Peninsula were, much more importantly, a tale of two cities. Jimmy's assessment of his own performance in Lisbon was astonishingly lukewarm. He was never slow to tell his son James that. The Italian full-back, chosen for the man-marking role, was the kind who seemed to have invented the on-field Velcro connection. 'He kept telling us that he hated the close marking. Burgnich went with him everywhere. "It was terrible," he would tell us. "They never let up, followed me everywhere and when you were near the box there were two of them beside you. It was murder." Don't get me wrong, when he signed things for people through the years it was always about Lisbon, as you would expect. He was proud of that and everything they did that day. But there's no doubt Madrid was very special to him, very special.'

He was never wholly satisfied with his performance in Lisbon, believing he could have done better, and is almost discomfortingly modest in underestimating his influence on events. That view, his special memories of that month, his achievements, the ultimately self-defeating obsession the Italians had of him, and his purring over the name Di Stefano needs to be put into perspective.

The Estadio Nacional in Lisbon is now a footballing shrine. In May 1967 it was simply a rectangle of turf about to be fertilised by what cynics, in that year, might have said were impossible dreams. But to watch the green and white legions swarming through Lisbon and along that sun-drenched stretch of road from the centre of the city to the hilly enclave surrounded by cypress trees that day, the idea of defeat seemed a wholly illogical outcome. Never have I experienced so much optimism surrounding so-called underdogs for this final against the former holders and Italian champions, Inter Milan. It is interesting to note that it was Jimmy who influenced one of Stein's basic tenets of preparation for the final; his ordinance that the players had to hide from the sun. Anybody found sunbathing would have been set upon.

The Palacio Hotel in Estoril had every inducement known to lotus-eaters: marvellous pool, beautiful gardens, acres of space for lolling about, and yet the Celtic players, apart from their training stints and their evening walks when the temperatures were cooler, were ordered to stay in the shade. All this was because of the scare they had received in the USA on their tour the previous year when Jimmy had been laid low twice with sunstroke, his fair skin being so susceptible to that. It was frustrating, but it was necessary, and leant a clue to the meticulous preparation which Stein had established.

Down in the bowels of the dressing-room area, cooler than outside, there were attempts at normality just before kick-off. But as others have already pointed out, Jimmy, on the verge of a crucial match, was inwardly a nervous man. This was all to the good, in the sense that with the adrenalin flowing and surging through him, those nerve-endings would turn into allies, sparking him into the sort of action that could wreak havoc. From his own mouth comes a slight admission of that state of tension.

'There they were,' he was to reflect some time later, 'Facchetti, Domenghini, Mazzola, Cappellini ... all six-footers wi' Ambre Solaire suntans, Colgate smiles, and sleek black hair. Each and every one of them looked like the film star Cesar Romero. They even smelled beautiful. And then there's us midgets. I had no teeth, Bobby Lennox hadnae any, and old Ronnie Simpson had the 'Full Monty,' nae teeth top or bottom. The Italians were staring doon at us and we were grinning back at them with our great gumsy grins. We must have looked like something out of the circus.'

Like all great self-deprecators, such sentiments hide the less apparent truth of the matter. For although you might read these words as coming from an awe-struck player, petrified by reverence towards men who had dominated Italian and continental football with their Argentine guru Helenio Herrera establishing *catenaccio* as the modernist, if negative, way to success, there is the alternative thought. Because of what eventually transpired, it was as if the Celtic players sensed there was something superficial about these towering individuals, that they were male models about to be shown the rough and tumble of life by a group of locals boys with a healthy disdain for aristocracy.

The Italian sports daily *Stadio* actually identified what the Inter side themselves were thinking when their correspondent described him as, 'A real pest of a player, a feisty and almost unstoppable little winger, the type of player apparently born to be the despair of full-backs.' In fact, he turned out to be the complete team-player that day. Stein had once warned him, given Jimmy's tendency to sometimes overdo it by deliberately beating an opponent several times in acts of self-indulgence and succumbing to show-boating, 'You play for the team, or you play for the reserves,' in that stark but cogent way of his. So Jimmy's performance in the Estadio Nacional fitted in to a pattern that had been set throughout a season, which explains much of what occurred in Lisbon, although at times he was somewhat perplexed by how Stein explained his expected role on the park, as Bobby Lennox explains.

'It was at one of the European games, before Lisbon, and we were having the team-talk. Jock was laying down what function we'd all have and who we were up against, since he was really brilliant at analysing the opposition. He turned to Jinky. "You know," he said, "You could help us win this game even without touching the ball. You could keep running about and drawing players here and there, and making space for others. That would do a lot of damage and you wouldn't even need to touch the ball." But when we were standing in the tunnel ready to go out, Jinky turned to me and said, "What was all that about? Is he aff his heid? Me no' to touch the ba'? That'll be bloody right."'

For whatever team conformity there had to be under the tutelage of the manager, Jimmy's sense of individualism which had never changed from his schooldays was never going to succumb to what he considered to be tactical prattle. And that is precisely how the Italians fell into the trap of spending so much time worrying about what damage he could inflict on them. He achieved that by being what you might call the accidental decoy. He never saw himself in that role. To him it would have been like looking into a carnival mirror and seeing a distorted image. But it was working. He and Burgnich went round the field at times, like they had an umbilical connection. The Italian was to admit many years later, 'I will never forget how that little man made me sweat that day in Lisbon. He was for me like a red-haired Houdini, there one minute, gone the next.'

That is exactly what Stein wanted. Space had been left for others like Murdoch, Craig and Gemmell to exploit the gaps, which they clearly did. He was up against one of the best markers in world football, but Emlyn Hughes, the former Liverpool and England player, nicknamed 'Crazy Horse' by the Kop, recalls that after facing Jimmy once, he had felt, as Burgnich himself must have felt, 'like a tin of spaghetti hoops.'

Watching the game from the commentary position I was never aware of Jimmy's influence being nullified by this marking, as he himself largely thought. Looking back I can only picture him popping up everywhere. There were the same bursts, the same sudden gyrations, the same explosion of pace, but although he feels he never really burst loose from the close-marking, to explode into something individually spectacular, which he dearly desired, he had done his job. The late John Rafferty of the *Scotsman* wrote, 'The speed of Lennox was disconcerting but understandable to Inter. But the play of Johnstone was beyond their comprehension. It would have taken a Glasgow man to explain to them that this was the intricate virtuosity of street football played with a tanner ba' and raised to the sublime.' *France Football* magazine hailed Johnstone as 'Le Roi de Lisbonne' ranking him alongside his childhood hero Stanley Matthews, Garrincha and the Swedish player Kurt Hamrin in the pantheon of great wingers.

So that sunny day still lives on. I still see the flows of green and white jerseys, bleaching in the Portuguese sun, a seeming constant tide slapping against those darker inflexible figures chasing and harassing them. Back comes the memory of the jarring award of the penalty that put Celtic one down through Mazzola, which so aroused Stein, that at half-time John Fallon, the reserve goalkeeper, heard him accuse referee Tschenscher of being a Nazi and telling him that he was probably expecting a villa in the sun as ready payment for the award. Thankfully, the referee, even as a noted linguist, would have needed an interpreter for Burnbank English.

Stein had certainly been an admirer of Herrera after his visit to Milan years before. But in the tunnel at half-time they blew up together in mutual loathing. Stein lashed out at him for the negative and crude attitude of the Italians.

Back in Lanarkshire, at that time, in Calderbank House Maternity Hospital, near Uddingston, a swaddling babe was unaware of what all the fuss was about. Little Marie Johnstone was only days old. Her mother Agnes had had a visit from her father a couple of days before he flew out to the Portuguese capital. She noted that Jimmy was more uptight than she had ever seen him before and commented at the time that it was a good job she had given birth already, or else all the tension surrounding her would have precipitated it anyway. She could not travel obviously, like the other wives, so watched the first half in the television lounge before being called back to the ward to look after her baby. The progress for the rest of the final was then conveyed to her by nurses, one of whom nearly fainted watching the ebb and flow of the game. The game was being played during visiting hours, but Agnes had no visitors. She was sitting there on her own. Friends and family were at home watching the game.

That almost idyllic and fruitful environment contrasted sharply with Jimmy's involvement, there and then, in what was now developing into a bitter personal battle between two managers. That might also have been at the basis of what happened when Celtic came out after the interval and discovered they had to wait for minutes in the sapping 85 degrees heat before Inter appeared. Never did I think that Celtic would fail to score. There was a momentum there from the start of that half, which hinted at something positive to come, and had it not have been for an outstanding performance by Sarti in the Inter goal Celtic would have been in utter command by the hour mark.

Then came the goals. Tommy Gemmell's words to me, decades later, still paint the picture vividly, 'I was screaming for the ball. Screaming for it. I screamed three times for Jim Craig to square the ball to me. Then it came. If you watch a tape of the goal you will see something interesting. An Italian defender comes out to meet me. But then he stops about two yards from me and turns his back. If he had kept coming and kept facing me I would never have got that shot in and the whole history of the Lions would have been changed.' 1-1 after 63 minutes. Then a deft touch by Stevie Chalmers turned the ball away from Sarti in goal for the winner with only five minutes remaining. A mundane-looking goal, but invested now with historical significance. Personally, I recall that second-half in Lisbon as a celebration of the positive properties of sport, of a triumph of the master of optimism over a peddler of the dark arts.

Back in the hospital, with little Marie tucked in her cot and Agnes being told of the victory thousands of miles away, she pined a little for being left alone at that time. But she hadn't to wait much longer, for she was experiencing only a tranquil precursor to boisterous celebrations. The visitors came flooding in to see her after the final whistle in Lisbon. Her seven brothers, festooned in Celtic colours and waving flags, invaded the hospital like the riotous men in *Seven Brides For Seven Brothers*, singing and dancing around the ward. Agnes lay back and enjoyed the scene. 'They were all drunk. Happy as could be. They ended up chasing the nurses to try to get them drinking. I'll never forget it.'

So eleven Scottish lads, all born no more than an hour away from Celtic Park had done enough to retire on you would think. But, as a clear indication of the tireless, brooding personality of Stein, the following morning in the team's hotel in Estoril, the manager was answering a question by James Gordon, later of Radio Clyde, who was out there filming the *Celtic Story*. He had pointed out that it had been a marvellous season for Celtic, to which the man who had become British Manager of the Year, for the second successive season, replied. 'Yes, but what about next season?' Stein knew that celebrations had a time-limit. Not that he needed to convince his men of that, because in the banquet after the game there was no surge of triumphalism coming from the Celtic players as they sat at their table having a modest drink, and hugely enjoying themselves without any indication that they were rubbing any salt in the wounds of Herrera, who was sitting uncomfortably at a table close to them. The Argentine did not acknowledge Stein and left the restaurant before the soup course was over, showing – in the words of Jack Harkness of the *Sunday Post* – that 'This proud peacock of a man was showing himself to be a sawdust Caesar!'

All the lads wanted was to have a night out in the town, or back at the hotel, away from the manager for a while, as players do. I tried to talk to Jimmy to get a reaction from him about the whole day, but especially about being a father now. He was stone cold sober, but I don't think it had dawned on him how his life had so dramatically changed that week, both on and off the field, and the conversation, to be honest, was laced with lurid interruptions by his colleagues, now seeming like carefree kids on an outing.

Agnes, having been deprived of a trip to Lisbon, had a treat in store for her, as compensation. It came from a neat piece of handiwork by none other than the great Real Madrid player, the Argentine Alfredo Di Stefano, who took the trouble to come himself to the Palacio Hotel in Estoril to strike an agreement with Celtic before the final to play in his testimonial game in the Spanish capital. However, because the players had their minds on the task in front of them, and had understandably surrendered willingly to the boisterous, tumultuous celebrations over the succeeding days, some of them didn't realise they had to face up to a testimonial friendly until the following Monday morning, by which time they were back at training behind one of the goals at Celtic Park and the new European champions were bawled out by the groundsman Hugh Docherty for walking on to the pitch to collect stray balls. Such were the fruits of success.

You can imagine that some of them, looking forward to the reward of a decent summer break, were not wholly thrilled at the prospect of another game. Jim Craig had actually thought, on hearing they were to play in a testimonial match, it would be for a good cause like a lifeboat disaster fund out on some far Scottish coastline, the type of thing which Celtic readily did from time to time. But, Real Madrid! Were they really serious? Was this great club, record holders of the European trophy, planning an act of deflation, of imagining they could puncture what they thought was a new European balloon raised by these intruders into their special preserve? These thoughts arose naturally and would have been also in the mind of the manager who in no way was going to treat this as an ordinary friendly. In what you might describe as a subtle psychological move, he would make changes: John Fallon for Ronnie Simpson in goal, Willie O'Neill would come in on the left side of midfield, John Clark moving to right-half, Bobby Murdoch to inside-right and Wallace replacing Chalmers at centre-forward. This was a Celtic XI rather than the original Lisbon Lions. He was beginning to guard their reputation.

Wednesday 7th June 1967 in the Bernabeu Stadium was the night in which Jimmy really lived the dream. If you recall his personality, his uninhibited desire to be on a ball, his inclination to take on the role of soloist, and his love of the big occasion when he regarded a football field as much a stage as anything else, then that night in Madrid could have sub-consciously been what he had been waiting for all his life. Think of Sinatra at Vegas, or Pavarotti at La Scala in Milan and it gives you an idea of how he seemed to sense the power of the venue itself, and both commandingly and comfortably stepped into the limelight, entranced the Latin crowd, had them eventually shouting *Ole* to his every touch, and, if the organisers had allowed such a thing, would have come back on for an encore. So what did they see that was special?

Again, no more than Mr Mulligan saw from out of his window in St Columba's school, watching the five-year old keeping the ball off the hordes around him in the playground. Against some of the best in the world the appreciation was now of a higher order. Perhaps Jimmy gained inspiration from another incident which happened early in the match. Alfredo Di Stefano, much loved around the world, but particularly in the Spanish capital, played for only fifteen minutes before grabbing the ball, stopping the match, and standing with his arm raised in salute to the massive crowd before moving off. It was an emotional farewell for reasons other than the normal testimonial. For this whole evening was also an act of reconciliation between the player, the club and the supporters.

They had become estranged after he had left Madrid in 1964, denouncing his former friend Santiago Bernabeu for backing coach Miguel Munoz's decision not to renew the 38-year-old's contract. Bernabeu had declared that Di Stefano would never darken their doorstep again. But the prodigal was back. He was the man, after all, whose name was more synonymous with Real than any other, and in fact had become an iconic figure throughout Europe, as being the one who had twinned the cultures of Argentina and Spain to lift the club to unprecedented heights.

Ironically Celtic had tried to sign Di Stefano after his parting with the club. In August 1964, manager Jimmy McGrory, accompanied by John Cushley, not only a player with the club but also a language graduate, who would act as interpreter. But when they got to Spain they had discovered he had already signed for Espanyol. Many years later he told the Spanish newspaper *AS* that he preferred the city of Barcelona, 'more enticing than the rain and cold of Glasgow.' Jimmy told me much later, of that night, 'I felt choked. It was really sad in a way to see this man finishing with football. Here was a man I hadn't seen much of, but had heard enough about him to know he was one of the greats.'

You have to wonder if the scene that night in Madrid was a source of inspiration to the wee winger, there and then, in that he always believed inwardly, and without any hint of arrogance at any time, that he could be one of the best in the world.

It is not as if this was a bland football match. Bertie Auld and the Real inside forward Amancio saw to that. In the culmination of a running feud between the pair, Auld, who had been having his jersey pulled and his ankles tapped, blew a gasket and threw a punch at the Spaniard who retaliated and both were sent off. But although not bland, it was certainly more open. There was not an Italian marker in sight. Real wanted to play open football, and so did Celtic, which was a cue for Jimmy to run the show. Released from Burgnich, the gaoler, he turned this relative freedom into a series of runs which bewildered his opponents. He was the ultimate Jinky.

He would beat them once, and then torture them by going back immediately to see if they had improved any. They hadn't. He would jink his way past several players like Steve McQueen in *Bullitt*, weaving through the traffic of the San Francisco streets. They lunged at him, they tried to trip him, they tried to body-block, but he just wasn't there, he was always out of reach, in a performance that did indeed conjure up the illusionist Houdini. The crowd, accustomed to some of the greatest football of that era, understood he was now one of them, in the universal brotherhood of pure football, which up until then they had imagined was the sole preserve of the white shirts. Indeed at one stage during a match transmitted live on Spanish television, there was the amazing spectacle of the crowd booing Jimmy's immediate opponent, Pedro de Felipe, after the defender had bundled the wee man to the ground. Celtic's last goal of that overwhelming season was laid on by Jimmy.

Starting deep in his own half, he eventually fastened on to a pass, in the inside-left position, skipped past one defender, then wrong-footed two more, before slipping an enticing pass to Lennox who swept it past the on-rushing Junquera. 1-0. Celtic's 201st goal in a 65-match season. It remained that way until the final whistle.

Then came a replica of the Di Stefano farewell. Some people thought Jimmy had been presented with the match ball in recognition of his display. Well, he did get it in that sense. But not before he had acted himself. He admitted afterwards, 'I just saw it at my feet and lifted it up to the crowd who were great towards me.' That raising of the ball aloft to the crowd looked as if they had decided he was more than worthy to stand on the same podium as the great Argentine master. It was a performance and a result which makes it much more understandable why it even precedes the Lisbon memory in the Johnstone household's compendium of recollections.

For instance the *L'Equipe* correspondent Marcel Gillot, in his 8th June 1967 report on the match, revealed Real Madrid's stance in respect of the outcome of the contest – if they won they would trumpet the victory over the newly-crowned European champions, if they lost they could say it was only a testimonial match. Even though the Celtic players knew the astonishing attributes of the winger, and had seen it displayed countless times, they realised that they had witnessed something special that night, as Bobby Lennox declared in an interview with the Glasgow *Evening Times*, almost thirty years later. 'We murdered them 1-0. Jimmy Johnstone played out of his skin that night. It was a performance I can never forget.

'Real had been European Cup holders before we took the trophy and they made big noises in the Spanish press about how they were the real champions and we were just the pretenders. Jimmy took that personally and never gave them a kick of the ball that night. All the fans turned up to see Di Stefano but ended up cheering the wee man. I later heard that Real's directors asked big Jock about signing Jimmy, but he wouldn't agree. The wee man would have been a real hit in Spain.'

The final accolade came in the post-match banquet when Di Stefano gathered former colleagues like Francisco Gento, Ferenc Puskas and Jose Santamaria for a group photograph. The Argentine master then asked for Jimmy to join them. They stood together with the wee man for a photograph like they had just inducted him into an elite brotherhood. He looked a perfect fit for the men who mattered. No wonder, around the fireside in later years, it was that night which surfaced in his memory more than any other.

His wife Agnes, now enjoying the treat promised her, had watched him from the stands that night. It was one of the few occasions that she saw him playing. As she had missed the final in Lisbon, Celtic flew her out to Madrid in the company of director Jimmy Farrell and at the end of the game she and Jimmy were to embark on holiday. It was a departure which Jim Craig would never forget.

'There are many things I remember of that night,' he said. 'There was the breathtaking performance by the wee man. Just superb. There was Di Stefano's very emotional farewell. There was the massive banquet after, where I saw the biggest display of trophies I have ever seen given to a player, all dedicated to Di Stefano, from all over the world. And then there were the Johnstones. They had packed their bags for their summer hols. I helped them down the stairs to the taxi the following day, and I will always remember the look on the taxi-driver's face, after we had packed in all the bags, when I said to him, "Benidorm, please." He stood and looked at me in astonishment.'

As he might well have done. Benidorm was over two hundred miles to the south of Madrid, through the same torrid Andalusian heat which Don Quixote had to put up with when tilting at windmills. This journey was to be less sedate than the Don's.

'He just wouldn't fly,' Agnes says. 'I couldn't get him to change his mind, so there we were in the back of a taxi all that way. And we discovered the back door was being held together with string, so Jimmy was crouched down in the back, absolutely scared out his mind that the door would fly open. All that way to Benidorm. I'll never forget it.'

They survived, even though Agnes made sure she would not, under any circumstances, drive all the way back to Glasgow. They flew back with Jimmy not overjoyed at having to obey his wife. He was superbly fit when they returned. He seemed a mature man. He had a daughter. All in all, life seemed to be coming up roses. It was opening up vistas he had never thought possible. The household was stable. He was feted everywhere he went. But he was still the local man, and, to prove it, he would often go to a hut where the old men of the area would congregate to natter away and examine the issues of the day. Practically all of them were ex-miners. These sages were not backward in telling him off about his lifestyle, for word was getting around that he was spending much of his spare time in pubs. Most of such talk was only anecdotal nonsense, for his drinking at that time was merely of the modest social kind. But he was finding out that he was now under constant scrutiny as public property. He would sit there and take it all in, at least to show them that he could listen, if not exactly follow their advice on everything.

They came from both sides of the sectarian divide and he would love to chew the fat with them over that. They loved him. He felt at home with them. It couldn't be better. Or could it? For in late August he discovered, to his horror, that in the coming autumn a 14,000 mile return flight was facing him.

Spring 2002

Tears were absent, humour was everywhere. What others might have considered a form of abysmal imprisonment, a breakdown in a long, dark horrendous tunnel, Jimmy and his wife could illuminate, astonishingly, with shafts of wit that seemed to suggest that all they were facing up to were the sorts of quirks which life throws up to anybody. Nobody ever thought it was all pretence, but something fundamentally in tune with their own natures. They were on a learning curve, though, about how to cope with the disease and didn't know quite what to expect.

Agnes was continually fearful about what would increasingly cause problems. She knew there would be deterioration, but she didn't know by what specific stages, or what minute occurrences she would have to face up to. She was prepared for scares. Even so, one day she got a real shock.

As his running continued Agnes bought him a new black track-suit which he complemented, to increase his sweating, by wrapping himself in a bin-liner. He came back one day squealing in agony because he had wrapped himself too tightly. He had been sweating profusely. As she had now to wash him all over, because his arms and hands could not assist, she was shocked when she took off his trousers. His testicles had turned pure black. She took fright. 'Oh, my God! What a shock I got. Is this what happens to you when you've got this condition, I thought? I panicked. Even he got a right scare as he looked down at himself. Then I applied the soap and water and I saw it coming off. It was the dye from the track-suit. I tell you, we killed ourselves. We couldn't stop laughing.'

But there were now times when laughter could not possibly suffice. They attended the funeral for a friend one day and Jimmy was eager to show that he was perfectly capable of attending any public event, to demonstrate that he was still a stalwart of the community. Everything seemed to be working perfectly until they came out of the church. He was walking just behind Agnes who was about to open the car door when she heard a loud thud. In attempting to raise his leg over the kerb he had tripped, and his dangling arms could not save him, so his head slammed into the kerb. There was blood everywhere again. All the strength in his legs was, at times, a trap being laid for him if he could not, at the same time, have the counterbalance of his arms. He was screaming in pain. The last thing he would have wanted was to attract attention, but he was beyond Agnes's individual help. She had to call for some men to lift him and put him into the back of the car. She knew it was that which pained him more than the fall, which was bad enough and required five stitches in his head. It was the indignity of it all which really got through to him. It was the first time she saw him deeply dispirited, and as she puts it, so 'fed-up with himself,' in not being able to avoid a public display of this crippling weakness.

When I paid him a visit at about that time, I saw him trying to lift a cup to his mouth using the inside of his wrists and you wished it would get no worse than that. But it did. Even that movement became impossible. A simple mechanical aid therefore became indispensable: a straw. It became a symbol of the struggle to remain independent.

Jimmy was not so perverse as to imagine he could do without a great deal of assistance from time to time. But he was fiercely determined not to be seen to be utterly reliant on others. Anywhere he went in the early stages the straw would prevent the indignity of him being seen to be spoon-fed. In the house, and in the local pubs, to which he went for some modest drinking, they would have the straws ready for him. That which we would

Winning came early to the wee schoolboy. Even before he was ten, silver was reflected in his eyes.

...mmy (above right) and (right) with ...s classmates at St. Columba's Primary ...chool in North Lanarkshire.

Under the strict disciplinarian of the man on the left, schoolteacher John Crines, Jimmy flourished as a player.

His period as a ball-boy at Celtic Park gave him the taste for jubilation and triumph but it did not satisfy him. The desire to actually play on a Saturday soon got the better of him.

With proud parents Sarah and Matt, and the jersey he wore against Wales, in 1964, the first of his 23 internationals.

Willie Henderson and Jimmy were rivals all the playing days but it forged a lasting friendship.

In the early days with the Hoops he still had to resolve doubts within Celtic Park about whether he had the physique to sustain a hectic professional career. Had it not been for an injury crisis within the club, his debut on March 27th 1963 would have been delayed.

Never the best of travellers he had to put aside his fear of flying to participate in the widening European and global footballing scene.

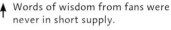

Words of wisdom from fans were never in short supply.

1 his wedding day on the 16th June 1966 in John's Church, Uddingston, Jimmy wore ecially built-up boots and Agnes, his new fe, wore small heels to ensure the illusion equal stature.

In the shamrock jersey in 1962, to indicate his involvement in the trial match in which he gave the seasoned defender, Jim Kennedy, as he himself admitted, 'the run-around.'

GW-SMS
CELTIC OUTSIDE RIGHT JIMMY
JOHNSTONE

In April 1969 he was scaling the heights. But, in opening a bar in the middle of Hamilton, he was both exploiting his fame and tempting fate.

Jock Stein supported Jimmy's right to make a living outside of football. But standing beside Jimmy's wife Agnes, his manager's countenance does not suggest wholehearted enthusiasm, and even betrays a little scepticism over Jimmy becoming 'mine host.'

The man who beat Vince Hill, of *Edelweiss* fame, in singing contests as a teenager in Jersey, never lost the impuls to serenade the worl

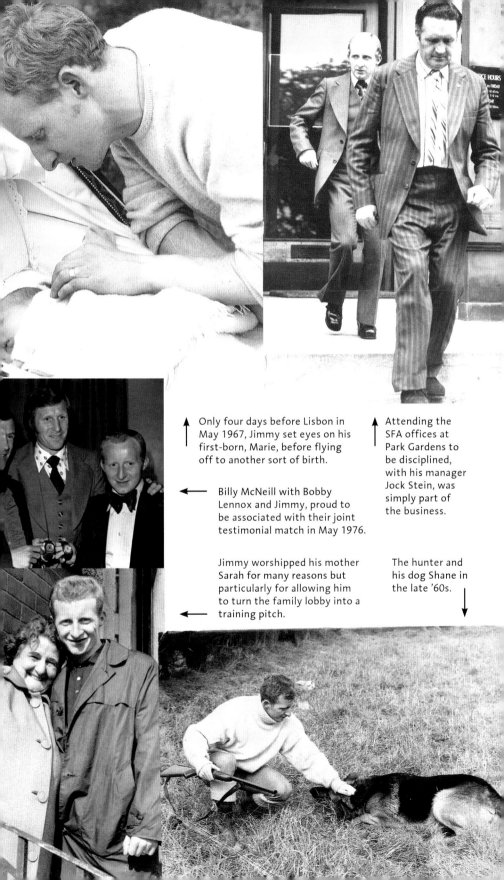

Only four days before Lisbon in May 1967, Jimmy set eyes on his first-born, Marie, before flying off to another sort of birth.

Attending the SFA offices at Park Gardens to be disciplined, with his manager Jock Stein, was simply part of the business.

Billy McNeill with Bobby Lennox and Jimmy, proud to be associated with their joint testimonial match in May 1976.

Jimmy worshipped his mother Sarah for many reasons but particularly for allowing him to turn the family lobby into a training pitch.

The hunter and his dog Shane in the late '60s.

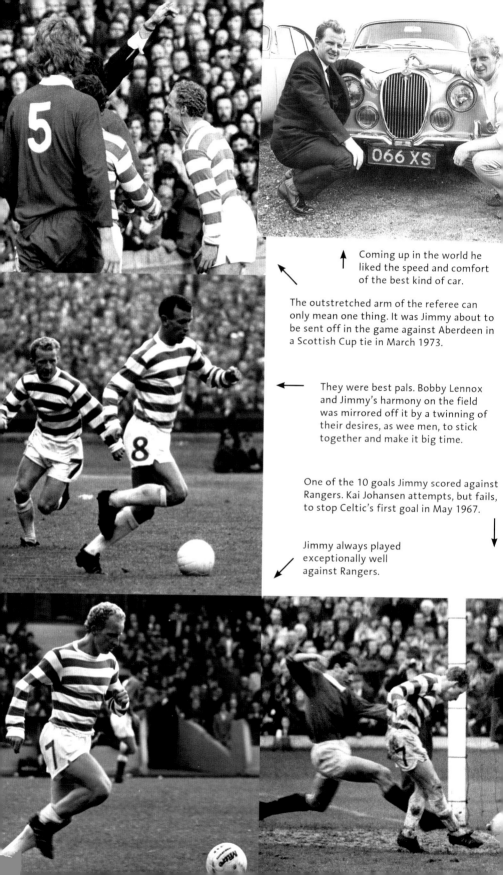

Coming up in the world he liked the speed and comfort of the best kind of car.

The outstretched arm of the referee can only mean one thing. It was Jimmy about to be sent off in the game against Aberdeen in a Scottish Cup tie in March 1973.

They were best pals. Bobby Lennox and Jimmy's harmony on the field was mirrored off it by a twinning of their desires, as wee men, to stick together and make it big time.

One of the 10 goals Jimmy scored against Rangers. Kai Johansen attempts, but fails, to stop Celtic's first goal in May 1967.

Jimmy always played exceptionally well against Rangers.

illy Mochan, seen here,
ght sometimes have
spected the wee man
d had a rough night
t he also knew Jimmy
rked nothing in training
e morning after.

the night of violence
Celtic Park on April 10th
74 in the first leg of the
opean Cup semi-final
ainst Atletico Madrid.

e last appearance of
e Lisbon Lions on May
1971, set against the
construction of the
nd at Celtic Park. Clyde
re honoured to be the
ponents on the day.

e Big Yin and Jimmy
re in mutual adoration.
y Connolly's presence
a Celtic dressing
m (as he was here
h Kenny Dalglish and
my before the joint
timonial match with
oby Lennox), was always
estament to his stature
hin the club.

With Billy Bremner
in the game
against England at
Hampden in 1974.

← The iconic image. The arm raised in triumph after that first Celtic goal at Ibrox in May 1967.

Small though he may have been he had the extraordinary ability to leap above taller men like Airdrie goalkeeper McKenzie and full-back Jonquin to head Celtic's second goal in the 3-3 Scottish ← Cup semi-final draw in April 1971.

Almost as a replica of the way he sat with his school team years before, Jimmy with the men who won everything in season 1966/67.

Turmoil. Jimmy prostrate after being hacked dow by a Racing Club Argentina player Hampden Park in October 1967.

Surrounded by the Lisbon Lions, Jock Stein (below salutes the crowd before his testimonial matc against Liverpoo in August 1968.

throw casually into a bin after sucking out of a carton, was for him a lifeline. The mind still brimmed with thoughts and sent tidal waves of sharp, witty conversation around a room. This was making the contrast between his sharpness of thought and the immobility of the arms, so much more aggravating, not only to him, but to all of us who saw him in that period sounding like the Jimmy Johnstone of old, but wrapped in this damnable cocoon. It was just that the brain seemed to be in denial that he had upper limbs, and was shunning them, for whatever mysterious reason.

Watching him with his straw was like thinking of him as a kid again, when he would sip his milk the same way in the classroom. What people were witnessing was the cruel reversal of nature – that he was being sucked back to infancy, in front of their eyes, his increasing lack of movement seeming to deny him a place in the adult world. But that world, in many strange ways, was about to offer help and sympathy.

SEVEN
Counting the Bruises

Celtic crash-landed at Ibrox on September 16th 1967. They lost 1-0 in their second league game of the season. It pained them. Losing any derby game contains its special mix of indignity and suppurating desire for revenge. But after Lisbon the expectations had soared. With a European upset coming so close to that, those unsympathetic to the club were quick to draw the inevitable conclusion that a bubble had been burst. Stein had not created a bubble though, he had poured reinforced concrete into the foundations of the club which might occasionally suffer tiny cracks on the surface, from time to time, but he knew that the more perceptive in the media would not be drawing analogies with seismic cataclysm when there was an occasional tremor under Celtic's feet.

Not that Jimmy had slipped into anonymity. In the very first game of the season, a League Cup game against Dundee United, he had scored the only goal of the match practically on the final whistle and although he missed the first league game of the season against Clyde, which Celtic won 3-0, when Chalmers filled his role, he was in the side for that defeat against Rangers. Indeed, he had given Celtic a marvellous opportunity to score a last-minute equaliser in that game when he broke through the Rangers defence, but failed to square the ball to the better-placed strikers Chalmers and Wallace. The anguish of these two strikers was plain to see at that moment. If that was not bad enough to suffer, one week later on September 23rd he was sent off at Celtic Park in the 37th minute, in the 1-1 draw with St Johnstone after an incident with Kenny Aird, during which a fist was reportedly raised, leaving the latter, '...in the next instant, lying flat on the turf, apparently out for the count.' Was a punch thrown?

You can draw a conclusion from the account of his friend Billy Donald who took a call from Jimmy that same evening to ask if he would drive him to the Royal Infirmary in Glasgow to the Accident and Emergency unit. He couldn't understand why that was necessary until he discovered that Jimmy had been wearing a signet ring which had almost become embedded into his finger. The ring obviously had not achieved that feat in a vice. It was much more likely that Aird had now a signet ring tattoo on his chin. Case closed. Now anybody who goes into that Royal Infirmary unit of a Saturday night will know from experience it can lend the impression that civil war has broken out, with queues of the maimed and inebriated looking as if the entire NHS system is having a nervous breakdown. The waiting room can seem like the nurses and doctors have fled into the night, never to be seen again. But it was here that Jimmy was to enjoy the plus of celebrity status, for a Florence Nightingale recognised him, and despite the broken bones of the other casualties lying there still to be attended, she shunted him in quickly for attention.

The plight of the signet-ring-damaged finger was, at least, an illustration of how committed he was to securing Celtic's supremacy. He was suspended for three weeks on the back of that, which deprived him of a third successive League Cup winner's medal. But given the extreme efforts they had gone through in the previous season, there was not the same verve about Celtic's early performances. And they knew that Rangers, deeply hurt by being elbowed out of the way as the major club in the country, would be ferocious battlers. That was shown in three encounters with them in five weeks at the start of the season which drew average crowds of over 85,000. Celtic knocked them out of the League Cup with an away draw and a home victory in their sectional matches. But Rangers victory in the first league derby of the new season, 1-0, meant that the Ibrox club would stay at the top of the league until the latter stages of the campaign.

Social changes were affecting the players. By now they all had cars. This gave John Clark the opportunity to chat to Jimmy when he drove him to the ground for training and games. They were opposites in many ways, and Clark was rueful about their differing approaches to the game. The brilliant defender was one of the most meticulous thinkers in the game. He was also a non-drinker. 'I would study pictures of our opponents,' Clark said. 'I would look at ways of how to cope with this player and that when I sat in the house through the week. I would go to bed on a Friday night at 9 o'clock. Then I would drive to Jinky's house in the morning to take him to Celtic Park. He would rush out eating a bacon sandwich that Agnes had made up for him and with his mouth full he would say something like, 'Is it Dundee United today?' He hadn't been sure who we were to play that day. He would then go on and play brilliantly, win the Man of the Match Award, and after the game he would ask me to drop him off at the Noggin Bar in Uddingston's Main Street, for a bevvy. I had to look at my own approach and ask myself, 'Where am I going wrong?'

But Europe had captured the imagination of the Celtic supporters, and every Celtic player I have known ever since admits that, from 1967 onwards, win, lose or draw, on European nights they were invigorated in ways which made the domestic scene so mundane by comparison. Not that they would leave the pitch on the evening of September 20th with eager thoughts of the bonus money. For they had suffered their first ever home defeat in European competitions at the hands of Dynamo Kiev who won 2-1, even though Celtic had been camped in the visitors' half for the entire second half, but never looking like gaining the equaliser. It was on the very day that the public had witnessed a special event at John Brown's in Clydebank, which prompted Hugh Taylor in the *Daily Record* to use an analogy in his summary of the game, 'Horrifying! It was as though the Queen Elizabeth 2 had turned over at her launching.'

They took out their frustration over that eventual European Cup exit, by turning vigorously on their domestic opponents and scoring twenty-five goals in the next five games, including a 5-3 trouncing of Dundee in the final of the League Cup on October 28th which bolstered their dented confidence and set themselves up for two matches which had excited the Celtic public because of their unique nature. For the supporters were about to witness an entirely new footballing culture, after which their team might possibly be claiming to be wearing the colours of world champions.

The dates had been set for the 1967 'World Club Championship' against Racing Club of Argentina, the South American champions. Celtic had no conception of what was about to face them, in travelling south of the equator for the first time in the club's history. Jimmy relished the prospect of thousands of miles up there in the sky like he would having his finger-nails extracted by pliers. But there was no ducking out of it. The first game on 18th October at Hampden Park had not turned out to be the kind of cultural exchange which could endorse the old sentiment that 'We're all Jock Tamson's bairns.'

Racing were from another planet. Perhaps we were all naive to think that they would come to try to win a match. Their football was shaped to lend the appearance of a cul de sac, through which for Celtic, they hoped, there would be no passage. They were fully aware that the Scottish and European champions had floored Partick Thistle 5-1 at Firhill on the previous Saturday, with four goals by Bobby Lennox which crystallised Celtic's power, and reliance on pace, as an expression of their natural instinct to attack. So the South American champions became obstructive, negative and nasty, with elements of crudity thrown in to suggest that this was a mere hors d'oeuvre for what would be served up in that elegant, but sometimes wild, city of Buenos Aires. The goal by Billy Mc Neill with a typical header from a John Hughes corner-kick in the 69th minute was the only advantage the club had to take with them in that long flight south.

All this flying was an ordeal for Jimmy, but he had to mask his concerns and tried to sleep for much of that journey. Argentina had identified his talent, and the clear indications were that in a country where t-bone steaks were guzzled in the cradles, he would be as welcome as foot and mouth disease. In fact, he became target 'numero uno.'

He admitted himself, later, that they were given ample warning at Hampden of what might occur, and this was illustrated by their first hours in the country when the Catholic players in the group were surrounded by police with guns and batons as they made their way to celebrate Mass, with the church only a couple of hundred yards away. And so it was wherever they went: shopping, sight-seeing, it made no difference. In such an undemocratic state as Argentina, ruled by a military *junta* even more viciously than Salazar ruled in Portugal, the country which had given them right of passage to South America, the brutality of the governing forces was the insidious glue which held the country together. Sport was no exception. A subjugated people, therefore, could take any advantage of public disorder, and football was the perfect excuse to vent fury of all kinds. Add to that the Latin temperament and you get what turned out to be the encouraging background for the Argentine players to try to create mayhem. Football, therefore, in such an unbalanced country was often riotous.

The Celtic players had a foretaste of that before the game when water-cannons were used on some belligerent fans who tried to approach the team bus as it entered the stadium on 1ˢᵗ November 1967. Police protecting the visitors? Of course. But any crowd assembly then was an excuse for the authorities to demonstrate their power to those who might seek to use the masses as a political surrogate. Everybody was skilled in brutality, how to use it, how to avoid it. The 120,000 crowd inside were well geared up to take their cue from what happened outside. When you go into the Avellaneda Stadium, you become instantly aware of how precipitous the terracings are. From the top it induces vertigo. It is easy to throw things to reach the pitch. And as a small band of Celtic supporters were to learn, it was easy to urinate from the top as well, as they suffered a sudden downpour not mentioned in the local weather forecasts.

And it was from somewhere on high that the first blow was struck against Celtic, even before the game started. An iron bolt came from within the crowd behind the goal and struck goalkeeper Ronnie Simpson on the head, just before kick-off. He went down like a stone. There was no way he could continue. A harassed John Fallon, the reserve goalkeeper, had to be got ready in that short time-span for one of the most torrid games ever seen at that level, and in which he performed heroics. One thing was amply clear, the Argentine players had decided that there was a wee man there they could bully out of contention. As many before them had discovered, they were utterly wrong.

The first scything tackle made on Jimmy was the sort that even the most liberal of referees back in Europe would have deemed worthy of a charge of assault and battery. It was intended to maim, not to dispossess. Any other player might have decided that since discretion is the better part of valour, it would be healthier simply to stay on the fringes of the game. Jimmy was not of that making, and the remainder of the match saw him use all his skill in control and evasion, to maintain his menace, and shirked nothing, even though some of his colleagues winced at the treatment he was getting. He was at the heart of the most dangerous Celtic attacks. He had a goal chalked off, for offside, in the early stages of the game, and shortly after was hauled down in the box for what seemed an obvious penalty, but which was denied.

Then the Racing goalkeeper Cejas took Jimmy's legs from him so blatantly that even the politically myopic referee, who came from across the river in Uruguay, could do nothing other than award the penalty. In a sense it was surprising to the players that the referee did make the award, as he had turned a blind eye to most of the aggression, reminding one of what Walter McGowan once said of boxing in Italy, that for a foreigner to earn a draw in a bout you had firstly to knock your opponent out. Tommy Gemmell's conversion of it in the 22nd minute only incensed the crowd and a warring atmosphere ensued. Some of the locals had dubbed Jimmy, 'El Chico,' which is as near as you will get in Spanish for 'Wee Man.'

But if there seemed a touch of affection in that, it was not much in evidence, as the frenetic crowd simply encouraged the Racing players to continue their war of attrition. Celtic had not yet knocked them out though. What followed was not just the winning of the game by Racing through goals by Raffo and Cardenas, 2-1, but a major dilemma for Celtic in having to face up to even more hostility. It was a points system that was utilised for this final, two for a win, one for a draw, a system that had nothing to do with aggregate score or away goals. What appears to us now as a quaint system meant that the third game had to be played on the other side of the River Plate, in Uruguay, and not Racing's preferred choice, Chile: principally because the proximity of these two nations, on either side of the river, caused political rivalry and continual social point-scoring off each other. In fact they were great rivals at almost any level in life, but especially dating back to the pain of 1930, when in the first World Cup, Uruguay beat Argentina in the final game 4-2, in front of 93,000.

But there was little doubt that Buenos Aires would export its hysteria across the water. It has become clearer, through time, that the Celtic chairman, Bob Kelly, did not want this third play-off game to go ahead. He was proud of the tradition of the club, that of striving to convey the purest of intentions in winning football by attacking skill. That did not mean that Celtic players could not rough it with the best when the occasion demanded. Indeed Stein had instilled that very toughness in them. But Bob Kelly thought that this was going too far, that the level of intimidation was such that even the most disciplined could hardly turn the other cheek under such provocation. Jock Stein effectively overruled the chairman. Bobby Lennox once confirmed to me that the manager had the backing of the players.

'We felt we were a better team than them and they could be beaten,' Lennox said. 'Maybe we were a bit naive to think it would be a straightforward match. But we wanted to go because we felt that outside of Argentina we could do it. If we were allowed to play it was going to be all right. But it wasn't about football though. They made it a battle and we fell right into their trap. Maybe we were naive about it all.'

Stein was to admit to me, in later life, that he did feel for the safety of Jimmy in particular but that his player was brave enough and absolutely adamant that nothing would prevent him from teasing them again, as he had recovered from the bruising of the first game. The chairman had been right though. As this was not yet an official championship, FIFA were keeping their distance from it, but should have intervened more firmly on all counts. The upshot was that the Celtic players, acting under extreme provocation, which made the first game seem as harmless as dancing the *Grand Old Duke of York*, could restrain themselves no longer and fought back.

Jock Stein had given a hint that he was prepared for the worst to happen, despite his desire to play this game, when he told the Glasgow *Evening Times*, on the day of the play-off, that his players would, '...give as much as they are forced to against the Argentinians,' adding that, 'We want to win the title, not so much for ourselves, but to prevent Racing from becoming champions.' In the match in Montevideo on 4th November 1967 in the Centenario Stadium, six players were ordered off, four from Celtic (though Auld refused to go), two from Racing Club and twice the police had to be called in to restore order on the field, when the three South American officials from Paraguay looked as though they could not control a tea-party in an eventide home. Jimmy was not the only one at the rough end of wild tackling or illicit shirt-pulling or sly digs in the kidney region.

At least the Argentines believed in democracy on the field as they shared out their cynicism in equal measures. One such was spitting. There was so much of it that at half-time Jimmy had to wash his hair as it was matted with spume. Tommy Gemmell, who was so incensed by the antics of the brutal and constantly spitting winger Raffo, decided to take revenge and skirting around a group of players, took aim with a kick which he described himself to me. 'I did a tip-toe through the tulips and I hit him one almighty kick in the bollocks. I can still hear him screaming to this day.'

Of course this is not what the Celtic management wanted to see, but privately they could quite understand that restraint can break down when men become painfully aware that anarchy exists all around them. Jimmy was still the target, and in trying to prevent being chopped in half in one skirmish, he had to push at the player who had him virtually in a half-nelson, and in so doing was promptly sent off by referee Rodolfo Perez Osorio. It just seemed to be in the South American script that such absurd moments would occur. In *Miroir Du Football's* seven page coverage of the final, Francois Thebaud, the completely neutral correspondent of the French publication, used the word *astounding* to describe his reaction to Jimmy's sending off. Its front page headline read, 'Racing of Buenos Aires, World Champions of Violent Play, Cheating and Gamesmanship!'

Stein, who throughout the game was beginning to realise that his chairman had been right in wishing to decline the game, said afterwards, 'It was evident to me at half-time that Jimmy Johnstone was our number one marked man. He could go round any Racing man on the park. They were out to get him, but I didn't think they would succeed three minutes into the second-half.' This sending off occurred when the winger was recovering from a 'sleekit' kick in the ribs he had had to endure, just before half-time, when the Racing goalkeeper ran all of forty yards, supposedly to commiserate with Jimmy, as he lay on the ground trying to recover from another assault, but instead, when the referee turned his back, kicked him brutally.

If anybody had any doubt about the lack of control by the official, then it came when Bertie Auld was ordered off, but blithely told the referee he was going nowhere, so stayed where he was.

Because, apparently if he had gone off, in effect it would have meant the referee would have had to stop the game because there would not have been enough Celtic players on the park. Bertie remained to the final whistle. To make matters seem more bizarre, after that Auld incident, the referee restarted the game with a free-kick to Celtic. The record baldly states that Racing Club won the World Club Championship by scoring the only goal of that match through Cardenas in the 55th minute. The whole sad saga was plundered by the media, as they sought to untangle the reasons for the chaos.

I recall having a drink with Jimmy about two years later with his friend Joe Reilly and even then he was stinging in his remarks about the South Americans, but equally so with the British media. 'They didnae give us a chance,' I recall him saying. Jimmy never sounded as sharp as others could be, when it came to dishing out criticism, because he was by nature a more trusting man who tended to look on the brighter side of life. But there is little doubt that he was affected by what the players, and particularly the manager felt, that the English media, and particularly Kenneth Wolstenholme's BBC commentary at that time, had a lack of understanding about what Celtic had to face up to in both games.

The English commentator had already been taken to task by the Celtic manager for the BBC's refusal to have live coverage of the first match at Hampden Park. Aggravated even more, Jock Stein went on the rampage after he came back home, particularly against the BBC, and refused to record any interviews with them for fear of them being editorialised, and would only speak live on the air. There was understandable anger, but it was also a means to build a public campaign to defend the image of the club, which some in the media had felt had been besmirched. On the other hand, when you spoke to Jimmy, you knew that this was not an orchestrated attempt at spin, but that since he had been battered and bruised in the process, this was genuine frustration that people simply could not understand the degree of provocation that had existed.

John Rafferty seemed to strike a balanced view, when he wrote in *The Observer* of 12th November, 'Their main condemnation is that they lost the championship of the world because they lost their heads, and that is the thought that they will have to live with, but in the circumstances to condemn them for this, and to pillory and castigate them and to forget their astonishingly good behaviour of the past year is shameful.'

They returned to Blighty, like soldiers from a campaign. They were to be fined by the club for breaches of on-field discipline. This was done by withholding the £250 pounds due to them, after their 5-3 victory over Dundee in the League Cup final prior to the trip. Jimmy certainly didn't complain about that, and indeed went so far as to say this, eleven years later, 'I must be mellowing in my old age because I find myself defending the referee who disallowed the goal I 'scored' in Buenos Aires. In his position, with a tribe of mental Argentinians in the ground, I would have thought twice about allowing it to stand. The people I cannot defend are the English press.'

Jimmy had been an eye-witness to a scene in Montevideo Airport, which he related with relish much later to me, when he claimed to have seen the Scottish journalist James Sanderson executing a perfect left-hook to the chin of an English journalist Peter Lorenzo, after some disparaging remarks about Celtic's lack of discipline had been made. It seemed to presaged the turbulent passage he and his colleagues would have to negotiate as they tried to work the nasty virulence of South America out of their system. That punch delivered to an English jaw seemed to summarise their own feelings of discontent about the entire trip, not least some of the media's reaction to it. It was Stein's task to redirect this frustration in the right direction. It was Jimmy's task to balance the demands of a restless manager with the responsibilities of being a father.

By now, though, there was barely such a thing as a private life for him. He was about as universally a recognisable figure, with his red hair and his bouncy appearance, as Charlie Chaplin's little man with the cane. He lived up to the effervescent reputation, and nobody could have been better company in a crowd, at that stage. He was popular in the dressing-room and in a pub. The Celtic players would congregate in some of their favourite hostelries after the game, as many others around the country with other clubs would do.

The bevvy was as natural a follow-up to a Scottish football match as a shower or a bath itself. Total sobriety after a match, for most players, would have been considered performing an act of penance for some reason or other. Drinking as the first means of relaxation after a game was, and still is, so ingrained in the after-match culture that little thought would be given to what the excesses of that might bring upon anybody. Harmony was essential in any dressing-room and, spilling over into companionship off the field, the route to the bar was driven by that herd instinct. The Celtic players in particular had every reason to look for relaxation, whenever they could, after gruelling experiences at the rarefied heights of world football. Although when I addressed this issue to Stein many years later he was as uncompromising in his views, as he was then, and spelled out his opinion graphically.

'I told my players from time to time that they should look round the Celtic terracings and ask themselves what all these people do that pay to watch them. They work down the mines, they work in factories, they put in a hard day's work just to afford to come and see all of you. I told them to keep that in mind if they felt like moaning about what they were asked to do.'

However, Jimmy in particular had special cause to ask to be wrapped in cotton-wool, and put out to pasture for a while, for mental and physical recuperation. He had suffered the debilitating fear of flying twice over an ocean that had given him a serious scare before. He had been hacked and kicked and spat upon in South America, and been singled out almost as if he were a piece of vermin. And during this season he was to endure the indignity of being barracked by so-called Scotland supporters, playing against Wales at Hampden, on November 22nd 1967, just a few weeks after their return from South America, out of their habitual dislike of his club. But there was an added dimension to it for he heard the name 'Henderson, Henderson' being chanted at him, simply because he had been selected instead of that Rangers winger. (It should be pointed out that he and Willie Henderson became very close friends eventually.)

Against all that he hadn't flinched. At least, on the surface he hadn't. But he would have been utterly inhuman if, sometimes, he hadn't felt despair at all this and looked for ways to anaesthetize himself against the recurring hostilities in life. Is it any wonder that he felt like that when he had the evidence of it scarring his body? For on the day after he arrived back from South America he went to see his old friend Billy Donald who could scarcely believe what he saw. 'Jinky took me with him to see his mother, old Sarah,' said Billy. 'When we got there he stripped down to his underpants and showed us his body. It was unbelievable. He was a mass of bruises, on his chest, all down both sides of his body and big welts on his thighs. And I remember him saying to me, "See these South Americans, they cannae take tae being nut-megged!'" His wit was a tried and trusted way of absorbing the blows. Joining his pals at the bar was becoming another.

Summer 2002

Willie Haughey was learning the hard way about Motor Neurone Disease. He was watching Jimmy's gradual deterioration with the special sadness which wells up from being a helpless bystander, desperately wishing he could do something to stop the erosion of his faculties. All he could do was provide everything possible in the way of creature comfort for him. His generosity, though, allowed him to pass judgement on others who trooped to the Johnstone household with the offer of remedies. As Haughey said, 'I never realised how many people there were in the world who think there is money in grief. I never saw so many witch doctors coming out of the ground. I saw so many people giving him false promises. So throughout his illness a major job was keeping the parasites away. There were great people who came to advise and offer practical help. There were others who just wanted to exploit him or send him on a wild-goose chase.'

Haughey also admits it was tricky to handle this, because he did not need to be told that here was a man who had been sentenced to death in effect, and who was perfectly entitled to seek out any source which offered a possible solution. One thing is evident. The word 'cure' rarely passed over Jimmy's lips. Much as he wanted to pursue any line of investigation, in all the suggestions and specific treatments put before him, he clearly did not want to articulate what his friends might see as a pathetic rejection of medical science, of the patently clear verdict that had been passed on him. Every so often he would contact the Motor Neurone Disease Association in Northampton by telephone, and talk to its top researcher Dr Belinda Cupid. She would simply tell him the facts.

'It is not our policy to advise people to avoid any particular treatment or so called cures,' she said. 'They are perfectly at liberty to do so. What we do is to let them know we are prepared to look at any evidence and assess it scientifically and by that method inform them of its suitability or if they are wasting their time. We do know how important it is for someone suffering this disease to keep trying for solutions.'

Her calm, studied approach was actually a source of comfort to him, albeit she was far from telling him that at any moment a shout of 'Eureka' would be heard from amidst scientific circles.

There obviously were others who more than implied that they could lead him to a cure. It was his open nature which made him susceptible to the 'witch doctors' as described by Haughey. He was not only prepared to listen, but to act, if he felt a case could be put to him that sounded credible. If someone tells you they can cure you then that is a huge incentive if you are lying there hoping to defy the odds. But one woman slipped through that guard. In the early stages of the disease she made contact and assured him that she had 'cured' someone who had suffered similar symptoms. It is not clear if she ever mentioned the success in relation specifically to Motor Neurone, but Jimmy was eager to listen, then try what she had in mind. It is difficult to see how any of us, under his similar circumstances, would simply reject an offer of this kind. Agnes recalls what happened.

'There were two women who came. They had this box, which looked like a small television set. They propped it up in front of Jimmy's face. She claimed that it sent out rays or something like that which would penetrate the body. The wee man just sat there talking away kindly to the women as this machine hummed away. But right in the middle of what they were doing in came Roddy Macdonald the Celtic doctor. I can remember the look on his face. He just couldn't believe what he was seeing. He got really angry with the two of them. He harangued them. When *they left, he lectured Jimmy about taking on what he thought were charlatans. But what could you say to the wee man? You couldn't bring yourself to stop him from trying anything.'*

Such a scene in that house crystallised the agony of the diagnosis of a terminal illness. On the one hand there is the delivered certitude of medical science. On the other there is a world of infinite possibilities, which range from the possibly miraculous to the fraudulent and, while there is still life in a body, the human spirit will navigate itself down even the weirdest route for survival. Jimmy did not want to offend his medical advisers but had he been of a more mean-spirited nature they might have taken a harsher line with him. It was because he was the irrepressible Jimmy that it prevented any lecturing turning into constant hectoring about what he should or should not do to combat the scourge. And Agnes would repeatedly say in explanation of his attitude, 'Jimmy being Jimmy, well you know what he's like...!'

That almost said it all, in his unswerving optimism. He was up for anything and his good nature shielded him from the censures of his doctors. This attitude produced bizarre moments and even, sometimes, hilarious outcomes, which rendered everybody present, despite the circumstances, laughing as if they were at a cabaret performance but not listening to a seriously ill man.

One such was when it was decided to administer a drug called Tamoxifen, which topped up Riluzole, the drug he was taking to slow down the process of deterioration. Tamoxifen had had some limited success in clinical trials and was primarily associated with victims of breast cancer. When Jimmy heard what it could do he was determined to try it out. Again Agnes has to resort to the phrase 'Jimmy being Jimmy...' in explaining the outcome.

'He decided he would double the dose he was supposed to take,' she says. 'He just kept swallowing this drug and felt it was doing him good. But then one night we were sitting watching television and I suddenly noticed something was happening to him. He had turned a strange colour, all over. I thought there was something

wrong with my eyes. I could hardly believe it. I got him a mirror to let him see what he was like. He burst out laughing and so did I. So I phoned a man who was very close to him, Ian Henderson.'

Henderson was shopping in Glasgow at the time and took the call on his mobile and could hardly believe what he was hearing, 'It was Agnes. She was laughing. She said, "You'll have to come out here Ian, this daft wee man has taken too many of these pills." Suddenly Jimmy came on the line, "Haw, sir, you'll have to come out and see me. What colour would I no' ever want to turn? What is the last colour in the world I would ever want to be. I've turned bloody orange!" He was still laughing when I got there, and as sure as I am sitting here, I can tell you he did indeed look like the Jaffa Man. Bright, bright, orange. We just sat there and laughed. What else could you do?'

There was a slight worry in the background that he would be left permanently looking like a grand marshal on an Orange march, but these were eased when after dramatically reducing the drug intake his natural skin tones returned. But once again humour had shunted out any other emotion. The man he had phoned was now to be his principal support throughout the illness. Given the ebb and flow of people and the varying recommendations for this and that treatment, dramatic or merely palliative, there had to be a responsible conduit through which much of this would pass. To call Ian Henderson a conduit would tend to imply some mechanical relationship. He was much more than that. His intimate friendship sprang from having shared with Jimmy severe personal problems with drink, which together they set out to conquer and which will be examined later. But, nevertheless, he was the man through whom much of the external relationships with Jimmy were conducted.

Many others were helpers, but Henderson was on hand at all the crucial moments of the battle against the disease. It is a role which will affect him for the rest of his life since his companionship meant he experienced, profoundly, the swing of moods between hope and despair. Indeed, Jimmy set the tone of the relationship by saying to his friend and helper one day,

'See if you read anything bad about this condition, son, don't tell me about it. I don't want to know.' It was his way of rejecting a constant negativity. However, Henderson remembers the occasional moments when Jimmy, despite the cheery disposition he displayed to everyone, had private moments of doubt and pessimism. 'You didn't get Jimmy downhearted very often. But naturally when you get your head on the pillow at night, it seems like an absolute nightmare. And he would say, "How's it going to be for Agnes, son?" And he kept on about that. He kept telling me about his worries for the family, everybody, right down to the grandchildren. He said to me one night, "What good am I to Agnes, son?" He was petrified she would leave him. That was preposterous, of course, but the thought was preying on him. When she went to her club for bingo he would always ask me to collect her. He wanted her looked after all the time by trusted friends, as if he was letting her down not to be able to do it himself. All these wholly unfounded fears stemmed from these moments of depression, but it did show you how this brave wee man kept his worst anxieties well-shielded from most people, including Agnes.'

Henderson did read something positive in all the literature which was now coming into the house. It was about a piece of research which Jimmy seized upon with enthusiasm, as it was coming from a really credible source. The information, and recommendation, came from Caroline Rafferty, now married to the broadcaster, 'Tiger' Tim Stevens, who had been a regular visitor to the home to offer alternative therapies including herbal treatment. There was a snag though. It would mean crossing the dreaded Atlantic, to New York City.

EIGHT
The Big Deal

The unique relationship between Jimmy and the massive Celtic support around the world was not simply because he could cast spells over a game and send them into raptures. They also knew, instinctively, he was one of them. He came from their own ranks. He seemed to represent them personally on the field. To be sure there were others who had signed up at Celtic Park as avowed supporters of the club. But this seemed to be different. He was a boy who had grown up to respect the institutions of school and church, seemed to have no airs and graces, and showed undisguised pleasure in watching the green legions in the throes of celebration. Furthermore, they had often seen him bullied, but watched him stand up to his detractors. Many of them wouldn't have known that, as a schoolboy, he had once stood up to three pupils in a playground fight and was still giving no ground before the headmaster intervened, and that when he had started work, in his teens, he was once given an ultimatum by his employer to cool his aggression after he had been found rolling over and over in the dust with a fellow apprentice as they tried to settle a feud. He knew how to defend his corner.

So nothing could have better defined the ideal figure to represent the value of true grit, which is the core attraction of a man in a highly competitive game. But he needed to live a personal, if not entirely private life, that was of his own making. For instance, he had become an avid hunter, so, he and Billy Donald would take to the wilds, with the simple but rather indiscriminate objective of, as Donald put it, 'Shooting any animal that moved.'

However on one occasion they went on to the Duke of Hamilton's estate, in Douglas, Lanarkshire, Jimmy with a Beretta 5-shot repeat rifle and his friend with a Russian single-barrel gun, which they had been able to buy at Lanark market for one pound each, and proceeded to blast away at anything with four legs. The problem was they had no permit. They had also forgotten that hunting has its own referees, with powers exceeding any invested in the men in the middle. So as the two of them, blasting away in the woods, were not entirely inconspicuous, they were nabbed by the gamekeepers and reported to the authorities. One of Scotland's leading lawyers, Joe Beltrami, managed to have any charge quashed and the hunting passion had to be subdued. From that you can deduce he badly needed outlets to discharge the tensions that football brewed within him.

He, also, had to ration the nights he spent at supporters' clubs or else he would never have seen his family, which between the Lisbon week of 1967 and January of 1971 would see three kids being born: Marie, Eileen and James. But as he regarded the fans as the salt of the earth he did make numerous journeys around the country to please them, which provided him with ammunition to criticise some of the players of later years who certainly never went near these functions. The hospitality put within his reach, therefore, was overwhelming, but in the late 1960s he could be described as a social drinker of no real consequence. It was not to remain like that though, as somewhere in that period he began to juggle the twin passions, that of his football, and his love of a hearty, raucous night in a pub.

The pace on the park had been relentless in fact. Rangers had gained a decisive advantage in the two-horse race when they had come away from Celtic Park on January 2nd 1968 with their two point lead still intact after a 2-2 draw which, you could say, had been gifted to them by a bad mistake by goalkeeper John Fallon, two minutes from time, to allow Johansen to score, a blunder from which Fallon's relationship with Stein never recovered. The manager was equally upset at referee Bobby Davidson's tolerance of some savage tackling on Jimmy by a variety of Rangers players. He was not the only one. Gair Henderson of the Glasgow *Evening Times* wrote, 'The Rangers tackling on Johnstone was both ruthless and reckless and Celtic won free-kick after free-kick when the outside-right was forced to pick himself up off the turf.'

Celtic's first goal in fact had come from an 18th minute free kick by Bertie Auld after Jimmy had had the feet 'swept clean away from him' some twenty yards out. The same writer also insisted that Rangers had employed a 'Stop Johnstone At All Costs' policy, '...from the start of the game he was hit hip, thigh and on almost every part of his anatomy, and it says a lot for the outside right that he took such punishment without retribution or loss of the temper that has so often landed him in trouble.'

That last phrase takes into account the occasions when he could stand it no longer and lashed out. You could say that the dilemma Celtic faced at that period was the degree of expectation that had been built on the success of the previous season. So after Celtic were knocked out of the Scottish Cup at home by Dunfermline, 2-0 on January 27th 1968, with their European Cup exit and their South American experience still painful memories, came that pivotal moment, which occurs in any season, when the initiative might seem to be tilting your way, or sliding inexorably away. When it came to appreciating this hint of a serious downward trend, Stein had the sensory ability of a smoke detector. He called a meeting with the players, a couple of weeks after the Dunfermline cup defeat, in which they were offered the opportunity to speak their minds about any team matter.

Knowing the certitude of Stein about the way he handled matters, I think he would have regarded this more as a group therapy session for the players, rather than allowing them to shape any significant team policy. Jimmy admitted publicly that, like a number of his team-mates, he had been off-colour for some months, when he spoke to Ken Gallacher of the *Daily Record* in March 1968, just before playing for the Scottish League against their English counterparts. 'For a spell I seemed to lose a lot of interest in the game. I know that sounds a bit silly, but it happened. Now it's all over. I've got back my appetite for football... All I know is that I want to play, and when I'm playing I want the ball.'

An echo of his very first day in school, no less. It contains the simplest of philosophies. To paraphrase words from another famous mouth, 'Give me the tools and I'll finish the job.' That is precisely what he did. He even stole the show in that League international even though, because of some goalkeeping errors, the Scottish League side went down 2-0. Up he went to Dundee on March 30th, with Rangers still narrowly in front in the league, and turned on another master-class of effective dribbling, not the self-indulgent sort, but that which tears holes in defences, inspiring Celtic to a 5-0 victory against United. A week later, against Hearts at Tynecastle, he out-jumped giant defenders and headed a goal which seemed impossible for such a wee man, and of the rest of his game Bob Patience of the *Daily Record* wrote, 'The wee redhead pirouetted and danced around opponents with such ease, it left one wondering about the two supermen [Florian Albert, the Hungarian, and Bobby Charlton] who managed to keep him down to number 3 footballer in Europe this season.'

The champagne was deservedly drunk in the East End Park dressing-room on April 30th 1968 when Bobby Lennox scored a couple of goals to clinch the championship in their 2-1 defeat of Dunfermline, in front of the stadium's record crowd of 27,816, thereby confirming that Celtic were not just three-in-a-row league winners but a new exciting phenomenon in Scottish football. They were there, in front, for the long haul, even though it had been a desperately close-run thing, with Lennox scoring a goal in the final seconds of the penultimate game against Morton to win 2-1, and Rangers being defeated in the very last game against Aberdeen at Ibrox, which was their only loss in the competition that season. It was hereabouts that Stein showed his hand to the squad about how he would treat Jimmy.

He decided to release him from travelling to the USA for a close-season tour. He had taken into account the fear of flying and the fact that Agnes was pregnant again. But he knew that this priceless asset needed to have his bruised body rested, his batteries recharged. Stein told the press, 'He had a very eventful season in several different ways, he was ordered off twice, he had those games against Racing Club when he was pretty badly treated, and there were other things too... All in all, it was a pretty heavy year for Jimmy.'

Relaxation was difficult for him though. He couldn't walk the length of himself without being waylaid, either in a friendly, hospitable way, or being pestered by those who simply wanted to be near him. He was, therefore, grateful to the manager for resting him from an arduous tour and his colleagues could see the benefit of that in the pre-season training when he returned. Although Rangers were to win their first game at Celtic Park since New Year's Day 1964, with a 4-2 victory, on September 14th 1968, Jimmy helped Celtic through that depressed aftermath with a performance which unfolded in a bewildering manner at Celtic Park on 2nd October 1968.

Celtic had returned from their first leg game with St Etienne in the first round of the European Cup two goals down. It was time to unleash himself again. The French were torn to shreds in the second half, when after Tommy Gemmell had scored from the spot just before half-time, Jimmy initiated a series of mazy runs, one of which in the 67th minute will be remembered for the number of opponents he left floundering in his wake, before squaring the ball to Steve Chalmers to score Celtic's third goal and thus put Celtic ahead for the first time in the tie, from which they were to go through on aggregate 4-2. It is time to dwell on that third goal and interpret it in the context of how, on so many occasions, a dominant Celtic side looked as if they might be battering themselves against a brick-wall, without any sign of a breakthrough, until their wee winger would come up with a manoeuvre the Wizard of Oz could not have bettered.

You might deduce, therefore, that Stein would have consigned a chauffeur, a valet, a masseur, and a podiatrist especially for Jimmy, just to keep him happy and indeed on the basis of performance-related results, who could have denied him the deluxe treatment? However, we were about to see in the short space of six weeks, after the St Etienne game, that Stein was not that kind of soft touch, nor was Jimmy of a mind to expect the cushioned life as a matter of course. He had to earn it. Their relationship, particularly defined in that autumn of 1968, goes down as one of the most absorbing in the history of football anywhere.

Stein had not wasted his early years in the mines of Lanarkshire in examining and absorbing how men related to one another. He had developed a respect for hard work, for camaraderie, for the necessary consensus among men about how to cope and survive thousands of feet underground. He brought that back up with him to the surface. He had only the most rudimentary education, and yet that early life experience gave him an uncanny perception of how men could think, and act, in all kinds of circumstances. He could back the right men ... if not the right horses. Even after that faltering start in 1965, when he thought Jimmy was not cut out to be in the new Celtic, and almost lost the winger to another club, it had become clear he was banking on the wee man making it big.

More significantly he had come to appreciate that he simply could not do without Jimmy. That was the bottom line. He was indispensable. It is not something Stein would ever have admitted to in such stark terms. But he didn't need to. His actions spoke eloquently of that. This was revealed to players and public alike in the next few weeks after the French side had been defeated. The manager was certainly beginning to hear talk that his winger was burning candles at both ends. He remained largely tight-lipped about that though, for Jimmy was performing acceptably well and had turned the tables on St. Etienne spectacularly. So media, players and public together, were ill-prepared for what happened on October 5th 1968.

The league game against Dundee United at Celtic Park on that day was flat, with the European hangover a kind of ghostly presence. Jimmy looked as if he was merely going through the motions. Perhaps there was also something in his play that suggested he was an untouchable, that he couldn't always be at the pinnacle of performance, but, that even in mediocre form, his position was secure, and that barring injury he would see out any game. That is exactly what Stein sensed Jimmy was assuming. But stories were being continually brought to the manager by various sources that Jimmy was spending too much time at the bar. This was fermenting within Stein. He had to believe that at least some of them were true. It was a delicate situation, just waiting to ignite, and it did. Stein had wanted to employ the over-lapping full-back tactic which he felt would destabilise United's defensive set-up.

This required Jimmy to part with the ball to Jim Craig coming up behind him. As Craig has alluded to, in an earlier chapter, sometimes the wee winger just wouldn't co-operate. And that day he was clinging on to the ball like a leech, leaving his full-back exposed too often. The team-talk had gone in one ear and out the other. Stein pulled Jimmy off with only twelve minutes remaining.

I will never forget the particular scene which ignited what had been a rather tedious afternoon. From the commentary position in the old Jungle I recognised that momentary hesitation of disbelief passing through Jimmy, as he tried to comprehend what was transpiring. Then when it sunk in, there was the quick spurt over the touchline, the jersey being snapped clear over his head, then the deliberately diagonal run towards the dug-out and the sudden angry throw of jersey straight into Stein's face. As I knew you couldn't even throw a surly glance at Stein without a volcanic response, my immediate thought was that the manager would end up in court later on a manslaughter charge. For he leapt from the dug out and, with that heavy-limp of his, set off in pursuit of the disappearing winger up the tunnel. The invalided Jimmy sitting, propped up in his seat in his house, years later, talked me through the sequence.

'As soon as I did it I thought, 'My God, what have I done?' and I belted up the tunnel as fast as I could, but I knew he would be right behind me. My first notion was just to run straight out of the front door without changing and head down London Road and just disappear for ever. But I got into the dressing-room, slammed the door shut, then locked it. I was about to dive into where the big bath was and shut that door when I heard him kicking the dressing-room door, then battering it with his fist. I knew then I was in deep shit. I stood behind the door ready to put my shoulder to it if needed, and then I knew I had to say something. I shouted out, "I'll let you in if you promise not to hit me!"

'Then the battering suddenly stopped, and there was a kind of silence, and would you believe, he burst out laughing at what I had said. He just laughed and I heard him walking away, because the game was still going on out there.'

So there was no blood-bath, thanks mainly to the quick-witted Jimmy, who did more than bar the door, but also I think gave the equally street-wise Stein the opportunity to defuse this in a personal sense. It was not that he could get off scot-free. He was suspended for seven days after that. But you had to ask the question as to what would have been the consequences for any other player to have committed that apparent act of *hara-kari*. There were some of the players, afield that day, who didn't need much convincing that, if it had been anybody else, they would have been shown the door for such a public act of flaunting the authority of a man whose public image was one of utter dominance. Stein had never been treated like that before. If ever an incident revealed the inter-dependence of two men it was this.

The manager simply had no intention of ridding himself of an individual who, with no disrespect to the excellence of his colleagues, was the conjuror, the special one, the one who could dance through a minefield with impunity. Stein did not want to see this wither on the vine which he was cultivating. Brian Glanville, in his history of the European Cup, actually tells the tale of Stein visiting his own mother who, allegedly, lectured him by saying, 'I think you are awfy hard on that wee fellow.'

Importantly, Jimmy knew that, however hard he was, the Big Man had the best of intentions. Performances in Lisbon, Madrid and more recently St Etienne were in the fine print of Jimmy's insurance policy against being ditched. But he was more the sort to want to pay back his debts to this big man, whom he also readily appreciated as being no fool and could read him like a book, rather than cynically exploit his exceptional tolerance. Jimmy was about to add a spectacular clause to his policy. It is when you come to the evening of November 13th 1968 that you feel that the special inter-dependence not only worked to perfection, but justifiably has passed into folklore.

And like all tales which do that, there are elements which either have been ignored or exaggerated, or simply have become part of myth. It is about how two men made what was described eventually as a 'secret' pact. Red Star of Belgrade were about to be destroyed by this stratagem. This is what Jimmy had to say to me some thirty years after that event. 'I was in having a pee at half-time in the Red Star game, when the big man came in and stood beside me. There was nobody else there, just the two of us. He just said quietly to me, "Wee man, if you go out there and change the game for us you won't need to fly to Belgrade for the next match," so here he was giving me a way out of what was always bloody terrifying for me. Now, he didn't tell anybody else what he had offered me.' In actual fact he had.

Stein, I learned few years later, had told the readers of the *Sunday Mirror* exactly what his plan for Jimmy would be, in his weekly column ghost-written for him by journalist Rodger Baillie. This is what he announced, in that article, on Sunday November 10th 1968, *three days before the home leg*, under the heading, *Jimmy Can Stay At Home, If...*, 'I have made this bargain with Jimmy because of his dislike for flying... If the score is less than four goals obviously we could not afford to take a chance and let him stay at home. But if he and his team-mates can crack the four-goal lead, then I am prepared to allow him to remain behind in Scotland.'

You have to bear in mind that it was thirty years later that Jimmy talked to me about it, and perhaps what he really meant was that at half-time, he was reminded quietly, about what they had already cooked up. The story has become legendary as an impromptu idea that sprung up at the half-time break; a version accepted as gospel by all and sundry. As the newspaper editor in the Western movie *The Man Who Shot Liberty Valance* said, 'When the legend becomes fact, print the legend.'

Whatever its origin, Jimmy sprang into dynamic life, after having that half-time chat, and as he described to me himself. 'I don't think I have ever tried harder in a game, and of course we thrashed them with four second-half goals, ripped them apart. I scored a goal only two minutes into that half, for I was really meaning business. In the last ten minutes I was back practically on my own goal-line, kicking and heading the ball away when the score was 4-1, for I didn't want to concede a goal and make it narrower or the Big Man might have changed his mind. And Billy McNeill was screaming at me, "Get down the field, you wee bugger, get out of here, get back up front!" because he didn't know about the deal Jock had struck with me, and I was damned sure we weren't going to lose another goal. Well, I did get back up the field in a breakaway, and when I scored the fifth goal and started running back up the field I was screaming at the top of my voice, "I don't have to go! I don't have to go!" and they were all looking at me as if I had lost my marbles, because they weren't in on this.'

His own description of his final goal is far too perfunctory and modest in that last quotation. It was one of his greatest, vying with that left-footed drive of his on the mud-heap at Ibrox, as the best of all time. His run at the Red Star defence, with only nine minutes remaining, in which he simply bewildered two defenders before lashing it into the net, put the tie beyond dispute. He had had a hand in all five Celtic goals in their 5-1 victory, scoring twice and assisting in the rest. Gair Henderson, in the Glasgow *Evening Times*, found himself struggling to do justice to that feat. 'Words run badly short when it comes to describing this individual performance. This was the night when he could beat half a team in one run. This was the night on which he produced every one of his conjuring tricks – and a few more that the public did not know he had up his sleeve.'

Even in the dressing-room, although the players were in awe of his personal contribution, they could not understand why he kept on about, 'I don't need to go! I don't need to go!' So stunning was his performance that less attention was paid to the fact that Bobby Murdoch had probably one of his finest games for the club that night. Looking back on the game, the driving force and accuracy of Murdoch's passing created the base for Jimmy's extravaganza. Not that Murdoch or any other Celtic player would begrudge the wee man the credit and praise that was heaped upon him. However, the deal over the exemption of a trip to Belgrade was entirely another matter, for which there were decided reservations.

As Jim Craig says, 'We were delighted with this result and Jinky was immense. But when we heard he had done a special deal and that he didn't need to fly to Belgrade, there were some who were far from chuffed about it. Remember there were others in the side who were far from keen on getting on to an aircraft.'

John Hughes puts it this way. 'Big Jock made that arrangement with the only man in the side who could respond that way. That sums it up in a nutshell.'

The deal had worked. What remains is the mystery of how the players pleaded ignorance of this when it had been announced in their own manager's widely-read column days before. Either they did not read the *Sunday Mirror*, for which they could hardly be blamed, or perhaps they were too scared of what they might read in the column, for fear of getting an unfavourable mention, which again is probably understandable. Some of the players felt they could have been left out of the trip as well, since they were so far out in front they were hardly likely to suffer a surprise reversal. So why would the manager need to pick his strongest side? Jim Craig, whilst holding the utmost admiration for the special performance they had witnessed, teased Jimmy about this.

'I told him that perhaps Red Star would produce a great performance from that marvellous winger Dragan Dzajic in the return leg, and do the damage to us that he had inflicted on them. So it would be safer for the right result if he went along. But he didn't buy that.' Stein himself took that teasing to a different level as Jimmy himself recalled to me once. 'The following day, when it was known by everybody what had happened between him and me, and it was even in the newspapers, he came up to me and said, "Look, the Red Star coach thinks it would be a great attraction if you played in Belgrade. He thinks the crowd would love to see you. I think he's right. I think you could turn it on there as well." Then he just walked away as if he had changed his mind about me flying. I ducked and dived for the next couple of weeks thinking the worst, but he was just having me on. He did like to take the mickey out of you. But he was true to his word. I never saw Belgrade.'

The fact is, the Serbs didn't want to see any more of the wee man. They were well and truly scunnered by now. The morning after the Celtic Park match the Yugoslav news agency *Tanjug* had commented that a team which their supporters, only the day before, had been calling 'The Greatest in Europe' had 'been buried alive by the exceptional player Jimmy Johnstone,' and a foreign correspondent for the *Evening Times* observed 'A City in Mourning,' describing the mood in the Yugoslav capital. 'Some of them refused to believe that the score-line was right.'

Disbelief was obviously difficult to disperse out there, as John Hughes recalls, 'You know they couldn't believe we didn't bring Jinky. They looked for him as we arrived at the airport. Honest to God, because they couldn't see him, they thought he had been packed away in one of our hampers and would suddenly appear at the game.' In his absence Celtic drew the second-leg 1-1, after having been in the lead through a Willie Wallace goal in the 76th minute. The demolition process had really been achieved in Glasgow. It is not that Jimmy had won the game single-handedly, but it certainly confirmed the fact he had won the hearts and minds of football lovers everywhere, on that purely individual level. It was now right to exploit that burgeoning fame. Time to cash in. He chose a route that was well trodden by footballers of his era wishing to make an honest pound or two. It is a pity he did not choose the 'one less travelled by,' for in going down the road of copying his contemporaries he made the mistake of a lifetime.

Mid-Summer 2002

On Sunday 4th August 2002 Jimmy boarded a plane to take
him to New York City. He was accompanied by the man who
was now guiding him through his battle with the disease, Ian
Henderson. They were now so closely attached that even though
the medical consultation was always available, he needed a
separate conscience, somebody who could guide, advise, refute,
agree, disagree with all the various routes they could follow, or
the types of treatments which might surface in an admittedly
tangled, complex world of pure science and alternative medicine.
Henderson had to strike the right balance between the orthodox,
represented by the doctors, and the unorthodox, which surfaced
from patently obvious charlatans, but also from many sincere
folk who wished to help.

His sole concern was to prolong the optimism which had made
Jimmy so astonishingly buoyant. So knowing that Jimmy would
baulk at no suggestion, but examine it and be willing to try
anything, there had to be an adviser close to his ear. Henderson
was the perfect fit. He was prepared to go to the ends of the earth
to help the wee man. Manhattan was not exactly at the ends of
the earth, but it did surprise many that Jimmy was prepared to
fly over the Atlantic again, given the previous scare which had
affected him for the rest of his life.

But he and Henderson were now excited by a project being
undertaken at one of America's leading research hospitals, the
Beth Israel Medical Center on First Avenue in Manhattan. They

were instigating a study into the effectiveness of a drug called Indinavir, which apparently had some success in dealing with Aids, given that it was thought that Motor Neurone Disease had a viral basis. The hospital was to administer this drug, and a placebo, to one hundred volunteers. Jimmy was to be the only patient from outwith the USA. Nothing, not even the icy waters of the Atlantic, and the inherent feeling that he was an Icarus-in-the-waiting, could hold him back from wanting desperately to participate in this.

To help him allay his anxiety about the flight they allowed him to search for what he thought would be the safest carrier; Jimmy selected Aer Lingus. He had heard from a source that the Bishop of Dublin had blessed their planes, so that was good enough for him. Thus fortified, they set out on a journey for which they had to 'beg, borrow and steal' as Henderson put it, to finance. Willie Haughey had been a great source of moral and financial support for him, but Jimmy and Agnes's pride would not allow them just to resort to the businessman every time they needed cash. They were met by a man called 'American' John, a member of the AA, who had been helped in his alcohol problem by Jimmy years before in Lanarkshire, and was only too eager to assist.

So in New York they felt content in having jumped the first hurdle. The money sorted out, the Atlantic crossed, the hotel secured, they now entered the Beth Israel Medical Center, amidst the towering skyscrapers, with high hopes. His spirit was exemplified by the way he had left the luggage hall, by resisting any offers of help, and despite the inertia of the arms, he was able to link two fingers round the handles of the bags, and with an obvious struggle, but triumphantly, he reached the friend who had been waiting to drive them into the city.

Jimmy was put immediately at ease by discovering that one of the two doctors leading the research, Dr Daniel McGowan, was a Dubliner, who knew everything about Jimmy. Nobody had needed to inform the doctor of Jimmy's status as a folk hero. The other doctor, Stephen Scelsa, explained in detail what would be involved: four separate visits over a year to assess the effect of the drug they were experimenting with. Jimmy would not be told if he had been administered the drug or the placebo. It was later understood that he had, in fact, been given the drug. The ambivalence of this he readily accepted, realising that any selfish motivation had to be subjugated to the need for discovery. The methodology was clearly explained to him. The seriousness of his physical state and the gradual encroachment of the disease was spelled out distinctly without any undue gravity.

This approach seemed to settle Jimmy, even though it had not carried any mention of possible cure. The fact that they were actively working on him was at least a positive sign. When they put it to him that they would need to take him into a special medical room and give him a lumbar puncture, he told them he wanted it, then and there, in the office. A lumbar puncture being perhaps the only technique in modern medicine which reminds you of a mediaeval torture, Henderson feared the worst. Out came the cold steel, and sitting in front of an office desk he had it inserted in him, without a whimper. The doctors could tell, from that one act, that he had guts. From then on he seemed to be in the mood for inspiration, from any source, and one of those near the top of the list was a place which could be called a sporting shrine.

They made their way up to Mickey Mantle's bar near Central Park. He wanted to see how one of baseball's greatest players was still revered amidst the commercial hurly-burly of this massive city. It was the memorabilia surrounding the walls which he appreciated most of all. There they were, Mantle's jerseys of triumph, proudly encased in glass, and all of them with that startling number which carried that special meaning for himself, No 7: Mantle's imperishable number, which no one was allowed to use after he had left the Yankees. The club simply retired that number. And Jimmy lent the impression to Henderson that the special number bonded these two in a kinship of the elite. This secular cathedral offered other affinities.

Mantle had had severe problems with the bottle before, during and after his professional career, and Jimmy did not need to be told that the fight against alcoholism required a special kind of strength. He drank only Coke inside there. There is no doubt that he derived great satisfaction from simply being in a kind of monument to somebody who had entertained so many, and suffered the consequences of celebrity status, like himself. The whole packed day, the jet-lag, the strangeness of the city, the consultation, the visit to Mantle's place seemed to have a profound effect on him, because he suddenly asked Henderson if he could be left alone for half an hour, because he would like to sit in prayer somewhere. They crossed to Central Park, and there in a quiet spot Jimmy sat down under a tree and bowed his head. Henderson left him there. Looking back over his shoulder he saw this tiny, almost crumpled figure, dwarfed by the immensity of the park, motionless, all the fighting jauntiness gone, simply communing with the God in whom he passionately believed. When he returned to get him, there he was, the smile on his face back again, and up for the fight.

They were now tourists. Jimmy took flowers he had had blessed in St Patrick's Cathedral and laid them at Ground Zero on a balmy August evening. They were in the downtown area around Wall Street, and looking upwards, as you tend to do amidst the all-enveloping skyscrapers, Henderson took his eye off Jimmy for only a few moments, and when he turned round he had disappeared. Gone. He looked up and down the street. He was nowhere to be seen. Henderson began to panic. Agnes had said before they had left, in keeping with her perky humour and which he now thought was prescient, 'If you lose him, you lose him!'

Jimmy might have been in a good mood again as a result of this first consultation, and, within the obvious limitations, full of vitality, but he was still a severely handicapped man in the city which boasts it never sleeps, and sometimes is not slow to take advantage of even the fittest tourist. Henderson had had instructions to phone Willie Haughey to report any news of the consultation. 'News quite good, but by the way, I've lost Jimmy,' was the message that he was now mentally preparing. Then he heard a sound which was very familiar to him. It came from an Irish pub he was just passing, as the panic in him was increasing.

It was the sound of the Viewpark interpretation of Lionel Ritchie's 'Once, Twice, Three Times A Lady.'

Inside he found Jimmy propped up in a seat, the arms squeezed to his side, with a drink in front of him, which he could still bend down to sip, and regaling the patrons of the bar with the still dulcet tones of his voice. On his head he was wearing a commemorative New York Firefighters' helmet in recognition of their bravery during the 9/11 terrorist attack. The sense of relief which Henderson felt was compounded by the astonishment he was to experience, when a bar which had few patrons in it, at that time of day, suddenly filled up, as for some reason the word had been spread that he was in there, in person, and before long he was singing to a much bigger audience of Manhattanites of Celtic persuasion. Given the undertaking he had made to take this trip, Henderson felt Jimmy deserved some time to relax and just do what he could manage to do, and be allowed a drink, without it getting out of hand. That is precisely what happened.

There was a day to come, though, which would linger in both of their minds as they resorted to the role of tourists, but little realising they would come across a series of uncanny coincidences, of the sort that make you wonder what, if any, message they might convey. Or whether you are simply ingenuous to put meaning to them. They had been given a lucky American dollar coin for the trip which they noted was dated 1967. The safety box in their hotel was numbered 1967. Later that day they met a man outside St Patrick's Cathedral, who wanted Henderson to take a photograph for him. In the conversation with him, they discovered he had fled to the States from Czechoslovakia in 1967.

After attending Mass in the Cathedral, Jimmy discovered a plaque which stated that the Cathedral had undergone some renovation in 1967. When they had attended the Beth Israel Clinic, they were told the unit had been founded in 1967. Then when they had bought a lottery ticket in that Irish Bar they had been in, it was revealed that it was for a poor children's charity, founded in 1967. Indeed they also recollected that the flight number on their outbound passage ended '67.' A total of seven coincidences. 'Spooky' was Jimmy's pawky response to all of that. But Henderson felt that the wee man was experiencing something deeper than conveyed in that glib initial response, and was in fact seriously affected. Nobody can really tell what those coincidences inspired in his mind.

It was perhaps as if New York was whispering in his ear that in Lisbon, in that year of 1967, Celtic were the underdogs and, outside of their own support, nobody gave them a chance. Such a thought might have touched on his own intransigent fight against the overwhelming odds, and given him even more reason to repeat his continual mantra, 'Ah'm gonnae beat this!'

Three months later, when they returned to New York for follow-up procedure, Dr Scelsa told Jimmy, in a voice much louder than a whisper, a startling fact, which made flying over the Atlantic seem like the thrill of a lifetime.

NINE

Pride and Prejudice

With a zeal which you could only associate with the old panhandlers of the Klondyke, Jimmy leapt at the chance to start a project which he felt would assuredly lead him to the mother lode. For on April 22nd, 1969, the day Jimmy started a three-week SFA suspension for an accumulation of cautions that he had received, causing him to miss the Scottish Cup final four days later in which Celtic beat Rangers, comfortably, 4-0, he had embarked on his first major business venture. Some would now say, in retrospect, that his opening of a large pub in Hamilton was to cost him even more dearly, in the longer run, than a three-week suspension from football. He had decided to link up financially with Scottish and Newcastle Brewers, to install himself as 'mine host' of a large pub in the middle of Hamilton, in Townhead Street. It had been called *The Met*. It was to be renamed, *The Double J*, months later. Most of the club's players and the manager came to the official opening, and photographs abound of what was a supportive and merry evening.

Billy McNeill joked to the local newspaper the *Hamilton Advertiser*, 'Jimmy will become as rich as the boss.' Stein, as one of Scotland's most famous teetotallers, nevertheless had had no reservations about mixing with drinkers, as some of his best friends were fond of a dram or two. But he had mixed feelings about this enterprise though. Undoubtedly he would have wanted the wee man to do well. He deserved everything coming his way. That is why Stein was there, smiling to camera, alongside virtually all the Lisbon Lions. After all, this was a natural route then for a professional footballer to take. Most of the prominent players in those days knew that alcohol plus the cash register could equal a summer house on one of the Costas or the Algarve. The pub always looked a safe bet. Stein, though, admitted to me that he felt this environment of punters, plus alcohol, would be as therapeutic to Jimmy as flights over the Atlantic.

Equally he knew he had no grounds for advising against a man who wanted to make an honest living. And he also knew that Jimmy was no fool. He certainly had chosen the locale well, and the brewery sponsors were backing one of the hottest personalities in the sports world. It seemed like the perfect combination. This was no sawdust hostelry, but was big enough to contain a public bar, a cocktail lounge and a function room which could be developed into a restaurant-cum-dance hall. There is a huge Celtic-supporting population in and around Hamilton, so when you sat there in the early days watching the crowds squeezing in, attracted by the name and the new facilities, the inescapable conclusion was that Jimmy had created his own gold mine.

Harry Hood, who became an influential and prolific scorer with the club and often played alongside Jimmy, also turned out to be one of the most successful of all ex-players in business, with various pubs and hotels that he owned. He could tell what the potential was here. 'Jinky had an absolutely amazing business, drawing fortunes in these days. It was always mobbed.'

Hood also knew Jimmy could not grasp the reality of what he had got himself into. 'He would take money out of the till for his own use. He was perfectly entitled to do so, but that's no way to run a pub business. You had to make sure you were covering your running costs or have someone there who was watching out for you, what was coming over the counter. And, you know, if you start taking money out of the till then it might encourage some others to do the same. I learned a lot in the business through Kenny Dalglish's father-in-law, Pat Harkins who ran various pubs including Kenny's. And there is one fundamental rule I learned. Don't run the pub as if it is yours, that you can do anything with it. Jimmy just couldn't approach it the right way. And this should have been the best place in Hamilton. It was the place to be seen.'

There is a world of difference between being no fool, and having the business acumen to run a place of this sort. Indeed, the bar came to be a reflection of the kind of personality Jimmy was. He was too kind-hearted and generous with his money, when he had it. This became open-season for an array of freeloaders who were attracted to Jimmy like moths to the flame. It was one thing to crowd round him for autographs, it was quite another to see them being transformed into spongers who took advantage of his hospitality, mercilessly. And as drink itself began to operate as a major factor in his life, Jimmy began to be one of his best customers: not classical business technique. So this was no Klondyke. This was the sinking of the Titanic, not just in financial terms, but in social habits.

You could not believe that a place with nightly throngs of folk, attracted by his name, could possibly fail. But eventually it was to gurgle slowly under the waves of financial debt, and had to be sold. It was only in the selling of it that it produced a benefit for him. An illustration of how he simply could not handle money, and of how his generosity was exploited, was on an evening when he was being driven back from a function in Glasgow by his good friend Jim McInally, a successful businessman in his own right. Jimmy persuaded him to pull into the Celtic Supporters' Association premises in London Road for a drink. Before they entered, Jimmy persuaded McInally to lend him £70, as he had no money on him. Inside the bar, supporters surrounded him, as you might have expected. Jimmy then proceeded to buy everybody in the place a drink. The £70 had disappeared in a flash. When McInally delicately brought up the subject that it was his money that had just vanished Jimmy replied, 'These people are the salt of the earth. They helped pay my wages in the past. I can't do enough for them. They had nothing in the first place.' McInally pointed out, jokingly, that Jimmy had had nothing as well when he had started that evening, but he also knew that he could hardly decry the gesture. McInally got his money back. This was no one-off phenomenon.

One night long after he had stopped playing, he asked Ian Henderson for £500. He was drinking at that time, and Henderson thought that he was going to blow it all on the booze and that he would never see it again. What, in fact, Jimmy did was to take the money and pay for the local Old Age Pensioners' Christmas lunch at the pub/restaurant owned by Harry Hood. Every penny was returned. If you multiply those acts of generosity a hundred times over in the time he was a licensee, you can see he was engaged in a slow process of self-immolation. Stein's nervousness over that whole project was well-founded, even early on. For it was also becoming clear to him that Jimmy was enjoying himself too much in his own new premises; that this great player was working into the wee small hours and occasionally with his pals. Something had to give. For all the genuine support he had given this enterprise, Stein was lying in waiting.

So almost like the eruption from a dormant volcano, the Stein-Johnstone relationship hit the headlines only a few weeks after the manager had lent broad smiles to the Hamilton venture. Any conflicts which had occurred at Celtic Park, had normally been handled delicately, even the tunnel-chasing incident, suggesting that Celtic could deal with these matters internally, without too much public fuss. But not this time. Curiously it was not over a matter which directly involved Celtic, but something which Stein felt did reflect on the club's reputation. It was when his winger had decided to leave the train at Waverley Station in Edinburgh and return home when he should have carried on for the game with England at Wembley in May 1969.

If a manager takes the trouble to come to the Scottish squad hotel and delivers boots to a player, who has inadvertently left them at the club, then it means he has serious intentions of making sure his player will represent his country. That is exactly what Stein had done for Jimmy on that occasion. But with one foot on the London train, he turned back. He had pleaded sickness. He had taken the trouble to phone the Scotland manager Bobby Brown, from Edinburgh, to tell him he could not make it. When he arrived home to Lanarkshire a message had been left to phone his manager at the park. Stein was fuming and ordered him to report to the club with a medical certificate. Bluntly, Stein simply did not believe him. Remember this occurred not so long after the jersey-throwing, and the suspension which cost him his place in a cup final.

Jimmy, at home, opened the *Scottish Daily Express*, and saw this headline, 'Jock Stein-Amazing Attack on Jimmy!' The writer John Mackenzie then went on, 'Jimmy Johnstone, Scotland's controversial, unpredictable winger was branded as 'unreliable' in a sensational statement from his own boss Jock Stein of Celtic yesterday. Mr Stein's bombshell came after Johnstone had been mysteriously pulled out of Scotland's Wembley squad.' And then added, less portentously than he had assumed, 'With that brief statement the international career of this brilliant, but mercurial winger may have come to an end.'

Later, Jimmy himself admitted that the meeting with Stein that morning left him sicker than when he went in to see the manager. He received the full wrath of the Big Man, which, truly, could be awesome. Think of a Niagara of bricks falling on top of you and you get near what a Stein outburst was. Why did he not believe him about his sickness? Why did he tell Bobby Brown personally that Jimmy was undependable? Why did he make his rebuke so public, like putting him in the stocks? Jimmy himself claimed, at the time, that the anger was only because Stein had been annoyed at playing the role of errand-boy with the boots, and should have been told of his sickness at that time, and certainly not have heard about it at second hand, as he had. No doubt that played its part. But it was more than that. Stein's deep affection for the wee man was largely something he kept under wraps but when it emerged it was like the greeting of the Prodigal. That being so, he wanted him to fulfil all his potential as a player, and part of that was showing off his wares on one of the best stages in the footballing world, Wembley Stadium. It would also have reflected great credit on Celtic Football Club. Stein was genuinely excited at that prospect, and essentially thought that only bubonic plague should be the reason for a call-off. He felt Jimmy's action was like an immense personal rebuff to himself. And you personally rebuffed Stein at your peril. There was also another factor which his wife Agnes and the manager both particularly understood, and indeed had the greatest sympathy with, but neither would say too much about. Jimmy did not really enjoy the experience of playing for Scotland. He never had. He played, of course, but not with the relish that was so necessary to his playing style. And that was result of the barracking he had received from so-called Scotland supporters, who simply hated him because he wore the hoops.

That did affect him more than people realised at the time. Stein, when he talked to me about that matter, regretted that, but his attitude was that the player should go out and prove himself, and, indeed, have the ability to turn the tables on the bigots. He might have seen Jimmy's reluctance to play in that game as rooted in wishing to avoid another bout of hostility. And as a culmination of the frustrations he had suffered trying to control the player that year, the manager had decided to change tack and hand out a dose of public humiliation to bring the wee man to his senses. Stein, in these situations, was always a careful calculator of consequences. As Jimmy later admitted, 'I must admit that I have given him a lot of trouble and worry in my time. Maybe it was his rather odd way of trying to teach me a lesson.' But the factor of booze can negate the best of lessons.

For, on May 25th 1969, only two weeks after that unprecedented public reprimand, and just a month after opening his new pub, a car failed to stop at a special roadblock which had been set up by the police in Hamilton. A high-speed chase had ensued and when the car was eventually stopped they discovered Jimmy at the wheel. He was breathalysed at well over the limit. The fact that it was a former Rangers player turned policeman who directed this operation, gave rise to a feeling amongst his family that this had been a deliberate ploy to get him: a sting, in other words, prompted by somebody phoning from his own pub to let the police know he was on his way. It may well have been pre-arranged, but John McKelvie, a former police superindendent, and friend of Jimmy's, insists that there was nothing as sinister as that behind the operation. 'They were only doing their duty,' he said.

In any case, unintentionally, the alcohol limit had been well exceeded. Jimmy himself felt that the book would be thrown at him, immediately, by the manager after that Sunday in May. According to Jimmy's words to me, when much later he had time for reflection, it certainly was not. 'He wasn't too happy about it, which I can understand, but he was great with me. Whenever I got into a bit of bother he would sometimes tell me to take a couple of days off, or he would say, "Don't worry about things. You just think of football. I'll handle things, I'll see about the polis." You know I think he had the polis in his pocket. They all respected him. It was astonishing.'

There is no doubting that Stein had influence in all sorts of quarters, but on this occasion the only success was that the punishment might have been worse, but for Stein ensuring he had the best legal aid. In July of that year, on the back of that incident, Jimmy was fined £50 and banned from driving for a year. However the *Hamilton Advertiser* of October 24th 1969 reports on

Jimmy's application for a new licence for *The Met* and the official reaction to that, 'Police mentioned Johnstone's conviction in July for driving with more than the permitted amount of alcohol in his blood. But Chief Superintendent James Campbell said: "We had no reason to say that he was an unsuitable person." Then he added, "Of course, Mr Johnstone knows that, as a licence holder, there would be serious consequences if there was any repetition of this conduct." The three magistrates – Provost Alex Reid, Bailie Hamish Wilson and Bailie John Blainey – all backed his application.'

But Stein had not been entirely forgiving of the incident, despite his initial sympathetic reaction. For he had dropped Jimmy for the first three League Cup matches of season 1969/70. You can tell from the report of the application that there was a great deal of local sympathy for Jimmy, albeit he seemed to be on a last warning. It is the almost mollifying sound of Stein's first words to Jimmy, in respect of the incident, that are of interest. They are not managerial, they are fatherly. That image persists. They are the mix of concern and frustration, but clearly influenced by his need to ensure that a talent was not being squandered: that this wee man had to be protected from himself, as well as from other influences.

Many of his friends who grew up with him believe that Stein was the resolute father-figure that Jimmy never had in his upbringing, capable of fluctuating between the stern and the considerate. His father Matt had been a decent man with the best of family intentions but clearly did not impose himself on his son as he might have. For if Jimmy's words are accurate, and there is no reason to think they aren't, then Stein, in private with the wee man, could be a more conciliatory man. Or, on the other hand, that he had come to conclude that Jimmy simply could not be tamed, even though at times he felt he could strangle him with his own bare hands.

Stein even used the phrase which I have heard echoed constantly among his friends and colleagues down through the years. 'Jimmy, being Jimmy...' You accepted these three words as a neat pen-portrait of an immensely likeable, but incorrigible free-spirit, answering only to his own instincts, and to no other. But there is another aspect to the relationship which John Hughes is certain about. 'Truly, I don't believe Jinky feared big Jock. Don't get me wrong, he respected him and all that, and Stein was a big strong man.' Hughes went on to repeat the mantra 'Jimmy, being Jimmy, he would just take Stein's outbursts in his stride and just shrug them off.' Bertie Auld goes further.

'I don't think he feared anybody. He had great respect for Jock Stein. But Jinky in his prime with Celtic was built like a middle-weight boxer. On the park he couldn't be intimidated. You might have thought that the likes of Bobby Murdoch, who was as tough as nails, could look after himself. Believe you me, nobody could look after themselves better than Jinky.'

There were others who were given the impression he did fear Stein, but perhaps they were influenced by their own feelings about their manager, who had a pair of hands on him that could strangle an ox. At times Jimmy might have shown what appeared to be fear, like the incident when he was chased up the tunnel. But these moments were fleeting. It should be stressed though, that even as the stories accumulated about his drinking, the players only recognised Jimmy as a dedicated pro who never showed any laziness in training sessions, nor shirked any responsibility on the field.

The season they had just played through, 1968/1969, leading up to the opening of the pub, had not turned out as they had expected, after that astonishing night against Red Star. For they were the victims of a smash and grab act by an Italian side whose main tactic was luring Celtic into a dark alley and then slipping the stiletto in. That's how it appeared, and indeed how it must have felt, when in the second leg of the third round of the European Cup, on March 12th 1969, at Celtic Park, after a goalless draw against AC Milan, in Italy, Prati, a lean, skulking figure, took advantage of a Billy McNeill slip, broke away, and slid in the only goal of the tie in 11 minutes. The pain inflicted was all the worse, for the Italians barely moved out of their half in the entire game. It was defeat by stealth.

By contrast with his spectacular nights, such as those against Red Star, Agnes relates that when he returned from any defeat, although there were not too many, Jimmy was almost inevitably surly and withdrawn. He hated it. He would skulk around the house not saying much. This was in marked contrast to his natural ebullience. Or, in later times, he simply would not come back at all, and head for the pub. Jimmy's mood on that day indicated that he cared deeply. There is nothing unusual in good players being bad losers. But it wasn't petulance. It was a revelation of the cradle supporter in him, that sense of faithfulness which many Celtic players had, of feeling personal betrayal to the cause, if you were on the losing side. He would shrug it off within a day, or perhaps even quicker than that, in the latter part of his career, when he would end up in one of his favourite watering-holes.

He had a particular regret that season, in having experienced a special defeat against an AC Milan side which typified the sort of negative football, contrary to everything the current Celtic side stood for. So, despite the glare of publicity, the talk of his drinking, the disputes with a manager who simply could not do without his exceptional talent, and being ousted from the main European competition by stealth, he still believed Celtic were in a class of their own in Scotland.

In fact Jimmy, along with his opponent from schooldays, John Hughes, had had an exceptional season, with nine and 16 goals respectively, along with innumerable assists, helping to bring Celtic their sixth league and Scottish Cup double. In their 4-0 victory over Rangers in the Scottish Cup final on April 26th 1969 they had inflicted on the Ibrox club their first Scottish Cup final defeat in forty years, and did so without Jimmy, who had been suspended for the game. Rangers must have felt they had been blessed in hearing that he was not playing, because shortly before, on April 5th 1969, in Celtic's 6-2 League Cup final trouncing of Hibernian, he had produced a performance which inspired Gair Henderson of the *Evening Times* to write, 'A demonstration of magic and deadly dangerous football... His best ever for club or country... This was football artistry at its best and the 74,000 crowd was entranced.' There was no danger though that the scribes would run out of superlatives, since more was to come. But not the sort they had hoped for at the end of the following season.

In that following season, 1969/1970, when Celtic just missed out on a quartet of major trophies, Jimmy would often excel, most memorably in a game which many thought exceeded his performance in Madrid. It was against Dundee United at Celtic Park on a chilly 17th December 1969 evening, in which he led the opposition to such a merry and calamitous dance that the Pied Piper of Hamelin came to mind. He piped the tune, while others scored, in the 7-2 victory. The fact that he unselfishly laid on the victory, without scoring, underpinned his value as a team player.

It was so impressive that the Dundee United player, Davie Wilson, renowned Rangers winger himself and Scottish international, waited by pitch-side at the end of the game, and lifted him aloft, as the ultimate gesture of admiration from one who knew better than any what the value of great wing play was.

However, Celtic's 3-1 Scottish Cup final defeat by Aberdeen on April 11ᵗʰ 1970 rankled. They felt they had good cause to be nursing their wrath about this because Celtic had undergone trial by referee. The official was Mr R.H. Davidson, who had a relationship with Jock Stein that was beset by permafrost. There had been some crowd trouble after the match, and Stein's voice afterwards could have been heard on the other side of the Himalayas as he lashed into a criticism of how the game had been handled by the referee. Lest there was an immediate response that this was simply sour grapes on Celtic's part, Hugh Taylor of the *Daily Record* reflected the general view of the press when he wrote, 'The highly arguable decisions of the referee, however, were shattering for Celtic's morale and there is no doubt they had an effect on their play afterwards.'

Celtic, as a whole though, were now greatly experienced at all levels, and their flint-like resolve had been exemplified best when Jimmy scored the final goal two minutes from time, in the Scottish Cup Third Round tie against Rangers at Celtic Park on 21ˢᵗ February 1970, to put it beyond dispute at 3-1. It was Jimmy's goal which sparked off a furious reaction at the Rangers end of the ground. For in the ensuing crowd trouble, and the arrests around the ground, the SFA were prompted to summon all 22 players, and the managers, to appear in front of them to lecture them on their behaviour, for indeed it had been a game fraught with wild tackles. It did seem odd, though, that if you score a decisive goal, as Jimmy had done, you are somehow implicit in inciting disorder. But leaving that aside for a moment, what was the result of that judiciary sit-in with the players? Jimmy was there, in the dressing-room, when next they played Rangers and witnessed the scene described by Jim Craig.

'Before the match Jock came in with Sir Robert and asked us all to be quiet, that the chairman wanted to say something. He spoke in a dignified manner about how Celtic did not want its reputation besmirched, that the eyes of the world were upon us and that under no circumstances would he condone any bad behaviour by any Celtic player. He wanted us to be fair and that our good name was at stake. Then he turned and walked out. Jock kept the door open and peeked out to make sure the chairman had disappeared and obviously out of earshot, slammed the door shut, turned to us and said, "You can forget that crap. Get stuck in. Any fifty-fifty ball will be yours. Anybody drawing back will be answerable to me!"'

But ambitions had risen above these parochial squabbles. You could tell that winning in Scotland was not enough for them, even though, on their way to winning the championship, they lost only four matches, with Rangers left a massive twelve points behind. They were openly drugged by the heady atmosphere of European nights at Celtic Park. They could not get enough of them. The motivation to sustain that level of achievement was almost overpowering. Over and above that, in March 1970, Jimmy's widespread popularity around the Continent was demonstrated on the night Celtic got around to playing in Florence, against Fiorentina, in the quarter-final of the European Cup second-leg.

They qualified for the semi-finals with a display in which Malcolm Munro of the *Evening Times* recognised that the winger had come of age, with a mature display, by working in tandem with Bertie Auld to help relieve the pressure on the Celtic defence, running with the ball deep into enemy territory. Celtic, three up from the first-leg, did go down 1-0 in the Stadio Comunale, but watching from the commentary position I could tell that Jimmy was adhering to the game plan, and that his side were never in any danger of relinquishing their Celtic Park lead. But that was not the only factor I noticed, as indeed did Malcolm Munro. At the final whistle I saw the extraordinary spectacle of the ball-boys swarming around Jimmy imploring him to surrender his jersey as a souvenir. Flaunting the convention of swapping with opponents, he relented and surrendered it to one of the urchins, who, as Munro noted, in Glasgow parlance, had to 'stick it up his 'juke' and run for his life.'

That night, in the streets of Florence, kids could have swapped about twenty cigarette cards of any of the local players, for one of Jinky. That Celtic had won through to that game in Italy by virtue of the toss of a coin, in the referee's room in the Stadium of Light in Lisbon, after an aggregate 3-3 tie with Benfica, perhaps indicated that Celtic had their name on the trophy again. But now they were threatened by invaders from the other side of Hadrian's Wall.

Winter 2002

The words which slipped out of the mouth of Dr Scelsa in that second visit to New York, four months later, were absorbed by Jimmy like he had just partaken of the elixir of everlasting life. The doctor first explained the term for the condition from which he was suffering. 'Brachial Amyoytrophic Scelerosis,' which to the wee man could as well have been the names of the half-back line from the Azerbaijanian national side. He preferred the colloquial, if equally chilling description, the 'flailing arms syndrome.'

In the States it was known as Lou Gehrig's Disease, so named after the famous baseball player of the inter-war period. Then he went on, 'Nobody we know with your form of the disease has yet died of it.' The words lifted him. Hope. Spelled out in huge letters. He clung on to that single sentence of the neurologist to the bitter end. It was exactly the sort of evaluation Jimmy wanted to hear, but in that respect, without the slightest trace of cynicism, Ian Henderson, sitting beside him in the Beth Israel Medical Center wondered if they were dispensing some kindness to him, and that this might be a bit of spin being put on the matter, in the sense that what they had said was the truth, but only so far, and that there was still no cure. It was at least a peek at survival.

In any case, the delight at hearing that was enhanced by the thoughts, still lingering in their minds, that it was a trip they almost had to cancel. They had run out of funds. Their personal cash had dried up and they did not want to go pleading to Willie

Haughey again. They had been let down by one source only the day before they were due to fly. They disliked begging, and thus they just had to wait until a benefactor appeared, who turned out in this instance to be a cousin of Willie Haughey, John, who funded the trip at the last minute.

New York did not have the same appeal to them this time. The tourism aspect of it was subordinated by the need for them to submit to more tests, which included extensive muscle testing. It was clear from the examinations that he was weakening in the upper body. 'You could see he was wasting away. He was skeletal from the hips up,' Henderson noted. And the trip was tiring him more markedly from the previous visit only four months before. In the plane on the return flight Henderson admits that Jimmy had a drink. 'Just a wee one. He was perfectly all right. Except for the fact that I wakened up at one point and he was trying to convince an American couple from Boston, who were going to Ireland for the first time ever, that there were such things as leprechauns. Honest to God, he had them believing in them. I think he had convinced himself. He was happy. That was the most important thing.' Instead of going straight back home Jimmy insisted he be taken to Baird's Bar in Glasgow's Gallowgate. They knocked at the door of the pub at nine o'clock that morning. He wasn't there for a cup of tea.

His real sense of contentment was when he was back with his own people though. Viewpark was a stockade, within which he felt secure, knowing he could talk to people who understood him. That was obvious to anybody who came from outside the area, and could recognise the balance between the drudgery of the illness and the indomitable spirit which seemed to be aided by the folk around. Therefore, he could never resist the urge to visit his old friend Billy Donald. They did drink together, even though Agnes disapproved. But the disapproval was muted. She knew Donald was part of the continuity of his life. If Billy Donald was still around, then all's well with the world, as it were. Indeed when the local doctor came in to give Jimmy an injection one day, Donald was there, chatting away and offered to leave the room while the injections were being given, but the doctor put it bluntly, 'You stay where you are. You're doing as much good for him as this injection. Just stay where you are.'

During his visit to New York Jimmy had actually phoned Donald and asked him, quite improbably, if he could join him there for company. One day, back in Viewpark, when he visited that same friend, it provided a conversation of sheer delight for Jimmy and for his pal, listening in. In the earlier days he would be able to walk his way to Billy Donald's house, which was next door to where he was born. In the latter stages of his illness he would be driven up there. He would sit back in his seat, and he would sip through his straw and they would reminisce. But on this particular afternoon Jimmy had felt compelled to phone 'Luggy,' John Clark, at Celtic Park, and knew the number of the boot-room, which Clark regarded as his 'office.' But being unable to use his hand and arms, and so as to make sure they could hear each other properly, Billy Donald held the phone up to his mouth for him and put it on to loudspeaker. As clearly as his pal can remember, this is how the conversation went.

JIMMY: Hello, is that you Luggy?
HENRIK: No. It's Henrik, Henrik Larsson.
JIMMY: Henrik! It's Jinky here. Great to talk to you. How's it gaun? Are you still drinking? What I'm looking for is a signed top for a charity.
HENRIK: Right, Jimmy, I'll get it signed for you and sent out.
JIMMY: You're doing great. How's your house down in Bothwell? What do you drink anyway, Henrik?
HENRIK: Oh, I don't drink spirits, Jimmy. I don't socialise much, I don't go to functions much in clubs or hotels.
JIMMY: Well, I'll tell you what. Me and my pal Billy here, we'll come down and visit you. What do you like to drink, I'm askin'?
HENRIK: Well, I like a good champagne and a good wine.
JIMMY: No bother. That'll be no problem. Tell your wife to put up a marquee in the garden and we'll come down and have a party to celebrate the way you've been playing. And it'll last for a few days!
HENRIK: Oh, you're more than welcome, Jimmy. More than welcome.

They wished each other well and the conversation stopped with Donald wondering how the comparatively ascetic Swede would take all of that. But, as soon as it had ended, Jimmy turned to Donald and said, 'Go round to the Co-Op and get some of the pomagne stuff. Henrik won't know the difference!'

The visit, of course, never took place. The conversation was priceless though. Two great wearers of the number 7 jersey, two men from different cultures, contrasting personalities, both adored by different generations, who although having different tastes in sipping from a glass, had definitely been bonded by the same thirst for success and the ability to achieve it. They were also men who did what they had to do without boasting or bragging. For instance, Jimmy took absolutely no account of the wonderful statistics which reflected his great stature in the game, as many assumed he did. His good friend Willie Henderson phoned him one night from the pub the former Rangers player owned in Broxburn. Henderson was taking part in a pub quiz, and he had slipped out to the phone, surreptitiously, seeking information on a couple of quiz questions which were coming up, in order to take advantage of his opponents.

'How many games did you play for the club?' Willie asked. Jimmy replied, 'I haven't a clue.' 'All right, how many goals did you score for the club?' 'I couldn't tell you that. Wait and I'll ask Aggie.' To which a demented Henderson, thwarted in his intentions, replied, 'Jimmy, did you actually play for the bloody Celtic?' Jimmy really wasn't the kind of veteran who boasts of battle honours and can count the shots he fired. But he certainly hadn't forgotten the battlefields. And the most famous of all, in Lisbon, was about to be revisited thanks to the initiative of a documentary film-maker who started his adoration of Jimmy in January 1968, in the 2-2 game with Rangers, when, after his long journey from the south and watching a bitter game with a wild, physical dimension, he realised immediately that he was now hooked on a small figure with number 7 on his back.

TEN

Disaster Days

Don Revie was a kind of Caesar of his day. He manipulated and schemed and translated orthodox football into new formations, like the 'W' one he had almost sought to patent while with Manchester City as a player. That sort of thinking established him as innovative and ruthlessly ambitious. And all innovators are extended a special status which can sometimes create mystiques. But, undoubtedly, he was an influential thinker who, along with a battery of stars around him, was thought by the English press, many of whom had reportedly booked rooms in the city for the event, to be a shoe-in for the 1970 European Cup final in Milan.

Some of his colleagues reading this now might not wholly agree with my assessment that these two games against the English champions are simply associated with Jimmy's name. If we return to Stein's ploy against Red Star we are talking about how the norms of the game can be stretched, almost beyond belief, by extraordinary individual ability, which the manager realised was unique. The Swiss philosopher Henri-Frederic Amiel best described it this way, 'Doing easily what others find difficult, is talent. Doing what is impossible for talent, is genius.'

There was talent in abundance for Celtic against Leeds, but there was also that genius. Of course it is a team game, and you cannot dismiss the rest of the Celtic side as simply the *corps de ballet*. But Jimmy's personal duels with one of the finest defenders in Europe, the Leeds left back and English international Terry Cooper, typified Celtic's sense of superiority which took the English side aback. They had felt their reputation would have been intimidating for Celtic on both sides of the border.

So, on the evening of April Fool's Day 1970 at Elland Road, Jimmy inflicted on Cooper such a roasting that it verged on humiliation. The *Scottish Daily Mail*'s John Fairgrieve recorded the damage that Jimmy did to the English side's collective psyche: 'He had that much vaunted Leeds defence in such a state of chaos that, had it not been exhilarating, would have been just a bit embarrassing. He murdered their confidence by making them look foolish, and displayed exceptional courage by ignoring the rough stuff handed out in desperation.'

Tommy Gemmell heard the response from amongst the Leeds players. 'It was so pointed a 'doing' Jinky was giving them that we heard Norman Hunter, Leeds infamous 'hard-man' shouting blatantly to Cooper to chop him down, and Cooper shouting back at him to come and try it himself if he wanted. He did. They swapped positions, and Jimmy just did the same to him and ran him ragged.' All in all the English media were perplexed. They had felt that George Connelly's goal, which came in 45 seconds, was something of a freak which the great 'thinker' Revie would be able to overcome. Leeds, however, never recovered from that blow to the solar plexus. The last thing Cooper wanted in travelling to Hampden to try to retrieve their 1-0 deficit from the first leg was to face Jimmy again. He must have been hoping that the wee man had been struck down with the flu. He had no such luck. Not even the marvellous 30-yard strike by Billy Bremner in 14 minutes to level the aggregate 1-1, in front of the European Cup record crowd of 136,505 on April 15th, could insulate Cooper from another 'doing.'

One of Jimmy's great rivals, the ex-Ranger Jim Baxter, outdid anybody in the media when he suggested that the humiliation heaped upon Cooper '...should have been prohibited by an act of Parliament!' The English media, some of whom were probably hoping now to sell their rooms in Milan to their Scottish counterparts, were struggling to come to terms with the manifestation of Celtic's superiority. The *Daily Mirror*'s Derek Wallis wrote, 'I cannot recall seeing Leeds so confused and bewildered by the intensity of the attacks launched with conviction by a team so certain of the ultimate outcome.'

Great credit went to Jimmy's schoolboy opponent on the other side of the park, John Hughes, for the hunger he showed in the game, scoring with a glancing header two minutes into the second half and then rampaging about, as only he could, with the more bludgeoning style compared to Jimmy's rapier. But the combination was too powerful for Leeds, especially when it was the wee winger who devastated them again with a match-winning run, colourfully described in one newspaper as '...jinking and dodging along the right, trailing defenders in his wake like some green-and-white Pied Piper' before he squared the ball to Bobby Murdoch, who came thundering up to blast the ball behind substitute goalkeeper Harvey to make the final score 2-1.

I recall the press conference afterwards as an almost incoherent Don Revie tried to find the right words to explain his failure. And I certainly remember, some years later, going to interview Revie in his garden in Kinross where he stayed with his Scottish wife. This time he talked almost reverentially about the wee winger, because he really did appreciate players of true stature. He did once describe Jimmy, publicly, as 'The world's greatest winger.' Then, that afternoon, his wife interrupted our conversation and said that it was time for his walk round the garden. He rose, and with the aid of a stick slowly made his way around the perimeter. I asked Elsie if he had a problem. 'He has Motor Neurone,' she said, calmly. It meant nothing to me then, but it does now. He died about a year after that on May 26th 1989 aged 61.

When Jimmy's illness was diagnosed I remember thinking of Revie and that night at Hampden, and feeling that it was such a tragic irony that two men who had contributed so much to the splendour of a football match in different ways – the one who planned an outcome, but failed, the other who destroyed his plans – were to attain this saddest of affinities by way of the cruellest of diseases.

To be fair to the English media, some probably did take up the options on rooms in Milan for the European Cup final against Feyenoord, fascinated as they were by this effervescent Celtic side. It is interesting to note that, despite the fact that Celtic had the Lisbon triumph behind them, the English were still not convinced that a side from the north of the border had the real credentials to usurp Leeds. But now that that had been achieved, they used their special regard for Leeds and for the status of English football to assume that the final had been won at Hampden Park. For what were Feyenoord compared to Leeds?

To be equally fair and blunt, that same assumption grew legs in Scotland. Celtic were installed, at least this side of the Channel, as clear favourites. Jock Stein did nothing to dispel that notion, and made the most profound misreading of the opposition in his managerial career. Jimmy was like the others in being swept away by the feeling that the 6th of May in Milan would be something of a formality against the Dutch. That it turned out to be nothing of the kind produced a soul-searching amongst management, directors and players. It is here that we find Jimmy out of tune with the rest of his colleagues, who afterwards were not slow to tell me of how much Stein had got it wrong. Here are the comparisons. The manager had told Bertie Auld that the left-sided Wim van Hanegem was 'a slower Jim Baxter with a right foot just for standing on.' In fact, his left foot orchestrated most of Feyenoord's midfield play, and he could waltz past players even though he had a lumbering style, and as Auld concluded about that player, 'He was just too good for me.'

Tommy Gemmell was also uncompromising in his analysis. 'I didn't agree with his team selection and neither did others. And as for his team talk, it was so downbeat you would have thought we were going out to play Partick Thistle. The man van Hanegem, who was supposed to be a one-footed weakness, was still running stronger than anybody in extra-time and pinging beautiful passes all over the field.'

However, Jimmy found himself almost in a minority of one in the debate that ensued, speaking up in defence of the man who once had chased him up the tunnel to get his hands on him. As he told me, 'Nobody can say a word about Jock on this game. We just didn't play well. If we had played to our strengths we would have won that game. We were nothing like ourselves, it was as simple as that.'

Few could argue with that sentiment. They weren't themselves. Jimmy had been marginalised in the game. John Rafferty of the *Scotsman* identified a major factor in the 2-1 extra-time defeat, 'With no steady service coming from Auld and Wallace, the tough centre to the Dutch defence remained undisturbed. Celtic's strikers were subdued. Johnstone tried to pull that formation apart, but he was no physical match for so unequivocal defenders who were prepared to topple him hard.' The wee winger was accustomed to close attention. Hadn't that been the reason for Inter being so obsessed by him in Lisbon that he had become a decoy, dragging Burgnich with him? But this time he looked flat and ordinary, although he had suffered an early ankle injury in one of the first crude tackles in the game. John Hughes tends to go along with Jimmy, in that they did not perform, but makes an interesting point:

'We were damned annoyed with ourselves because we all knew we were a better team than them.' And then, without actually contradicting himself, but in tandem with Gemmell's view, added, 'If we had really known about them we could have beaten them. If we had gone out again the following night with the same teams we would have won.' After all, when you put it into perspective, despite the admission by Jimmy and others that they had substantially underperformed, they did only lose the final 2-1 after extra-time. Celtic's lead through Tommy Gemmell in the 30th minute had only lasted two minutes before Rinus Israel equalised and Ove Kindvall scored the winner.

The tone for any inquest was set by Stein himself, when he became decidedly enigmatic in his explanation for what *Corriere Dello Sport*, the Italian sports newspaper, described as 'A Celtic in decline, their desperate resistance destroyed by Feyenoord.' The manager told the press that he knew the reason for Celtic playing so poorly. 'I know why, but I will tell my players – and no one else. I was surprised by my own side.' Then he followed that up with a statement a day later. 'We did not play to any more than twenty-five percent of our capability.'

Some players did not like the way in which they had had blame attached to them, knowing the manager himself had obviously understated the challenge. And there were decided reservations about the training preparations for this final, which included such a relaxed atmosphere in their former-monastery hotel on a hilltop outside Milan, that you felt the team were on a close-season tour. The contrast with how they had prepared for Lisbon could not have been more marked. The players even had an agent now, Ian Peebles, which showed remarkable tolerance on their part, as the man was steeped in the traditions of their greatest rivals. It all seemed so bizarre.

So why didn't they read the signs in advance? Because Stein's stock was so high he lent the impression of invincibility on these occasions, and the players had complete trust in his analysis of opponents. Jimmy's support for his manager, in his analysis, puts that special relationship into perspective. For in all the time I knew him, even though he might have had good grounds for doing so, I never heard him say an unkind word about Jock Stein, although many others did.

Jimmy did not travel to North America that summer with the rest of the team, an exemption based on the manager being unsure as to Jimmy's future, for he was now harbouring outrageous thoughts about leaving Celtic. However, if he was absent from the tour he certainly was not absent from the manager's thoughts. For in mid-tour, Stein suddenly disappeared, and headed back home on the very day a game against the Italian side Bari was getting out of hand. With fights developing all over the field, the manager, having had enough, jumped into the Italian dug-out and delivered a clunking fist to the jaw of the Italian coach who had been inciting his players to create mayhem throughout. With the coach flattened, Stein lifted his travel bag and headed for the airport, leaving Sean Fallon in charge for the rest of the tour, which caused some players to think they had been released from solitary confinement, and they stepped out of line, so much so that Bertie Auld and Tommy Gemmell were both sent home before the tour ended for 'conduct unbecoming.' Why the sudden departure of the manager?

Of the many reasons suggested for what appeared to be a dereliction of duty, by Stein's own personal standards, the one which had certain credibility was dealing with Jimmy. The wee man, on the back of the Milan disappointment, and having come through three or four seasons in which he had not only survived some specially brutal treatment, but had excelled, was beginning to grouse about his lot for the first time since he had joined the club. Bluntly he wanted more money. All the other players knew that walking in to ask this manager for an increase was like simulating a car crash. Bigger men had charged into Stein's office before with demands and had come out needing therapy. But 'Jimmy, being Jimmy...' to use the accepted mantra, disregarded the gale warnings previously issued by the others and raised the prospect of a better settlement for himself. But a confused picture was emerging.

On Wednesday 20th May he responded to an *Evening Times*

inquiry about the speculation which had linked him to a move to England by replying, 'I'm not interested. I'm happy where I am,' which was contradicted within twenty four hours when he stated that if he didn't get a new contract he would never play for Celtic again: which was another level of confusion, since a few weeks earlier he had stated he would never leave Celtic Park. It is worth a reminder here that by comparison with modern contracts those superb Celtic players of that era were paid bawbees. Stein had come from the mines where you had to battle constantly to gain mere ha'pennies of increases, and sometimes had to use union muscle for just minimal gains. This ethic affected the way he presented himself as the seeming controller of the purse at Celtic Park. Men had to be set standards of prudence, which paralleled the struggles he had had to endure to make ends meet working at the coal face.

All this was implicit in the statement he gave the press about Jimmy's position. 'Johnstone presented me with an ultimatum before we left on tour a fortnight ago. He made financial requests which we considered unreasonable. The next move is up to the player.' Such a cold and austere statement also betokened the fact that there could only be one winner in the so-called stand-off. Stein knew that Jimmy would rather cut off his right leg than leave the only club he ever wanted to play for. He was also aware that his wife was a level-headed person who spoke her mind bluntly, regardless of what Jimmy thought about it. She was hardly a shrinking violet, when she admitted to me what she had told him during this period. 'If you're thinking of going to England, then you're going yourself, because I'm staying where I am.'

Stein and Agnes together could not be messed around with. Even Arthur Scargill could not have got anything out of that duo on this matter. In any case, all three personalities involved in this knew that talk of moving to England was only a ploy to try to extract as much as he could from negotiations. A week after Stein had made Celtic's position clear, Jimmy smuggled himself in and out of Celtic Park, by a side door, to avoid the press. More or less, he had accepted the conditions of the current contract, with the abject humility of someone who, against all his fighting instincts, had been forced to raise the white flag: a toeing of the line reflected in Stein's powerfully brief and almost chilling announcement to the waiting press, 'Johnstone has come and gone. He will resume training with the other players on July 15th. All his problems have been solved.'

The formality of such a statement seemed to be an attempt to distance himself from any familiarity with a player who behind that stern facade he adored. For Jimmy it was a mix of surrender and an abrupt wakening to the fact that the only way you could survive with Stein was to employ common sense. It was also known that only Derby County had expressed passing interest in him, in a dual transfer deal with the also unsettled Tommy Gemmell. So, even the market was not taking his stand too seriously. What intrigued the media was that, perhaps for the first time, Celtic FC were feeling a sense of discord in the ranks, when a devoted player could actually talk of leaving the club, however artificial the posture was, and that others were echoing the same desires to better their lot, like Tommy Gemmell.

It could be said, that from this pivotal moment, relationships between Stein and his major players were never quite the same again. If not exactly the opening of a Pandora's Box, nevertheless Jimmy had led the field in breaking the mould of subservience, no matter that he had failed, and others were to follow suit in standing up for what they thought were appropriate awards for their services.

The manager, in the aftermath of the Milan disappointment, realised his players were not performing to their full potential. There was the hiccup which occurred on October 24th when, in a typically coupon-busting derby game, Rangers beat the hot favourites to win the League Cup final with the only goal scored by the 16-year-old Derek Johnstone. And there was now a different balance in Scottish football with Aberdeen coming to the fore, and actually leading the league in December of 1970, when Stein made surprising changes in the side for the game against Morton at Cappielow on Boxing Day. He dropped both Jimmy and Billy McNeill, suggesting that he had left them in the stand to help stimulate a return to their true form, remarking, 'If McNeill and Johnstone can be brought back to their best by sitting in the stand, the rest will have served its purpose.'

Billy McNeill uttered a cryptic statement, afterwards, which might suggest he was not wildly enthused about taking the air at the Tail of the Bank in winter, 'I think it's warmer on the field. We picked a cold day to be in the stand.' It was also an icy comment on being dropped. Jimmy, by now, was embroiled in trying to make his bar/restaurant a success and his financial affairs, and his increasing self-indulgence in the pub, in late-night closed-doors sessions, were engaging him in ways that could have been taking the shine off his play, understandably. He had actually asked to be dropped from a home game against St Mirren four weeks earlier, telling Stein that he was 'not mentally attuned' for domestic reasons. Whatever doubts were in the manager's mind about the wee man's personal problems, and worries about his form, by now Jimmy was the toast of the European press.

In the November 12th 1970 issue of the Milan-based magazine *Intrepido*, the writer, enthusing about the winger's mastery, ended by quoting the great Inter Milan full-back Giacinto Facchetti who attributed to him the nickname, 'Lo Scoiattolo Del Diavolo,' literally 'The Devil's Squirrel.' The little scurrying animal, whose redness was associated with the devil, had come to the Italian's mind as he watched a wee red-headed man, elusive and brisk, lead so many teams on a fruitless chase. As if to underline his European credentials, and as a preview of the European Cup quarter-final tie with Ajax Amsterdam, the Dutch weekly *1-0* devoted a four-page spread in late February 1971 to Jimmy.

They photographed him in his neighbourhood with all his family, and playing football in the local park with children, personifying him as the emergence of working-class hero who would never forget his roots. And, as if to show that his sort of football mirrored the modernising of what they might normally have portrayed as a resolutely Victorian industrial city, he was snapped looking up from the rubble of the old and notorious Gorbals district of Glasgow, at the rebuilding taking place in that neighbourhood. No other Scottish player had ever been feted in the Continental press this way before, nor had been shown representing a feature of a city determined to revamp its 19th century image.

However, the publication did more than that. They sent a photographer to see him in action in a game which they thought might capture the essence of his style. They got more than they bargained for. The game they chose was the derby match at Ibrox on January 2nd 1971.

It was the kind of misty, damp, bone-chilling day of post-apocalyptic nature. Over 80,000 were crammed in, indifferent to the weather as they vented the ritualistic hatreds. But the game itself seemed so flat, so negative, as both sides leant the impression that their sole concern was not to lose the game on a bone-hard pitch. Malcolm Munro in the *Evening Times* was entranced by the wee winger, as he was 'rounding opponent after opponent as if he were a statue – Wee Jimmy On Ice!' Then in the 89th minute Jimmy scored with a header as the ball rebounded towards him from the crossbar, which had been struck by a 30-yard shot from Lennox. Game, set and match, so it seemed. 60 seconds later Colin Stein equalised. The players left the field, and many supporters left the stadium afterwards without knowing that just after that final whistle, 66 people had been killed, and 145 injured on one particular staircase.

In all the introspection which goes on in the minds of the players who took part that day, there are nagging thoughts about what might have happened had Jimmy not scored, and had Colin Stein not responded so soon after, if events on that staircase would have been different. Would the 66 people who perished in the ensuing collapse still be living their lives? That awful theorising went through Jimmy's mind for months after, as it did other Celtic and Rangers players. Agnes actually remembers someone coming to the door, on some job, and asked her if 'Disaster Jimmy' was in. She was so shocked that even now she still doesn't know whether it was a sick joke or not.

However, those two late goals had little to do with the disaster. The official report blamed the particular structure of the staircase and tripping on the steepness of the stairs, and stated that the tragedy had happened a full five minutes after the last goal had been scored. It did show, though, that the players were sensitive enough to jump to the conclusion, as erroneously as most of the press, that there had been a causal link between goals and disaster. Even so, to this day that theory of the goals causing the disaster still holds sway. So 'Disaster Jimmy' he was not. But many of the players involved that day still retain a sense of unnecessary guilt about it. The aftermath also provided the possibility of bitterness between the factions subsiding. Which it did, for a time.

I saw Jimmy outside Glasgow Cathedral where a memorial service was being held, signing autographs for Rangers supporters who had turned up to hold vigil in the overspill outside. Nobody ever thought this harmony would suddenly sweep through the opposing ranks and end the hostilities for ever. But at least it was a pause for reflection.

The disaster overtook anything that the Dutch magazine had

wished to portray of Jimmy that day, in a game, which, although recorded by the BBC, has never been shown on television. But the Dutch coverage had posted enough warnings to their population about his threat in the European Cup. That threat mysteriously vanished in Amsterdam as Celtic were comprehensively beaten 3-0 in March 1971, a result which prompted Jimmy to admit afterwards, 'I simply felt I had let everybody down. I had such an ordinary game, anyone who read the pre-match stuff must have wondered what all the fuss was about.'

Although he did score in the second leg, to suggest a miraculous recovery was possible, his goal in 28 minutes was the only meagre comfort they could derive from a comprehensive out-smarting by the Dutch side which included the great Johan Cruyff, winning 3-1 on aggregate. This hurt Celtic deeply, given their increasing tendency to judge their progress in Europe as a more accurate barometer of their status in football, and not just the winning of the championship. Jimmy was personally upset by this, and again he asked not to be selected for the game against Cowdenbeath, three days after that.

For the first time in his life he had three main responsibilities, family, football and business.

He was a family man, immensely successful as a footballer, but at business he might as well have tried to pilot a jumbo jet over the Atlantic. The first tiny signs of worry about money were beginning to surface. Not so much that he was heading heavily into debt at that stage, but that he was being asked to think on his feet about the flow of custom at the pub, and the way it was being handled. For obvious reasons he wasn't always there, although he needed to be to supervise and keep an eye on what happened over the counter. Such thoughts can impinge on performance. It has already been stated that all you needed to do was throw a ball at Jimmy and the irresistible compulsion to play quickly stimulated him. But this was the season when he did show signs of indifference, when at times the sparkle seemed dulled. Being human it was impossible to reach spectacular heights in every game he played, but nevertheless there were occasions in this personally crucial season for him, as a budding pub magnate, when he seemed distracted. Fortunately for his manager and colleagues, he knew he could turn it on: the talent was always there, latent and easily recoverable.

In looking back over his record, a goal against Motherwell

in Celtic's 3-0 victory on April 12th reveals a quality which was largely overlooked in the general appreciation of his ball skills. It was described, thus, by Hugh Taylor in the *Daily Record*, 'It was the genius of Jimmy Johnstone which gained the vital points [Celtic had dropped a point in the previous game against Dundee United]. The wee man is right in the mood, practically unstoppable, a variety show all on his own.' And then went on specifically, 'he leapt fantastically' above defenders to head down a Lennox cross into the path of Wallace, who volleyed the ball past the keeper. That ability to out-jump players much taller than himself was something which came with preparation, dating back to his early teens, as Billy Donald recalls.

'We used to go to the local baths in Bellshill, as we were both keen on swimming. But Jimmy used to climb up on the topmost springboard and bounce up and down on it. What he would do is bounce as high as he could and then put the brake on the board using the strength of his thighs. From being like a seesaw he made it rigid in one movement. That must have helped build up strength in his thighs and gave him that extra spring in his legs.'

If you are willing to accept that as significant, then a season ticket for the Bellshill baths, in days of yore, was worth its weight in gold. For that goal he scored at Ibrox, on the day of the disaster, was only the first of four he would score with his head against Rangers in a total of ten he netted against his great rivals. So you can tell that he did respond with vigour to the sight of blue jerseys. It was these jerseys they would have to face again at the climax of the season in the Scottish Cup final, after having achieved one of their results of the year in the 1-1 draw at Pittodrie which gave Celtic a distinct advantage over Aberdeen in the title race. And nearly two weeks later, on April 29th at Hampden Park (with Celtic Park under reconstruction), with some of his colleagues appearing to be suffering the jitters, Jimmy lifted morale and inspired Celtic to the title, in their 2-0 win over Ayr United.

His display that day caused Hugh Taylor of the *Daily Record* to sound as if he had just feasted at a table provided by a master-chef, 'It was Jimmy the Dazzler, Jimmy the Magician. The baffled United defenders must have thought they were chasing a shadow as the wee man flitted here and there, the ball glued to his toes with his deceptive swerve and brilliant control. Johnstone was exactly what football is about. I can pay no higher tribute.'

Coming from a seasoned journalist like Taylor, who knew class when he saw it, you could truly say that Jimmy was not only helping to win a league with unique talent, but was also an evangelist for the way Celtic were prepared to play their football. Then came the game which he always claimed was his best ever against Rangers.

Summer 2003

Jimmy returned to Lisbon that year. The cameras followed him there. But before he went others were trying to raise awareness of this disease even further, two years after the initial diagnosis. One such was Joe Carroll from Dundee, who had set up a Jimmy Johnstone Motor Neurone Disease Fund and sent letters to some of the most influential figures on the world stage to inform them of Jimmy's condition. The year before Jimmy had been voted Celtic's Greatest Ever Player by the supporters, which carried its own significance. So, replies flooded in offering support. From the Vatican's Secretariat of State, on behalf of Pope John Paul II, came the message, 'His Holiness wishes me to assure you that he is remembering Mr Johnstone in his prayers.'

All the political leaders from all parties in the UK, including Tony Blair, the Prime Minister, responded with sympathy including his wistful and all too accurate remark, 'Sadly, there are too few players of Jimmy's calibre playing today.' From Ibrox Park came a response from the Rangers manager at the time, Alex McLeish, which understandably would have tickled Jimmy, because of his obsession with stem cell research. 'In this day and age of the clones, perhaps we could take a wee cell or two from Jimmy and these futuristic scientists can produce a replica!'

The family could see that this was of enormous therapeutic effect on him, as if he felt a comforting blanket of support was being wrapped around him. But it was obviously going to be hard for him to remain like that. There was no sign of remission *from the disease. Periodically he was, in fact, showing signs of deterioration. You could not have expected otherwise given the circumstances. He was involved in enterprises that others in similar straits would not have attempted. But they offered him new leases of life, and those signs of deterioration would then seem less obvious, temporarily.*

One such major venture was when he was approached to make a film documentary about his career. The man behind it, Jeff Healey, was born in Barrow-in-Furness, in Lancashire, but since he lived beside a Celtic-supporting family as a boy, he became fascinated with all things pertaining to the club and after his visit to an Old Firm game in 1968, became firmly hooked.

'I watched that game in 1968 and I could see that he just refused to be intimidated,' Healey said. 'John Greig was giving him a particularly bad time. But he just kept bouncing back up. So it was the very simple prospect of making a film about a hero of mine which fascinated me. We also knew that the family were coming through hard times financially and we thought a documentary would help in those circumstances. On top of that we had never heard of the phrase Motor Neurone, and when we discovered that it was an incurable disease we felt and hoped that while making this film some cure might emerge, and in any case Jimmy's attitude was simply that if time ran out on him then, perhaps, in what he came through and pursued, others in the future could be saved. But I didn't realise how affected Jimmy was with numerology, this fascination with numbers, because he told us that when we left an initial message with him on his answering machine to ask if he would co-operate to make a documentary, he didn't feel any inclination to reply to us. But something changed his mind. He admitted this to us. "What mattered was that I saw the last two digits of your phone number. 67. That did it."'

Healey at that time did not know about the recurrence of the number 67 in New York, nor could he have anticipated that Jimmy would respond to the trip like he was reliving the good times and that thoughts of easing up on life, because of his illness, were conspicuously absent. 'What people perhaps do not appreciate is that Jimmy had to battle against two diseases, Motor Neurone and something which he had fought valiantly for years, on and off, sometimes with success, then with regression – his alcoholism. This trip gave us special focus on just what he had had to face up to. Agnes had warned us that we had to keep Jimmy off the booze. Easier said than done. Ian Henderson acted as a kind of chaperone, since he was off the drink himself by then. But, you know, as soon as Jimmy left home he wanted to party. And party he did. Should we have had more control? I ask you, how could you not give a dying man a drink?'

Henderson kept close to him, and was there at all the meals, helping to feed Jimmy who was now beyond the point of embarrassment at being seen in public like that. The night before their visit to the Estadio Nacional, where they would retrace their steps of the famous 1967 afternoon, they had dined, alfresco, in Cascais, the charming fishing village just outside Lisbon. Earlier that day Henderson had taken a photograph of Jimmy standing in the village at the door of the small hotel, and when it was developed, on return to Scotland, they could see a street number in the background, 67. It had not been posed for effect. It just happened. But above all, Healey had to make sure he rationed Jimmy's drinks.

One thing led to another though, as it does, with so much preoccupying people during filming preparation, that it all led to the breaking down of what could be described as custodial protection. When Healey felt the rigours of the day catching up with him, he went to his bed, leaving his film crew with Jimmy to keep him company and also to enjoy a few beers on a balmy night, as film crews willingly do. Healey doesn't know how long he was there until he heard singing starting at the tables outside. He knew immediately that Jimmy was leading it. It got louder and louder. Everyone was clearly having a whale of a time, until somebody on a higher floor objected to the noise going on in the wee small hours, went to their balcony and emptied a jug of water on the table below, most of which drenched Jimmy. Healey indicates that there were some big men in the film crew who rushed up stairs, fuelled by drink and anger, and who were ready to do battle with whoever had doused them. The problem was that they went to the wrong floor, banged on the wrong doors, and all hell was let loose as other innocents were dragged into it, and it all ended up with the participants looking like they were acting out a farce on stage.

With the tumult in full flow, Healey went downstairs to the pavement and discovered Jimmy, soaked to the skin, but still singing at the top of his voice, U2's 'Still Haven't Found What I'm Looking For,' which had become something of an anthem in the on-going crusade for a cure. He was in his element. Wet to the skin though he was, Healey could see that here was a man who thought the night was still young, and was still fit enough to keep going until he had the background support of the dawn chorus. Jimmy, clearly, was blissfully unaware that it was the middle of the night and that he was due to face the cameras first thing in the morning. What astonished Healey about the following day was Jimmy's power of recovery

'He was in a terrible state, to be honest. You wouldn't have thought he would have been able to do anything. Admittedly he did spend a couple of minutes in the bushes at the stadium, at one juncture, to get rid of some of the previous night's indulgences, but when we were ready to film, from being an ill-looking man who looked wobbly, he became alive again, full of life, bubbly, and gave us just what we wanted. Amazing.' So with the cameras rolling Jimmy stepped his way into the well-remembered past. Henderson followed him as he walked through his paces. 'At the stadium we went into a deserted, darkened dressing-room area and then he took the walk down the long tunnel towards the pitch, climbed the stairs, and as Jimmy came into the daylight, a cameraman was pointing towards one of the goals, which caused Jimmy to intervene. "Haw, sir! Get it right. Point to that goal. That's where the three went in."'

They then managed to squeeze through a small hole in a thick, protective plastic sheet to film Jimmy in the position where Billy McNeill had been presented with the trophy, on the other side of the stadium, a view he had actually never seen before. It had been an effort and a triumph to do so, because of the wee man's condition when he had surfaced that morning. It was easy for anybody to tell though that he had been visibly affected by seeing the pitch, around which he had dragged Burgnich for 90 minutes. Thirty-six years on, his eyes were bright with remembrance. His only regret was that they were not able to take all the surviving Lions there to accompany him.

The following day he also responded positively to the anticipation of meeting the great Eusebio, who had asked to meet him when told Jimmy would be in town. For this they travelled to Lisbon itself to the original, and famous, 'Estadio da Luz,' the Stadium of Light, where the great Portuguese international had plied his trade to great effect in the marvellous Benfica teams. They met and were filmed on the pitch. Eusebio, you could say, was held in the same respect in his adopted country and back in Mozambique, where he was born, as Jimmy was at home. Thus, on that pitch two marvellous players simply enjoyed their brief meeting, acknowledging each other's brilliance. But the Benfica great had a little surprise in store for Jimmy. As they embraced each other Eusebio made an admission.

'I have a great friend in Scotland. You know him. Willie Henderson. Because of him I support his team. Sorry, Jimmy.' The wee man was disappointed that when the documentary was finally shown, that moment did not appear, for he would have liked to have included Henderson in a mention, being now so close to him. The reason for that was quite simple. The cameras had not been running at the time.

Then came the meeting which meant most to him. It was the third of the journeys with the production team and the one which had taken the most trouble to set up. The place, Madrid. The man, Alfredo di Stefano. It had taken Jeff Healey two years of gruelling negotiations to set it up through the intermediary, Emilio Butragueno, the man nicknamed 'El Buitre' (The Vulture), who played 341 games for Real Madrid and scored 123 goals, and netted 26 goals for Spain: a man whom you might say had a bit of clout, since, apart from that, he had been given his first senior game for the club by Di Stefano as manager. However, Butragueno had not had an easy task. He warned Healey that Di Stefano was now a grumpy old man and was difficult to deal with. For a time it hung in the balance, but eventually a deal for a meeting was agreed. So far so good.

It was decided to take Bertie Auld on the trip, who, as you might recall was sent off in the famous testimonial match in 1967. Bertie and Jimmy were very close, blood brothers as it were. Although they were consigned separate rooms in the hotel for the overnight stay, they ended up in just one room, swapping tales and enjoying the benefits of the drinks cabinet, like all night. Thus, they were late getting to the Bernabeu. This worried the producer, who was concerned about the 'grumpy old man' aspect he had been warned about in respect of Di Stefano. To hide this late-coming they decided to interview the great Argentine first, which they did with the benefit of the interpreter. Bertie recalls the meeting.

'There we were, Jimmy and I, in front of this magnificent stadium, taking it all in. We could remember the last time we had come to it. Just looking at it brought back memories. It was just magnificent to be there again. Then suddenly we saw this old man toddling towards us. As he got nearer, I swear we could see his spectacles were held together by sellotape. We thought, by the look of him, he must be the groundsman. And then suddenly he took off his cap and we saw it was Alfredo di Stefano.'

The doffing of the cap was no simple matter. What they had experienced was a phenomenon that even shook Butragueno. For Di Stefano to make the cap gesture out of respect for the wee man was unique, given his patriarchal stature in Spanish society. He had never done that before, even for the King of Spain. They embraced: the passing of the years evident, in ageing joints, the palpable weakness of both men, the facial lines and creases that reflected traces of occasional hardship, all nullified in one explosion of memory and the obvious mutual comfort they derived in simply having been able to survive to have a last meeting. But with Bertie Auld at Jimmy's side there was no room for gloom settling in over the passing of time, and both of them laughed their way through the trip, joshing with each other, culminating in a scene at Edinburgh Airport which almost caused a furore. When they landed Jimmy needed the toilet. Bertie takes up the tale.

'The wee man was very independent and wanted to go himself, although he could not use his arms. I heard a lot of cursing going on inside the area and when I went in, a bit alarmed, I saw that he couldn't get one of the doors open. I did that for him and then he turned to me and said, "You'll have to help me," I told him to get lost, I wasn't doing that for him. But he insisted because he was accustomed to getting help like that in the house. So here's me taking down his track-suit pants he was wearing, and then holding him on the vital part and saying, "All right then, pee!" When I noticed nothing was coming I said to him, "I think you're liking this!" He couldn't stop laughing. Just then the door opened and in came this big fella who couldn't believe what he was seeing, a man with his pants at his feet and somebody holding his weapon. All I could say was, "We're pals." And I'll always remember what he said back, "You would have to be!"''

There was no such thing as an orthodox life in coping with Motor Neurone Disease. It could produce those pantomime incidents like that one above. Such precious laughter lent the impression that Jimmy was levitating, rising above the problem, floating, liberated.

ELEVEN

Hanging On

After the Ibrox Disaster match there was a strange feeling that a shadow hung over the national game. It was not helped by noting that in the charity match played between an Old Firm select and a Scotland X1 on 27th January for the Ibrox Disaster Fund, there was a dispute when Harry Hood, by now a prolific scorer for Celtic, was angered by insults directed towards him by Rangers supporters in the crowd that night, refused to come off the bench, walked back to the dressing-room, and left the stadium in disgust. Celtic, though, were not distracted by any of this from the primary purpose of attempting to win their 26th Championship. Jimmy was now a partner of other emerging stars: Harry Hood, who would end up their top scorer with 33 goals; Lou Macari, who was not as prolific, but with the knack of scoring at crucial times; Davie Hay who could shine at both full-back and midfield, and the troubled George Connelly, whose name conjures up, sadly, the mystery of squandered talent, all now vying for attention, surrounding Jimmy with new assets and new rivals for top billing. He always relished a challenge but at the same time he was conscious of the absence now of 'weel kent' faces.

By the time the Scottish Cup final came along on May 8th 1971, the animosities which we had all hoped would at least have been muted, were still there, and so was Jimmy. It went to a replay and it is the second game which showed that Hugh Taylor of the *Daily Record* had not run dry on superlatives, when he described the winger as 'The Magic Man.' The first game had the look of a resolute Rangers, determined to achieve the cup double, on the back of their League Cup victory, and exuding the physical self-awareness of a side more suited to cup than league football. What Rangers could not achieve was the consistency which Stein seemed to be able to manage, with occasional slight bumps along the way.

He was the master of the deployment of players, selecting, dropping, switching roles, and keeping his own side, as well as the opposition, on the alert as to what he would come up with next. But in all of that there was one over-riding factor, and that was to keep Jimmy in the right frame of mind to unleash his talents, which was still at the core of any of their successes. It is impossible to over-state the effect his dynamism had on the other players, of which Stein, even with increasing doubts about Jimmy's personal life, was fully aware. So this replay re-emphasised how badly he was needed. What had annoyed Celtic was the fact that they had the winning of the cup in their hands on the Saturday when they were 1-0 up, from a Bobby Lennox goal, until the substitution which brought Derek Johnstone on with only twenty minutes remaining. The goal he scored was of such galling simplicity, using a touch of his head to a long ball hoisted into the Celtic penalty area, that all the tactical awareness which Stein always brought into a final was made to look redundant. That stung him personally.

That annoyance was compounded by the fact that Jimmy had sustained a thigh injury in the first game and told his manager that he would not be able to play in the replay. This was Stein's brusque comment after the replay, 'We had to persuade him to play in the game tonight.' Perhaps not down on bended knees, but nevertheless an open admission of his reliance on the winger. The persuasion was of obvious merit, for Rangers were then exposed to a full battery of Jimmy's attributes. Ex-Celt John McPhail in the June 1971 issue of the *Celtic View*, seemed to reflect Stein's inner thoughts on the wee man when he wrote, 'As so often this season on important occasions, Jimmy took the opportunity to display his remarkable skills and by the end of an hour's play it was clear Rangers players had no answers to the problems Johnstone had set them.'

The winger's thrust into the penalty area brought about a penalty only a minute after Lou Macari had scored the opening goal in 24 minutes. As Jimmy rose from the turf, he turned to the man who had hauled him down, Ronnie McKinnon, and gave him a quick, and almost congratulatory handshake, before Harry Hood scored from the spot for the winning goal of the game. The *Sunday Mirror*'s Rodger Baillie wrote that Jimmy had, 'put his imprint so conclusively on a game of that stature, that it will be known for ever more, not just as the cup final of that year, but as the game that belonged to him ... in this game Johnstone truly demonstrated that he is probably the only Scottish domestic player who could match the towering talents of the world-class giants, the Peles, the Eusebios, the Moores.'

Then Stein added his weight to the praise, but not without a certain cautionary note, when he told the above journalist, 'The little man struggled as badly as anyone in Amsterdam. It's the sort of situation in which too often in the past he would have retreated into his shell and perhaps faded out of the picture for the rest of the season. But he was superb. He was our most consistent player for the last three months of the season and you have no idea the pleasure it gives me to say that! He achieved the consistency of which I always felt he was capable, but so rarely produced over any length of time. I reckon that an on-form Jimmy Johnstone gives Celtic an advantage over every other club in Scotland – yes, and Britain too – for there is no one to touch him at his peak.'

Note that within that unbridled praise there are phrases which infer Stein's recurring reservations about the player. He added two other phrases to his *Celtic View* article, which further emphasised that relationship, by saying that the great form he had been in needed, 'A consistency that hasn't always been apparent.' And added, 'We will be looking for the same from him right from the start of the coming season.'

It was as if he made these statements with his fingers crossed, hoping that such an endorsement would spur Jimmy on to even greater heights. The wee man was never one to go looking for praise, but in the aftermath of that final it was he who handed out praise in a rather unusual way. His handshake with McKinnon, after the penalty incident, was like one professional to another, respecting each others efforts at giving their best for their clubs. Jimmy went a stage further than a handshake, after the game, when he complimented the Rangers players on the spirit they had shown and went so far as to extend that to their supporters for the backing they had given their team, but also because, as he said publicly, 'All the time I felt that they were appreciative of any good things I did.'

So that season had culminated in the prodigious effort of Jimmy to cement Celtic's position at the top of Scottish football, and in the Old Firm games in particular, he is indelibly linked with a dynamic presence which altered the course of events, from the Disaster game, through to the Scottish Cup final itself. And as you stand back from them now, you can recognise his almost unique status, in that dramatic context, because although Rangers supporters would like to have seen him banished to Devil's Island with the cell-key thrown away for the way he could torment their team, nevertheless, underneath that, there was respect, sometimes reluctant, sometimes with open admiration, for his skills. But there was the other factor.

He was seen as a wee working-class boy who had so much in common with supporters of all kinds. Wee, but plucky; wee, but a scrapper; wee, but honest, in the way he went about his business on the park. That is exactly what people saw in him locally, on both sides of the divide, and he most certainly firmly grasped the meaning of the whole Old Firm ethos and its life-affirming importance to people by simply having grown up amongst it in the Lanarkshire streets.

He was simply a Viewpark boy who never passed anybody without speaking a kind word to them, and despite the overarching tension of sectarianism which could cloud the area, it did not deter him from maintaining life-long friendships with men who supported his great rivals. This social dimension, which was supposed to define you one way or the other, and cause rifts, deterred him not one bit and was a complete irrelevance in relationships with people, although a devout Catholic and a passionate Celtic man. One day, not long after Lisbon, with his reputation at its peak, he was sitting in Billy Donald's house when they heard the Orange Walk approaching. It does not rank as even a spectator sport for Celtic men. Jimmy went to the window to look out at it, and in the narrow street he was as close as he ever would be to such an event.

'Come back from that window in case they see you,' Mrs Donald cried at him, more than slightly alarmed. He didn't budge. Suddenly they recognised him. 'There's Jinky!' somebody in the parade shouted and without any hesitation the men in the parade started to wave to him, like he was just a wee fella from the area who had 'done good.' Jimmy just waved back. Some of them he knew well, and had grown up with, and drank with. There was an innocence in this incident, devoid of the natural trappings of suspicion and hatred, which the cynics might have regarded as some freakish act of nature. It might also have suggested that familiarity breeds contempt of the traditions of hatred.

On the field of play it was, however, transition time. It was something which, for one principal reason, did not suit him. For throughout his life he seemed to flourish among people he knew well. Familiarity with folk was another way of defining what 'home' meant to him. On or off the field he responded better to this familiarity. However, those players he had reached the heights with in Europe were gradually disappearing from sight. Soloist though he could frequently become, he did need the right kind of support for his play, and above all the tolerance of his mates for the occasional self-indulgences.

The man who was most willing to accept him as he was, and who was to be so close to him during his illness, Bertie Auld, was given a free-transfer on April 30th that year. John Clark and Steve Chalmers would depart within the following few months. And in October 1971, on the eve of the second round first leg European Cup tie against Sliema Wanderers, John Hughes and Willie Wallace had been bundled off to Crystal Palace. Jimmy would miss them all, particularly Auld who was immensely talented, with an irreverence in his play which made you feel he was football's equivalent of a satirist, somebody who could both take the mickey and also hurt teams badly. But he did care about Jimmy, and was a frequent escort when the wee man needed companionship. Harry Hood, who played alongside him at this period, sensed this feeling of creeping alienation.

'Jinky missed the players he had grown up with at Celtic Park. There were fewer of them about and he liked to think that they were the best. As for my relationship with him, it was not intimate. Formal, you could say. He was proud of that number 7 that he wore, and it was a number I would wear when he wasn't playing. I think it made him uncomfortable with me. He definitely could be brilliant for spells, but I was becoming aware that they were not as frequent as they used to be. I was a great admirer of Jock Stein but if there was one flaw at that time I think it was when he would say, "All you need is one hour of Jimmy Johnstone." He kept repeating that, which shows you how good the wee man was. But, I think Jimmy began to believe that as well. And I think Jimmy thought he could cut that back to, say, one half of the game, then maybe half-an-hour. You could claim that the manager hung on to him longer perhaps than he should have. But on the other hand, if you take a crowd of 60,000 at Celtic Park, 59,500 came to see Jimmy. The other 500 came to see Harry Hood. Jock Stein knew the value of the wee man all right.'

This was underlined by the fact that many of the players felt the break-up of the Lisbon Lions came far too early, but that there was no way that the manager was allowing Jimmy to go anywhere ... at that stage.

The last appearance of the Lions was in the league game against Clyde on May 1st 1971. It was an emotional occasion, and although Ronnie Simpson did not play, he took part in the warm-up and shoot-in prior to the match. It attracted an above-average crowd of 35,000, for such a rather meaningless final game of the season, with the league already won. It was pure stage-craft by Stein. Three months later, on the 14th of August in the League Cup game against Rangers at Ibrox, sheer pragmatism took over. For only five of the Lisbon Lions were in the side.

The new era had begun, and was emphasised by a young man called Kenny Dalglish, who took his time to bend down and tie his bootlace before stepping calmly up, and scoring with a penalty with twenty minutes to go to take the score to 2-0, and put the result beyond dispute. That sanguine execution of Rangers did not mean that the newcomer had upstaged Jimmy. For again, in keeping with the hope of the manager at the end of the previous season, it had looked as if they might be able to rely on his consistency, as he and John Hughes ripped into the Rangers defence with maximum impact. Four weeks after Dalglish's entry into the big time, Jimmy clinched a 3-2 league victory at Ibrox when, in the very last minute he '...somehow managed to outjump the tall Rangers defenders to head the winner,' according to the report of the *Glasgow Herald*'s Jim Parkinson. He was already the stuff of legends, but there was obvious delight in providing even more evidence for generations still to come.

He was still a significant contributor to the Celtic cause, but it would be inaccurate to suggest that he was entering an exhilarating period in his life. His selection for games was now no longer assured and in Copenhagen on September 15th against BK 1903 in Celtic's 2-1 European Cup defeat he was ignominiously taken off at half-time. Then, having survived the tie and qualified to play Ujpest Dozsa, came a moment in the second leg of the quarter-finals (he had missed the first leg because of chicken-pox), which again underlined both the adoration of the wee man, and the increasingly uncertain relationship with his manager. The Hungarians had pulled the tie back to 2-2 on aggregate, when in the 54th minute, the East End of Glasgow heard a sound, from the terracings, which was akin to a flotilla of B-29s flying over Celtic Park. For there, on the track, was Jimmy, warming up to come on as a substitute for the injured Jim Brogan. Malcolm Munro of the *Evening Times* captured the emotional relief of the 70,000 crowd, better than most, when he wrote, 'I swear there were tears in the eyes of many as the Celtic red-head emerged on to the field.'

It was a pivotal moment, not only because he turned the fine balance of the tie into a rescue act, with agitated defenders so distracted by his very presence that, ten minutes after he had come on, Lou Macari was able to lob the goalkeeper for the equaliser to make it 1-1, but also because of a growing public scepticism over team selection. This very largely centred on the lack of consistency in the use of his wee winger. But Stein, who did not go out of his way to court popularity, except through the best way possible, winning trophies, was unaffected by any fuss about his winger even when, seven months later, he heard the response to one of his decisions in another European tie against the same Ujpest Dozsa in October 1972.

He substituted Jimmy, shortly after he had been denied a penalty, and heard Celtic Park ringing with boos at this unexpected exit. This was not a period of deep unrest, but of increasing scepticism, about the publicly unsteady Stein/Johnstone relationship. Where perhaps it made a significant difference was in European football, as indecision about Jimmy's role on the field was just part of an apparent decline in the self-confidence which had previously buttressed them against adversity. The sheer incessant nature of that kind of belief, which had propelled them to victory in the last seconds of their famous game against Vojvodina, was lodged in the minds of many as they faced Inter Milan in the second-leg of the semi-final on April 19th 1972 after the goalless draw in Milan, and kept the crowd in customary suspension, expecting the almost inevitable breakthrough, even well into extra-time. But there was something missing that night.

The sudden spurt of Jimmy which had brought about the corner against the Yugoslavs, which led to Billy McNeill's headed goal, was the element that was conspicuously absent: that flip, from the ordinary to the exceptional. The Italians had been taught bitter lessons from the past, absorbing much of the pressure with an almost elegant tactical know-how. Jimmy was Jimmy, without that extra spark. Malcolm Munro, a bit like Jimmy himself, in being a sort of non-conformist, and, believing in 'publish and be damned,' stepped into very contentious territory when he wrote in the *Evening Times* words which probably could have reflected the views of many in the support. 'If Celtic consider they have the best right-winger in Europe, why don't they play him on the right wing? Why play him in the middle – or allow him to roam all over the place?'

Few had ever dared to challenge Jock Stein on the matter of tactics. But Munro knew that he had an ace in the hand he was playing; Jimmy's popularity. There is no information of the specific Stein response to that article, although from hearing Munro speak of other encounters, one can guess it was not as fraternal as that of Stanley meeting Livingstone. So the historic penalty shoot-out, with the first taken and missed by Dixie Deans, costing Celtic their third European final appearance, was almost a valedictory gesture to a glorious era they had just left behind. The new era dawning was to be a turbulent one for Jimmy.

Billy McNeill, reflecting on the early 1970s, in a *Champions* magazine interview in 2005, with Kevin McCarra, attributed the relative decline in this period to the club's failure to hang on to outstanding young players. 'If players like Lou Macari and David Hay had been getting paid as they should have been, then there would have been the basis for mastery in European football for many years. The truth is Celtic were very often a selling club.'

You can see it was appropriate for Celtic's greatest captain to be looking back on an era when Jimmy could not spirit up the magic quite so readily to turn impending failure into resounding success. The squad badly needed fresher input. The famous Red

Star Belgrade night now seemed distantly nostalgic. That weighed particularly heavy on the minds of supporters who had to endure, stoically, a no-scoring draw, at Celtic Park in September 1973, against a Danish side, Vejle, which came from rural Jutland, famous for coastal sea-battles but not for football, and half of whose team were school-teachers. Those of them who taught history might have compared this indignity for Celtic to Troy's falling to a handful of men inside a wooden horse. What made it worse for Jimmy, whose appetite had not lessened for the great European nights, let us remember, was that in the absence of the injured Billy McNeill, he had been appointed captain for the night. He did not need reminding that he had just led out a team to debatably their most humiliating evening in European football, thus far, against rustic part-timers. Winning by a single goal in Denmark in the return match did not exactly spread fear and alarm amongst their potential opponents. Were they now a declining force?

That sort of question has to depend on the context in which it is asked. Certainly, people who were passionately devoted to the club were making a fuss about exactly that, but their anxieties have to be set against the fact that Celtic, by the end of season 1973/74, would equal the world record held by MTK Budapest of Hungary and CDNA Sofia by winning their 9th successive league championship, which entitled the club to rebuff the most biased interpretation of their situation eventually. However, if you bear in mind the European mentality which had flourished within Celtic Park since Lisbon, then there is little doubt that they were right to be concerned about standards. Celtic had become, understandably, elitist.

So there were misgivings about how much they had struggled to beat FC Basel from Switzerland in the quarter-final of the tournament. Swiss sides do not conjure up images of racy football, and mostly their game plans look like the internal workings of the cuckoo clock. But Celtic laboured against them in both legs, as if they were climbing the north face of the Eiger. They lost the first-leg 3-2 and in the second at Celtic Park, on March 20th 1974, it was 5-5 on aggregate after 90 minutes, and only a headed goal by Steve Murray for Celtic's fourth goal of the night, in extra-time, saw them through to what was to prove to be one of the most bizarre nights at Celtic Park, against a team from a city of which Jimmy had fond memories, Madrid. He was to be left with cuts and bruises decorating his body reminiscent of his South American adventure. This had Agnes and his family not knowing whether to laugh or cry over what appeared to be a sort of *fatwa* taken out against him, by certain people in a city which had once fallen under his spell, and in a season in which a good friend and former colleague was to suggest, strongly, that Jimmy was now past his best.

Autumn 2004

A house, understandably, can sometimes be compressed by illness into a tomb. The curtains can be drawn, the shutters put up, the light excluded, evidence of life outside diminished to tiny distant echoes and the atmosphere range from silence to hushed tones. This provides a kind of claustrophobic mustiness, like the reclusive Miss Havisham's room in 'Great Expectations.' The Johnstone household was as far removed from that as the sun is from the bowels of the earth. Even from the first day of his illness and the news of it spreading more widely through word of mouth and among the Lisbon Lions in particular, the Viewpark home had become as open, as busy, as vibrant as the main alley in a shopping mall. People came and went with regularity. Nobody was excluded. Except press photographers.

Jimmy drew the line at that. He didn't mind being snapped when he was outside at a function, but he didn't want to give the impression that he was hopelessly housebound. Apart from that there was no hiding from the realities of what they knew people would observe in coming to meet him personally. Anybody was welcome, in that regard. But there was a certain test that everybody had to undergo there. It was to overcome the initial shock of seeing the inert figure in the chair, completely distorting the image in the mind's eye of the spritely figure in a green and white jersey. There he was with a ready smile, but lying back in his chair, his mental agility totally unimpaired, but his arms unnaturally straight and still in front of his body in a posture that suggested he was in a deep-freeze, but minus the shivering.

You had to have a steely determination not to show how affected you really were. Jim Craig summarises the reason for that unease well. 'One of the tea ladies at the club used to say of that great group of players, in the 1960s and 1970s, as she served us some beverages at the park after a training session, "All of youse have goat ants in your pants." Jimmy, without doubt, was the one she would have singled out for most of her approbation. Jinky was always on the move. Not for him the chats in the dressing room after the shower; he would be in and out of the water in a flash and have his clothes on within seconds, desperate to get out and about in the wider world. I often thought he must never have been fully dry before the clothes went on. It was truly ironic that this mobility that he loved was eventually taken away from him by this dreadful disease. And yet never once did he complain about his lot in all the times I met him then.'

Albeit that the emotion was extremely difficult to describe when I first saw him, even in the earlier stages of the disease, and needing to disguise the shock, I was reminded of Abe Lincoln's story of the little black boy who stubbed his toe in the dark and admitted the complexity of that by saying, 'It was too sore to laugh, and I was too old to cry.' You were caught betwixt these emotions. One former colleague, Jim Brogan, had to turn his back and leave the house, and standing on the pavement break down in tears out of Jimmy's sight so that it would not disturb the wee man. He simply could not contain himself. Our greatest help was himself. He would banish the notion of invalidity within a few seconds, with his own irrepressible urge to make you feel at ease. One man experienced this, with particular force, although little known compared to the celebrities who came through the household over the years of the illness. Jim Simonette. They called him Simmie. He turned out to be an unsung hero of the latter part of Jimmy's life. He worked within the Willie Haughey organisation. He was asked by Haughey to go to Uddingston to help a friend of his who would need some assistance within the home, and to return with ideas as to how this could be made possible. He was told the address, and then when the name was mentioned he thought he was having his leg pulled. But he certainly was not prepared for his first ever meeting with the player he had so admired through the years of supporting the club.

'Honestly, I couldn't believe it,' Simonette said. 'This wonderful player lying back in his chair in that peculiar way with his arms tucked in beside him, so helpless looking. I was shocked and you know I am not sure if I did show that to him. All I can remember, of that first moment, is that he smiled and said, "I'm sorry I cannae shake your hand." I found myself walking across and kissing him on the head.'

What followed, after that emotional moment, was a practical examination of how they could adapt the house to make his life and the daily necessities of living much more bearable. The first thing Simmie could identify was that a toilet had to be at ground level and with adaptations made for a person without the use of hands and arms. Eventually they constructed a walk-in shower which started automatically on entry, but which was awkward to control when in full flow. There was decking to be installed just outside the room at the same level so he could slip out there without the problem of steps. Later they were to install an electric chair-lift to take him upstairs. This caused occasional hilarity when it would stick half-way up, for some reason, and Agnes would threaten to leave him there all day if he gave her any cheek. It was never followed through, although on one occasion he fell out of the chair trying to control it himself, and just lay there laughing at the seemingly preposterous nature of it all.

All these changes were set in motion after that visit and worked on personally by Simmie, who in that process was to become close to the wee man. But in all the years of working in the house Simmie dreaded one thing. 'Jimmy couldn't go to the toilet himself obviously. He had to be helped, and in the latter stages it was amazing to see how Aggie could lift him up and do the needful. But you know in all the time I sat with him I feared he would ask me to take him to the toilet. Me, take the great Jimmy Johnstone to the toilet! I just feared the time would come when that occasion would arise. It never did, curiously enough, in all that time. But, you know, by that stage, it wasn't Jimmy my great

*hero I was talking to but Jimmy the man who needed help. I felt...
chosen. I use that word advisedly.'*

*His arduous work in the house was helped by the light-hearted
mood around him when Simmie was never entirely sure if Jimmy
was pulling his leg or not. 'I came in one day when I was putting
in new flooring and he said to me, "You'll need to put new
locks in all the doors, we could be broken into." I told him that
there was little to steal since there was no evidence of football
memorabilia there. The only thing connected with football in the
whole house was in his display cabinet. It was a signed copy of
a DVD from his great pal, Willie Henderson. "I know," he said,
"Maybe I'm the only thing in the house they would steal. Did you
know they tried to steal Elvis when he died!"'*

*It was said with a smile on his face, but even yet Simmie feels
Jimmy did fear that the sanctity of the house would be breached
by some looney. But to make him more secure in his enforced
captivity Simmie alighted upon a brilliant idea of communication.
He would be asking Jimmy to use his magic feet again.*

TWELVE
Rowing Against the Tide

It was seven days before the cataclysmic Atletico Madrid night at Celtic Park that one of the most celebrated Lisbon Lions, Tommy Gemmell, voiced his reservations about the current form of Jimmy Johnstone on the eve of the semi-final of the Scottish Cup. Tommy was now captain of Dundee and had helped his new club beat his former one in the League Cup final 1-0, four months previously. He was entitled to assess the game against Celtic more favourably for his own side and did so with relish. In an interview in the *Daily Record* on the day of the semi-final, April 3rd 1974, under the heading 'Jimmy Who?' he was scathing in his criticism of his former mate, although certainly did not use the phrase of the eye-catching headline. Nevertheless, he was uncompromising. 'If wee Jimmy is playing, it will suit me perfectly. I'm not just saying that, by the way, I mean it. There is absolutely no reason in the world why we should worry about the wee man lining up against us. He hasn't shown any form at all this season and we have faced the best Celtic team available before [i.e. that season] and beaten them twice.'

Tommy was expressing a professional judgement, without any regard to his deep commitment to the Celtic cause in the past. He was also professionally focused, for most commentators had reached the conclusion that Jimmy had been well under par that season. But Tommy was also tempting providence, and should have realised that Jimmy had always relished the gauntlet being thrown down at him: that unpredictability was one of his prime assets. Others had tried to dismiss him as a decreasing influence. And suffered. There might have been some folk, reading Tommy Gemmell's words, left thinking they could have been put to the music of Peter, Paul and Mary, with the refrain, 'When will they ever learn...?'

For Jimmy won the match: not single-handedly, but almost. Not only did he score the only goal of the game from six yards, three minutes from half-time, but according to the report in the *Daily Record*, did 'practically as he liked with his former colleague,' and Alex Cameron spared none of Tommy Gemmell's blushes by writing, 'Johnstone tantalised and taunted well-beaten Dundee, ran circles round them and kept coming on with the ball at his feet.' Although Jimmy let his feet speak for him, he also went public, in print, when he told Alex Cameron in an interview on April 5th, 'After Wednesday night, I feel as if I'm starting all over again. A lot of people whom I thought were my friends have said a lot of rubbish about me being finished. John Clark and Neil Mochan at Celtic Park certainly didn't. They've given me tremendous help. They're the two I thank particularly. I'm going to screw the head from now on. I know in the past I've done a lot of things I shouldn't have done. That's going to change.'

That definitely sounds like closure on the rake's progress, does it not? But we have to recall that affectionate phrase used by his nearest and dearest, 'Jimmy, being Jimmy...' It was a rueful admission that predicting in which ways his personality would lead him, was as reliable as picking a Grand National winner with a pin, blindfolded. Certainly his boss was not holding his breath on hearing that, as he had listened to contrition before. All Stein wanted, five days after that statement, was for Jimmy to recreate a Red Star Belgrade performance for him again. But Red Star had tried to play football. This time Celtic's opponents renounced such a preposterous idea.

Murmur the name Atletico to any Celtic player who played on the evening of April 10th 1974, and you can sense they are looking back to a few hours when it was as if a beast had been set loose to stalk the streets of the East End of Glasgow, and was out to get them. You get a response which is a mix of disgust and frustration, spiced by anger. They now know, in retrospect, that in Atletico Madrid's efforts to brutalise the Celtic players on the Celtic Park pitch, they had been sucked into a massive con. Billy McNeill sums it up well, 'We shouldn't have got angry with all of this. But in many ways you couldn't blame us. We got too upset about what was happening and we started to spend a lot of time protesting, rightly. They knocked us off our stride. That was exactly what they wanted. They didn't want to play football that night, they wanted football to be stopped altogether. Nothing could be more cynical than that, but it worked for them.'

The poison emanated from South America. Their coach, the Argentinian Juan Carlos Lorenzo, had the dubious honour of leading Lazio to such outrageous conduct on the field in previous games, that UEFA had banned the Italian club from European competitions. This ought to have qualified him as a platoon commander for the assault on the Falklands, but not as a football manager again. Which, being the way football is run, is why he knew somebody would still take a chance on him. And assuming that he would need a supply of potential assassins he deliberately packed his squad with Argentines of his own nature. Lorenzo would have been fully aware of what happened with Racing Club in 1967, and probably assumed that intimidation was the better part of valour.

There was a man called Diaz fielded at left-back. Jimmy knew him well. Ruben Osvaldo Diaz had tried to maim him before, at Hampden Park when he played for Racing Club. About five minutes after the referee blew for the start of the game, Diaz tackled the wee man waist-high, in the manner of Jackie Chan slamming a drug dealer, but without Chan's cheery smile. That seemed to set the tone of the evening. Davie Hay, who could certainly look after himself, even against pit-bull terriers foaming at the mouth, puts a different complexion on this game he played in. 'Because of what happened in Argentina in '67 big Jock had warned us before we went out, 'No retaliation!' However, I think if just one of us had lashed out, at one of them, it would all have stopped. I believe we really needed to wallop one to prove they were basically cowards. I think that would have stopped it. I mean, they began to play keepie-uppie with Jimmy.'

Jimmy never once complained. As they surrounded and hacked at him, he just bounced back up and went at them again. The sequence of persistent fouling, tolerated by the referee, until it was too much even for him to accept, was the Atletico master-plan. It made fluency impossible. As foul piled on foul, the referee had to jump in to prevent serious injury, and perhaps even a riot amongst an increasingly angry and, at the same time, incredulous crowd, who could scarcely believe what they were watching. The booking of seven Atletico men and the dismissal of three, Diaz (barely surprising, although his performance was worthy of a report to the Procurator Fiscal), Quique (clearly wishing to keep orthopaedic surgeons in gainful employ) and above all, Ayala (a highly talented footballer who had just debased his trade in front of 73,000 witnesses), reflected the mayhem of the evening. John Clark, on Celtic's coaching staff at the time, said of him, 'The man with the long hair, Ayala, could be some player but that night he was the biggest culprit, the ring-leader. He was vicious.'

Davie Hay repeats a regret. 'You know I think it was a pity we left our retaliation until after the game.' It was, in fact, epic retaliation. Harry Hood recalls that the final whistle signalled bedlam. 'Suddenly all hell broke out on the touch line and right through the tunnel. Everybody was into it, kicks flying, punches thrown.' John Clark remembers it as if it lasted half-an-hour, but reckons it lasted only a couple of minutes. 'But you've never seen anything like it. Even the police were caught up in the middle of it, a milling mass of men just trying to hurt each other, right through to the dressing-room area.'

It was there, in the tunnel, one of the Atletico players ran at Jimmy and kicked him in the stomach, the final act of cowardice of the night, which, for the record, ended goalless. The shabby night had seen cynicism triumph. For Celtic it had been a miracle of survival. For Jimmy it was to be days of anxiety about his own personal safety in the return leg. There ought not to have been a return leg anyway, and it is astonishing in the passing of time to look back on that match, and still be bewildered as to how UEFA could have sanctioned a second game. Nowadays, Atletico would have been expelled, and perhaps served several years in the wilderness. But there were two reasons which predominated.

Firstly, UEFA did not have the crusading individuals in their ranks to drive through punitive measures against certain clubs from certain countries. Secondly, it was thought, with considerable justification, that the Latin countries had an undue influence on events in the corridors of power. So the return game had to be played. It was at this time that Agnes noticed that Jimmy was taking the negative build-up to the game quite seriously. He would make one or two jokes about it, but, underneath all of that, she noted that he was taking note of everything written in previews of the game.

As we have noted before, his normal mental preparation for any game was basic. A match did not exist until he was within sight of a stadium and then the urge to get out there and play was overwhelming. This time he was clearly apprehensive. After all, a noted Spanish newspaper *ABC* had pointed the finger at him when it castigated the Turkish referee, Dogan Babacan, as 'clearly anti-Spanish, an official who deliberately ignored the tricks and theatrics of the veteran Johnstone.' (Note, by the way, the use of the word 'veteran.' It is the first recorded use of that word in connection with Jimmy, whom we thought was a kind of Peter Pan, beyond ageing, and never used by the Scottish media, but perhaps a sudden reminder from the Continent that Jimmy was nearing thirty.)

It was ironic that this publication should write of him in such a way, since seven years previously, it had printed words of unbridled praise of the same player, after his performance in the Di Stefano testimonial game, writing of how he had 'slalomed' his way through the Real defence with ease. Thus admiration had given way to hatred, with *ABC* more concerned about pandering to the over-emotional Spanish public, than reflecting the infamy of their own players.

Celtic's sojourn in Madrid was like a re-run of their time spent on both sides of the River Plate in 1967. There was police presence everywhere. It was obvious that while this was perhaps for their own good, there is little doubt that players can find it difficult to throw off the feeling of restraint in their own performances in such an environment. Then there was the raucous background of noise which followed Celtic everywhere, and even sustained during the night at their hotel in the outskirts of the city. All this was provided by the belligerent fans of the home side.

The Atletico support is drawn from the southern working-class district of the capital. They are recognised as providing the passion in their Atletico stadium that the supporters of their city rivals Real cannot match, and thus they have accused their opposites in the Bernabeu of being *pechos frios* (cold-chested, but in truth was a slur which made them seem like shop-window dummies). The *rojiblancos* are far from being so, and even under normal circumstances Celtic would have been in for a torrid time in the Estadio Vicente Calderon. But the circumstances were far from being normal, as Jimmy himself recorded years later.

'The worse moment of my life came on the night before the match,' he said. 'I was rooming, as usual, with Bobby Lennox when the telephone rang about 2am. Bobby awoke first and picked up the receiver before handing it to me. Still half asleep, I answered, only to be greeted by a sinister Spanish voice which snarled in broken English, *"Johnstone, you are dead!"* Needless to say I had difficulty catching forty winks that night. The following morning rumours spread that a sniper was planning to shoot me at the stadium. I was petrified. After breakfast Jock pulled me to one side and revealed that he had also received a threat to his life. So we were both in the firing line. This certainly was not what I had bargained for.'

Whether the manager had received actual threats was neither here nor there, in the frenetic atmosphere which had been created, but what he was clearly doing was putting an arm round the wee winger, offering him comfort, with the thought that they were all in this together, by adding, 'Don't worry, wee man. You'll be OK. When you start to jink and jive out there nobody will be able to hit you. What about me? I've got to sit in the dug-out like a sitting duck!' He even offered Jimmy the opportunity to pull out of the game, which, not unexpectedly, was turned down.

Celtic did try to make light of all this, as Davie Hay recounts. 'On the team-bus on the way to the ground Steelie [Jimmy Steel, the highly popular and perennially jolly team masseur,] had got this toy machine-gun from somewhere. He started to go round the bus pretending to shoot at the police-cars which were escorting us. You could see the guns sticking out of the cars. It caused a laugh until Jock noticed this, and went spare, shouting at Steelie that you couldn't kid around with these people. I think that reminded us about what we were about to face up to.'

When they arrived there, Stein discovered that he was not in fact a sitting duck, but was more like a sitting mole, for they had escorted him to a dug-out which was in fact well below the surface of the pitch, and from where he could hardly see the game, while Lorenzo, the Atletico manager, sat on a touchline bench on the centre circle. It was a case of aggravating, consummate

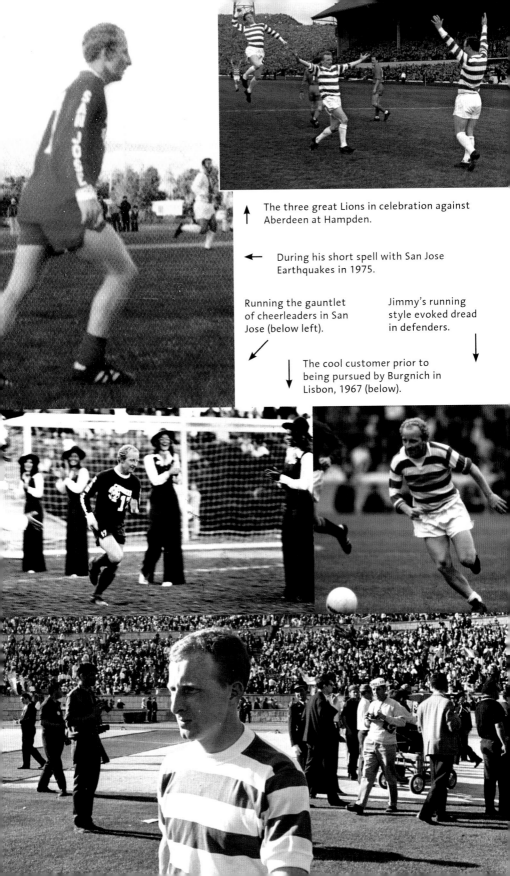

The three great Lions in celebration against Aberdeen at Hampden.

During his short spell with San Jose Earthquakes in 1975.

Running the gauntlet of cheerleaders in San Jose (below left).

Jimmy's running style evoked dread in defenders.

The cool customer prior to being pursued by Burgnich in Lisbon, 1967 (below).

In action against Tottenham Hotspu[r] at Hampden in 196[ ]

His colleagues did note he was on edg[e] before any game despite the calm appearances here.

He returned from Argentina in 1967 with bruises all over him. Physio Bob Rooney had his work cut out with the wee man, attending to his bumps and scrapes.

↑ He loved this area near the Clyde where he did much of his training.

← With the family after landing back from Los Angeles following his abortive sojourn there.

↓ Willie O'Neill, Bobby Murdoch, and Bertie Auld shared many a social occasion with Jimmy after their playing days were over.

↑ During the St Patrick's Day March in New York in 2006. The procession halted for a minute's silence outside St Patrick's Cathedral on Fifth Avenue to mourn his death.

Ian Henderson, the man who guided him through much of his illness, with his great pal Willie Henderson before one of their chat evenings for an audience in a hotel.

↓

His return to the hallowed turf in Lisbon where his memory of great events lifted his spirits even as his body weakened.

↓

...emory Lane. Unwell
...ough he was in
...003, he poses where
...e once stood in 1967
... the team's hotel,
...e Palacio in Estoril.

...mmy at Ground
...ero in New York.

...wo of the greats. The
...eeting with Eusebio
... 2003 was one of the
...motional highpoints
...f his Lisbon visit.

↖ ↑ Jimmy at home

With Agnes and the grown-up family, James, Eileen and Marie, who were a source of strength to him when his arms had totally failed and his neck muscles were weakening.

←

The Celtic Chairman, John Reid, seen here along with Ian Henderson, had cause to thank Jimmy for his intervention in Westminster matters concerning stem-cell policy

On the news of his illness
spreading, the Vatican
issued a sympathetic
response indicating Pope
John Paul II's concern about
the wee man.

s increasing debilitation
d not prevent him from
minding his celebrity
sitor, Rod Stewart, not
depart from his normal
nging repertoire.

he last picture. Stephen
cManus and Jimmy look
a happy frame of mind.
wo days later he died.

Vhen he could still use his arms,
ugging Henrik Larsson seemed
ke confirmation of their mutual
espect over the generations.

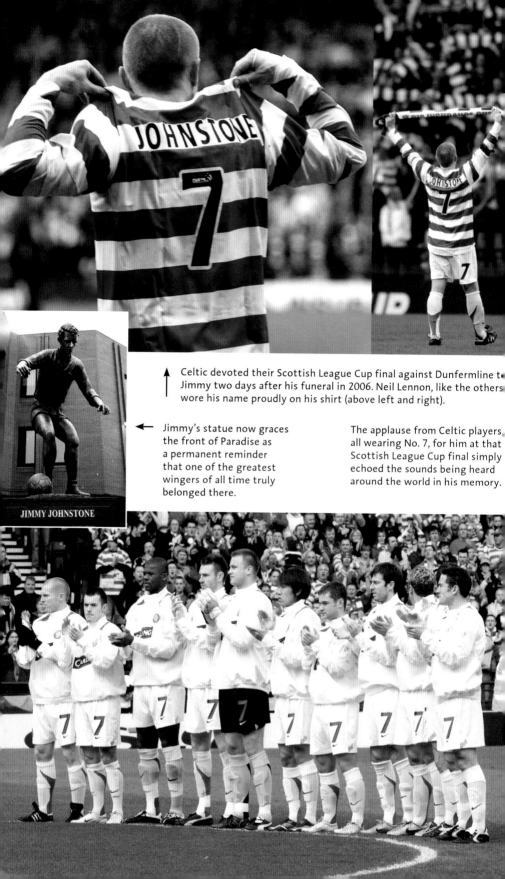

Celtic devoted their Scottish League Cup final against Dunfermline to Jimmy two days after his funeral in 2006. Neil Lennon, like the others, wore his name proudly on his shirt (above left and right).

Jimmy's statue now graces the front of Paradise as a permanent reminder that one of the greatest wingers of all time truly belonged there.

The applause from Celtic players, all wearing No. 7, for him at that Scottish League Cup final simply echoed the sounds being heard around the world in his memory.

JIMMY JOHNSTONE

gamesmanship. All in all, Celtic had been ruthlessly upstaged. The game was bland by comparison with the first leg. Atletico had brought back some of their more skilled players, who under careful official UEFA scrutiny tried to play some football, of which they were perfectly capable. Kenny Dalglish did have one shot brilliantly saved by their keeper Miguel Reina, (father of Liverpool's Pepe) but apart from that they lacked inspiration and went down, 2-0, to two late goals.

Jimmy did not leave the stadium unscathed. He admitted himself that he was 'non-existent' during the game, but was the victim of a right-hook delivered by his immediate opponent Jose Luis Capon, which was to prove to have a sad consequence. He came back with an eye blacker than a coal seam. There was one dissenting voice, amongst the supportive media expressions in the immediate aftermath, when much sympathy was extended towards Celtic for the physical hammering they had taken in the tie. It came from Alex Cameron of the *Daily Record*, when he wrote, 'The Lisbon Lions would have had Atletico for breakfast, no matter how hard or how often they kicked ... in the end they lost on ability in Madrid, and no amount of moaning about the bad sportsmanship of Atletico will change this.' Obviously the Lisbon legacy could inspire, but also haunt them.

That black eye was to cost Jimmy. Sorely vexed about losing out in Europe, his mood was not lightened by the injury to that eye, which meant he was confined to the substitutes' bench at Falkirk, three days later, and did not play in that historic landmark match, in which Celtic clinched their ninth successive league championship. Even more daunting for him was that he felt as if he were losing family members in that there were now only three Lisbon Lions left in the squad: Billy McNeill, Bobby Lennox and himself. He was not experiencing a sense of desolation about this, because he still had around him talented players. But he was not the Jimmy of the late 1960s. Of course, how could he be, you might ask?

Consider the many miles over which he had weaved, bobbed, sprinted in all that time since he had first established himself. There was also an even more human reason, as Harry Hood recognised. 'He was missing his pals, and I think he was beginning to feel a bit lonely, daft as that may sound.' To anybody who knew how Jimmy flourished among his ain folk in Viewpark, it was not so daft. That is why he looked forward so much to a different challenge in an entirely new environment – the World Cup finals in Germany that very summer of 1974.

But by the evening of May 15th of that year, there was little chance of finding a corner of the globe ignorant of the fact that a Scottish player, preparing for the World Cup finals, had gone to sea, without the means of navigation or of proper propulsion, and was saved only narrowly from a watery grave. That would be a synopsis of some of the reports which spread like wildfire around the news-wires, pointing the spotlight on a tiny hotel in Largs, and a wee man who liked a lark or two to brighten up the tedium of match preparation. The name Jimmy Johnstone was on the tongues of even those in Outer Mongolia who normally took interest only in polo matches with a bull's head. With the boozed-up Scottish squad, in the background, offering vocal support on the prom, acting either like a Greek chorus, depending on how seriously the incident was to be taken, or an encouraging rabble at a strip-club, Jimmy pushed out a rowing-boat and, standing amidships, started to wave the only oar he had, chanting with encouraging patriotism, 'Scot-land, Scot-land!'; his mates cheering him on, as the crowd had at Hampden the night before when he had played splendidly in the defeat of Wales in the Home Championship.

The boat was drifting out, not in, as they sometimes do. Of course, there were those there who encouraged the idea that he would end up having to go through customs at Manhattan, portraying the comical, whimsical aspect of the incident. But since they had to call out a rescue boat, eventually, to pull him back, it lent another shadier aspect to the wheeze. So which was it? A potential calamity, or just a wheeze that lent itself to media hype? To start with, it was 6am. And they were to play the Auld Enemy in a couple of days' time. Does it get any more serious than that? Albeit, we also have to relate it to whether Jimmy was in any danger or not.

Accounts of this differ though. Not the facts, simply the interpretations heaped upon the incident. This is Davie Hay's view. 'A few of us had just come out of the bar after hearing some of the fuss. It was now daylight and we could see him out there signalling, but not looking like he was heading for disaster. To be honest we only saw the funny side of it, and I think he did too. The whole squad were on the prom by this time, killing themselves laughing. I admit that we then began to think about doing something about it, so Eric Schaedler, the former Hibernian player and myself decided to go down and get a boat to see if we could go out and tow him in. There was a small leak in our boat and the word got around that we were going to put our lives at risk by heading out after him. But it was a tiny leak that was typical of these boats. And by the time we started to consider this, a call had been put out, and a rescue boat appeared on the scene. Now I know about all the jokes about how he was heading for America and all that. But this has been ramped up by after-dinner speakers and the media and such, and to be honest I never felt he was in any danger, for the sea was dead calm. There wasn't a breath of wind.'

It would be churlish to spoil a story that has gone the rounds so often, but it would appear that Jimmy, a strong swimmer, on a sea like a millpond, was in as much danger as he would have been being helped over Old Edinburgh Road in Viewpark by a lollipop man. What had been at stake was not his life, but his reputation. Controversial stories about him still clung to his record like barnacles under a rowing-boat, and he therefore became the prime target for ridicule and abuse.

Some of the media waded into the incident, portraying it as a national maritime epic, and heaped blame on this one man who they felt was utterly irresponsible and was defeating the purpose of preparation for the World Cup. It was a jape, for which, of course, he had to carry the can. Without excusing him, what was largely overlooked was the fact that almost the entire Scottish squad were up through the night drinking, and were still there whooping it up on the promenade as daylight revealed the boat incident. It would have been unusual for any Scottish side not to have headed for a bar after a match. Although it might appear as a blatant example of mass disobedience, there was, perhaps in rueful consideration, nothing outrageously different from the norm in their behaviour, except for the proximity of the sea and Jimmy's derring-do personality.

So, if he was at the front end of the pantomime horse in this escapade, then it should not be overlooked that any of the inebriated others could have been chosen for the rear-end. At least Jimmy could claim he had come out of the bar for a breath of fresh air and some exercise: a point that was not missed by Hay. 'I am not making excuses for us all, but that tiny hotel we were in at Largs was not fit for purpose. For example, the higher up your room was, the less chance there was of you getting hot water for a shower or bath. And after a game you just wanted a bit of relaxation, and it was just too small for that.'

Claustrophobia as the cause of indiscipline might be carrying excuses too far, but what is beyond doubt is that that inadequate hotel exacerbated the needs for players to let off some steam somewhere, whether one likes that or not. To a personality like Jimmy residing there would have seemed like doing solitary at Alcatraz. The stigma, though, was indelible. Even had manager Wille Ormond arranged a public induction for them all into the Trappist order, the harm had been done. What Jimmy had, inadvertently, kick-started, was as close a scrutiny of the behaviour of the Scottish players as they ever had had before, and which reached its demeaning baseline in the pre-World Cup tour of Belgium and Norway. There is little doubt that it also reflected on the fact that the genial Ormond, who had, in my view, the best Scottish squad for any of our World Cup finals when he took them to Germany in 1974, exerted minimal influence over his men. They certainly liked him. But too often you felt that he was seeking authority, rather than imposing it.

So the angry response of the Scottish players, including Jimmy, who was exonerated by Ormond, for what basically they all considered to be no more than high jinks, was not inspired by their manager's attitude. They now had an incentive to strike back at the press. Davie Hay points out that Jimmy was the most fired up of all. Destroying England three days after the Largs incident would be like the best damage limitation of all. 'Some might have thought all the adverse publicity would have put him off. But I had got to know him well enough and I knew he would stuff it up his critics. And, by God, he did. He was great.'

During that game he put his imprimatur on events by some typical mazy runs, being instrumental in bringing about the second Scottish goal by Dalglish in their 2-0 win over the Auld Enemy. He had performed an impudent back-heel to Peter Lorimer, whose cross was then turned past Shilton by Dalglish via a deflection from Todd. His performance that day was like a man shorn of all cares in the world, his close dribbling and speed amounting to a personal dismantling of a very professional England defence. In light of the bad press which had preceded the match it was astonishing that he could summon up such a carefree exhibition. At the end of the game, as they embarked on their lap of honour around the stadium, being the farewell party before departure for Germany, Jimmy waited until he was just below the Hampden press box, before issuing an imperious two-fingered 'V' sign to all of us assembled there.

The only people who might have taken offence were the English, for, after all, we had just beaten them, and what is more they had not qualified for Germany. At that moment, looking down on high at him, Jimmy was now the very epitome of the Scottish entrepreneurial spirit, prepared to be outrageous and take risks; he was now to us, a hero, a five-foot four embodiment of Andrew Carnegie and James Logie Baird, rolled into one; the torch-bearer of unorthodoxy who would set the World Cup on fire. We were all swept up in enthusiasm, and we would have had a whip-round to buy him fishing gear and a new boat if he had wanted. But one man would not have contributed. Mr Stein. For in the summer edition of the *Celtic View* that year, he showed his hand.

After paying tribute to the two remaining Lisbon Lions, Billy McNeill and Bobby Lennox, he said, 'Then there's Jimmy Johnstone. What can I say about him? He's an enigma. In the shadows for much of the season, he suddenly takes a tumble to himself, and there's all the old artistry and ball skills in full flower, so much so that he finds himself back in Scotland's colours and a Hampden hero in the win over England. However, Johnstone will need to show more dedication if he is to be of any use to Celtic next season.'

What had happened at Largs would not have endeared him to his stern taskmaster who was, nevertheless, still inclined to give him the benefit of the doubt, although with a sting in the tail. But that does not account for the fact that Jimmy was not selected for even one of Scotland's three World Cup matches. Why not?

Firstly, there was the factor of the pre-World Cup tour of Belgium and Norway. As I was an eye-witness to much of it, you had to admit the preparations were as assiduous and as therapeutic as a September weekend bus party to Blackpool. The free champagne dished out to all and sundry on the official flight to Ghent, and then, a couple of days later, repeated on the flight to Oslo, including, it has to be said, for the media at the back of the official plane, set the tone for those few days which seemed like a re-creation of the 'Roaring Twenties pre-prohibition' era. There was much drinking. Not by all the Scottish players, but by a section which you could call the hard core, including the captain Billy Bremner and Jimmy, the two of them mutually respectful of their abilities, both on and off the field. After a dreadful performance against the Belgians, in which Scotland lost 2-1, the party were domiciled in what was essentially a students' hostel just outside Oslo and of which, given the five-star residences they normally enjoyed with their clubs, they did not approve. The beer cellars were handy though.

One night sitting in one of them, with the English commentator, John Motson, Bremner and Jimmy appeared, made direct tracks for us, sat down in front of us, and the wee man started to sing at the top of his voice. Motson having been brought up in conventional English surrounds had never before been so close to two Scottish drunks. He reacted as if he had a sighting of the Loch Ness monster. He was petrified and gave the impression he was wishing to be back to the world of Morris dancing again. There was no chance that Jimmy was about to offer the Englishman a ditty by Noel Coward. Out came the lusty Viewpark repertoire which would have gone down well at the local miners' welfare. It was entertaining, it was largely harmless, but it was attracting the attention of the surrounding Norwegian students, and even if the two had been stone-cold sober, which they were not, and had sat down calmly to discuss world peace or the state of the economy with us, they were still in breach of the curfew which had been imposed on the players.

Bremner, it has to be said, was in a worse condition than Jimmy, who was his noisy but cheery self. The Scottish captain was the kind of surly drunk who believes the world is ganging up against him, and carrying the threat that if you had said a word out of place to him he would have slugged you. You could have scarcely believed that they had to prepare to play against Norway in a couple of days' time. Then we spied Ormond looking on at this scene. A storm was brewing, we thought. Instead, he turned on heel and disappeared. A couple of minutes later, in came the SFA doctor, Dr Fitzsimmons of Celtic, who had obviously been delegated to do the dirty work.

As a constant witness to how Stein dealt with such bravado, the doc did not mess about. His stern rebuke had them fleeing for the exit. That, in an instant, indicated one of the overall problems: the manager was probably more scared of them than they were of him. That is not a formula on which you can build a winning mentality. The manager's timidity could not justify two players breaking a curfew on such an important mission as a World Cup, but if managerial authority is off-loaded to someone else, as it was so blatantly then, and the word of that drifts back through the squad and the press, then discipline is at least questionable, and you are presenting an Achilles heel to the public. Although as a club manager Stein had to deal with players who liked to slip under his radar for nocturnal entertainment, if he had been in charge in Norway, such a situation would never have reached that absurd climax. It takes us back to the theme of how dependent Jimmy was on the rigorous attention of the Big Man.

Although Jimmy did play against Norway, and Scotland won 2-1 the harm had been done. The SFA had gone public and issued a statement saying that they had been on the verge of sending two players home, but had accepted their apologies. The players were unnamed but, by now, even grannies back home knew to whom they were referring. This episode and the rebellious nature of the Scottish squad who had declared war on the press, even resorting to ripping the trade-marks of the manufacturer off their boots because they could not reach a commercial agreement, and employing a so-called agent who had trained for World Cup duties by being a rep for the Playboy Club, all conspired to raise serious public scepticism about the prospects for the imminent tournament. All that junk behaviour trailed in the wake of the squad to Germany. It was there, to his horror, that Jimmy discovered that he was now being touted by the international media as a totemic figure of Scottish hard drinking.

He and the others were sitting one evening in the lounge of the Sporthotel Erbismuehle, just outside Frankfurt, a kind of old fashioned hunting or ski lodge reminiscent of the kind seen in the *Prisoner of Zenda*, when Jimmy's face was suddenly flashed up on the German TV screen, followed by a report. When it was translated for the squad they were shocked to learn that it was stating as fact, that Jimmy had been found drunk in his room and was about to be sent home. Ormond was enraged by this and issued a statement which simply said, 'Jimmy trained this morning and during the afternoon went on a shopping expedition and practised his putting here at the hotel. There's not a word of truth in these reports.'

The SFA even went to the extent of sending a letter to FIFA complaining about this and asking for all media outlets in Germany to issue a retraction. There was as much chance of getting the

German media to play ball as there was of demanding they impose a ban on sauerkraut dishes. For as anyone in the public limelight can find out, sometimes painfully, as Jimmy did in this instance, perception is all. If you are tagged with a dubious reputation, however inaccurate that might be, then it will cling, no matter how hard you work to deny and rectify it. He certainly thought the first step should be to take legal action. It did not come to that, and by then the harm had been done anyway.

So we arrive at the second factor of why he was not selected for any of the World Cup games: that is that Ormond by now felt, quite wrongly in footballing terms, that Jimmy was a PR disaster for the SFA; that to have him on the field would be to focus too much attention on him, and that it would suggest that disciplinary norms did not exist. The manager had become so influenced by the preceding events that he actually thought Willie Morgan was a better proposition than Jimmy. Without disparaging Morgan, he was not in the same class as Jimmy, at his best. This proved to be a kind of politically correct decision, eliminating the element of risk. Jimmy was too much of that, it seemed. But even more curious was the attitude of the Big Man. Stein worked closely with us as an analyst for the BBC, and at the same time met and talked to the Scottish players occasionally at their various hotels.

On one occasion I witnessed him savaging Bremner, in a hotel in Dortmund, before the opening match with Zaire, telling him to stop moaning about the SFA and Ormond. And more significantly I saw him walk Willie Morgan round the hotel grounds, before the Brazil match, deep in conversation, almost as if the winger had found a father confessor, and as if Stein was wishing to be seen endorsing him. By contrast, not once, during the entire stay in Germany, did I hear him mention Jimmy or his absence from the team selections. Managers usually like to punt their own players, with justification, but Stein was oddly silent on this issue. It was almost as if this was the beginning of a serious disaffection with the wee man; that he had already given him up for lost. For consider what he said prior to the Finals, in an interview with journalist Hugh McIlvanney.

'Most foreign opponents have never seen anything like him before, and they can lose concentration for 20 minutes trying to work him out. What will the black fellers from Zaire think of him? They'll take him for a leprechaun or a hobgoblin. Even the Brazilians have never seen anything like him. If Willie Ormond can keep a grip on him, Jinky may show some of the old stuff.' The slight inference of doubt about Ormond's viability, in that regard, hints at the deeper longing of Stein to have been able to be in there looking after his own player, and in that regard it did strike us that Jimmy, minus Stein, was like a rambler without a compass.

The third reason for Jimmy's non-participation is more bizarre. With Scotland having beaten Zaire 2-0, drawn creditably 0-0 with Brazil, they needed a victory against Yugoslavia to qualify for the latter stages of the competition. The men from the Balkans feared only one man. A spy sent to look at the Scots in their previous game against Brazil, spoke to Jim Blair of Glasgow's *Evening Times*, and said, 'People in my country still talk of Johnstone because of his fantastic performance against Red Star Belgrade several years ago. Why did Willie Ormond play Willie Morgan? Surely Johnstone would have done better in that role?' Of course he might have been spinning a line.

Although, if you think back to Lisbon in 1967, all the preoccupation with Jimmy adversely affected Inter, even though they kept him so closely marked. In that sense, the very prospect of having to cope with Jimmy might have distracted them. That had no effect on Ormond who made it clear his first choice would again be the Manchester United player, Morgan. Davie Hay, who had a marvellous World Cup, makes it obvious how he felt. 'If ever there was an occasion to play Jimmy it was in this game in Frankfurt. The Yugoslavs were a fine side, a bit mechanical, but their defence was solid. It needed flair to break through them and Jimmy was perhaps the only man in the squad who had the ability to do that. We needed something so different in our attack and it was a tragedy he didn't play.'

In fact, he almost did. Since the Yugoslavs required only a draw to qualify, they formed a nine-man barrier against a Scottish side quite unable to find the necessary penetration. When the Slavs scored the opening goal, though, in the 82nd minute, Ormond, in some desperation, decided to substitute Martin Buchan for Jimmy. The wee winger had warmed up and was now ready to come on, but down on the touchline, in the era before number-boards, the Scots bench could not catch the attention of the officials. The World Cup finale for Scotland was now turning into a scene from a pantomime, as Ormond and co were turned into bookies' runners tic-tacking frantically to get the officials attention. They failed.

Two minutes from time Joe Jordan scored the equaliser. 1-1 was not enough. Jimmy had, by then, sat back on the bench, a forlorn figure, thwarted by the lack of adventure within the management team. If that seems like absolving Jimmy from the blame for his own misadventures prior to Germany, then equally you could ask, why was Bremner, the much more troublesome of the two, still in a Scotland jersey?

Jock Stein refused to be drawn on that, in Germany, when he was subjecting himself to many other analyses in his role as a BBC pundit or when in private conversation with us. In fact, ominously for Jimmy, the Celtic manager was biding his time as he watched Scotland depart home, undefeated, but having failed to eradicate the overall impression that his player had contributed greatly to the perception of anarchy, from which the squad suffered throughout, and which, perversely, had prevented the wee man for redeeming himself in Germany as he had done against the English at Hampden.

There was little sign of anxiety about Jimmy when we met up with him and his family, by chance, on the island of Menorca, the following month. He was living in the villa belonging to his lawyer Joe Beltrami, who was representing him in a case where he had been accused of taking part in an affray outside the Casanova Nightclub in Coatbridge with some friends, which had attached unwelcome publicity to him as the press now felt that Jimmy could provide them with a controversy every week. Of that he was perfectly capable because of the drinking. If you compare the rather raucous but harmless drunken-singing in a Norwegian students' beer cellar with a punch-up outside a club in Scotland you can see the perilous environment he was slipping into as a result of being increasingly attracted to the bar. In February of 1974 he had been arrested after this fracas outside the club where in a confused scene there was charge and counter charges being made by the various parties. The trial had been delayed to allow him to take part in the World Cup, but in that very month of July he was found guilty and fined £50 pounds for assault. A move was made to appeal that decision because of the confused accounts, but was later rescinded. Relate that to Stein's silence on Jimmy throughout the World Cup in Germany and you might conclude that the manager was deeply wrestling with the thought that his wee winger, at the age of 29, and sliding into increased nocturnal activities might now be a liability. Knowing Stein's basic love of the wee man it must have been an anguishing notion to have to pursue. But on that Mediterranean island Jimmy seemed utterly at peace with the world, enjoying the attention of tourists clearly still in love with him, kicking a ball about the beach, swimming strongly as if to make a statement about Largs again, and being the perfect family man. And, it has to be said, enjoying a gargle or two with us and other friends. We had some pleasant evenings with him, including his serenades and impromptu swimming.

No questions were asked of him about Germany, and he volunteered nothing either. Jock Stein's close friend, the bookmaker Tony Queen was part of our social group on the island and you could tell he was keeping a close eye on Jimmy. Considering the harmless jollity we all enjoyed in those two weeks there, none us could have foreseen that the wee man was enjoying his last full summer as a Celtic player.

Spring 2005

The word of his illness had spread globally, and people from around the world wanted to hear about him, or even talk to him if they could. That, of course was the problem. The telephone had to be held to his ear. It needed someone to act for him, which essentially meant Agnes, but that was just too inconvenient. It was Simmie who solved the problem. In Willie Haughey's office there was a large telephone used for conference calls, with a loudspeaker, and a larger than normal keypad. They brought it to the house and placed it on the floor just in front of his legs. 'So there were the famous legs with probably the last demand to be made on them,' Simmie recalls. 'We asked him if he could use a toe to tap out the numbers, and using the loudspeaker he would be able to call or answer people.'

Jimmy felt a burden had been lifted from him and reacted to this with relish, tapping his toe on the pad with the delight he used to experience in trapping that ball coming at various angles from that corrugated wall in the school playground. The world was now at his feet again, as it were. But that in itself was antediluvian compared to what was to come next, by way of the Motor Neurone Disease charity fund: a voice-activated phone. This became not only a new means of communication but a source of gleeful entertainment as Simmie observed. 'He loved to show people how this would work. He would shout out "Bertie" and the phone would ring at Bertie Auld's, and he would cut it off. He'd shout "Willie" and the phone would ring in our office, and he would cut it off again. And so on. He would love shouting out the names and getting the phone to jump to his command. It was like a toy. At least until there were problems with the voice.'

It was a voice though, at that stage, which was distinct enough for him to express his views forcibly with a candour that again confused those at the receiving end of it. Nobody was above being toyed with that way. One night Simmie was there when they had a famous visitor. Through the window they saw this large car travelling slowly past the house and then reversing until it stopped just outside. When the doorbell rang Simmie answered and standing there was Rod Stewart. 'Is Jimmy in?' he asked, like a bairn wanting him to come out to play. In he came, to be welcomed by the standard greeting and smile, 'How you doin' big man?'

Stewart is hardly ever in awe of anybody, given the luminaries of Tinseltown with whom he keeps company. But it was obvious this was no mere visit, but a pilgrimage, respect and reverence shining out of his face. He reached down and gave Jimmy a cuddle. He had a gift for him. A box. 'It's my new CD, 'American Song Book.' I've signed it for you.' Jimmy looked up at him po-faced. 'Nae point in giving me that!' he said. Stewart looked puzzled. 'What do you mean?' he asked. 'Because it's shit.' Jimmy replied. 'It's what?' a perplexed Stewart asked. 'Shit. You're better going back to your old stuff you used to do, like Frankie Miller.'

All Stewart could say in way of reply was, 'But, Jimmy, it's made me lots of money. You've got to progress.' Jimmy looked him up and down and then said. 'Ach, I'll take it anyway. Just give me it. I'm only kidding you.' Stewart took it in good part, although since Jimmy was a genuine admirer of his buddie, singer Frankie Miller, he might not have had his tongue so firmly planted in his cheek, on that occasion. The point was, if you entered that room you were not dealing with a passive object glued to a chair, but someone who had tuned himself through the years to be elusive and teasing on the field, against some august opponents. Mentally this was like those occasions when he would beat the same player twice or even three times before showing mercy by leaving him behind, or passing the ball. In his mind he was still that player.

And he was still then a regular walker, despite the rapidly weakening upper-body, looking for victims to poke fun at when he met them. His friend Billy Donald recalls the time he heard a police siren approaching his house and the white patrol car stopped outside. Out came two white-capped officers and in between them was Jimmy, being escorted towards the door. 'God, what has he got himself into, I thought?' Donald recalls. The two police were wearing broad smiles though. The whole neighbourhood had been aroused by now, having heard the siren, and were practically hanging out of windows to see what had happened to the wee man. Jimmy walked casually in, asked for a drink, and blithely explained.

'I was walking up the road when I saw these two with the speed gun. So I stopped and said to them, "Have you no' got something better to do than try to catch motorists. Whit aboot chasing murderers and burglars? Would that no' be more useful?" So I just decided to keep chinning them about that until I think they were getting fed up. I was just going to stand there all day until one of them said. "C'mon, Jimmy, we're getting you out of here." They had to give me a lift just to get rid of me. They said they were Celtic supporters. Traffic cops Celtic supporters? Nae chance!' The last comment was probably based on experience.
But there had to be more serious conversations. When you are told you could end up in a wheelchair in four months from diagnosis, not everything can be played for laughs. The really difficult conversations were with people who claimed they could help him, alleviate the problems or even dare to say they could cure him. He was to dismiss no suggestion out of hand.

THIRTEEN

End Games

Jimmy played another kind of game in his last season at Celtic Park. You could have called it 'Hide and Seek.' Even his greatest admirers, still turning up in droves expecting to see the full repertoire of his skills, were never quite sure if the real Jimmy Johnstone would appear. He would run out with enthusiasm in the Hoops, and with it came that sense of anticipation you always felt watching his first appearance, even in the warm-up. But, where once the very touch of the ball would electrify him into a reaction, he was now giving the impression that a game was the equivalent of a domestic chore.

Furthermore he was now watching games from the bench far too often for his, or the club's own good. Harry Hood points to a factor that demonstrated Jimmy's special value to the club in domestic games, and was also a barometer of the wee man's mental and physical condition. 'The one game that he always gave something special to was against Rangers,' Hood said. 'He was always guaranteed to lift his game. It meant a lot to him. But even that started to change.'

Indeed it had. When Rangers won 2-1 at Celtic Park on September 14th 1974, beating Celtic there for the first time in six years, on the day George Connelly announced his retiral from football, it was Harry Hood who replaced Jimmy in the 82nd minute after the winger had been caught up in a poisonous atmosphere, his lapses of discipline prompting his withdrawal by Jock Stein. But these had been the conditions for many a derby game Jimmy had taken part in, and in which he had dominated and starred. We have repeated often enough that he was immune to intimidation, and had proved that on either side of the Equator. It would not have been lack of courage that caused his lack of influence on that game. It was that he had lost something within himself. His engine, too often, appeared merely to be idling, or erupting into unnecessary aggression, going nowhere. It could have been that he was feeling his years, although still only touching thirty. It could have been the niggling injuries which can complicate the life of a player as the years roll by. But more than that, too often he seemed drained: still-water now, compared to the carbonated fizz which his characteristic play always seemed to suggest.

That he was not even selected for the next derby match in January 1975 was a reflection of the waning trust in his abilities by the manager. (The last ever match, by the way, in which both clubs used only Scottish players). He did come on as a substitute for Harry Hood, in a reversal of the first match, but only late in the game. As Celtic lost 3-0, this substitution drew a withering report from journalist Ian Archer, who I know from personal experience was a wholesome admirer of the winger. Writing in the *Glasgow Herald* of the match, he wrote, 'Johnstone's anonymous spell as a substitute made no impression.' As a bald statement it gives a factual account. But it reveals something else, especially the words 'made no impression.'

With that expression you can tell he would like to have seen something irresistibly attractive, that he experienced the same sense of anticipation, shared by so many others, and that 'making an impression' was all that Jimmy had been born to do on a football park. Archer, sadly, like so many others then, was beginning to perceive Jimmy as merely a fringe figure, or at least a figure of anti-climax, someone increasingly incapable of fulfilling expectancy. And Celtic's constant employment of players of reasonable, but certainly not of outstanding quality, was now exacerbating Jimmy's sense of detachment from the past, which Harry Hood had identified in the previous year.

He not only felt increasingly isolated, but, more practically, none of the newcomers really could replace the service he had been accustomed to receiving from the likes of Bobby Murdoch, whose departure to Middlesbrough in September 1973, where he was highly successful, was one of the most seminal changes in the Stein age. This led to the most un-Jimmy like attitude, an apparent disinclination to help himself out of a rut. Or so it seemed, as, over this particular season he hopped between reserve football, the bench, and, increasingly, less frequent first-team appearances.

He had disappointed in the European Cup 2-0 defeat in Greece against Olympiakos in October 1974, after his manager had built him up in advance, by admitting he was, '...looking for something from the wee man. The Greeks know he is the one man who can win the game for us, with just a couple of minutes of magic.' He looked bereft of that magic, and was substituted after only an hour, as Celtic headed for an exit from the competition. But, in between all the mediocrity, there were brilliant flashes of his former self. In the League Cup final against Hibernian on the 26th October, he scored the opening goal, and then went on to carve artistic swathes through the Edinburgh defence to such an extent that in a game distinguished by two hat-tricks, one by Dixie Deans and the other by Joe Harper for Hibernian, Celtic ran out 6-3 winners. People rightly raved about his performance, particularly Jim Blair in the sports edition of the pink *Evening Times*, 'Celtic, inspired by the confidence and impudence of Johnstone, were now showing Hibernian the way home. Everything seemed to be channelled through Johnstone, who was hungry for the ball and keen to be involved in every department.'

Thus arises the notion of the game of hide and seek. For that superb image of Jimmy evaporated soon after, and he seemed to duck out of sight again for a while. As such, he again raised his head above the parapet at Dens Park in the 6-0 victory against Dundee in December of that year, where his performance and that of Kenny Dalglish began a long love-affair between the onlooking Rod Stewart and the green and white jerseys. But the manager was seeking consistency, not random rendezvous with the Jimmy of bygone days. For Rangers had risen from the apparent grave and were now threatening to take the last old First Division championship.

It is certainly true that after being knocked out of Europe by the Greeks, Celtic seemed to respond well. Their sixteen domestic matches without defeat after that flight back from Athens might have resulted in the view that they were full steam ahead for another title. However Jock Stein, the realist, warned against this optimistic view, that life was only coming up roses for them. In the *Celtic View* of November 6th 1974, he issued a stark warning. 'Any great team consists of exceptional players, serviceable players and good team men ... but of late even our serviceable players were below par.' The problem for the manager, as many ex-players have subsequently confirmed, was that he was denied appropriate funds by a board which even by the kindest interpretation, was considered parsimonious. As Harry Hood put it in an interview with journalist Phil Gordon for *Scotland on Sunday*, in 1997, 'They only gave coppers to Mr Stein.'

So, after the heavy defeat at Ibrox in January 1975, in which Celtic dropped from top spot, they lost seven and drew three of their remaining fourteen league games, during which Jimmy made only four appearances in the starting line-up. Inevitably, faithful supporters were raising angry voices as they watched Rangers stroll towards the title. They could not believe Jimmy had become so ineffective that he had to be sidelined, and began to feel that he was being blamed for the failure in Europe, and for the loss of league consistency. Affection for the wee man may have been clouding the judgement of those who could not stomach his absence, even though it was demonstrably clear he had been far from his former self, too often, in that season.

One supporter wrote to the *Celtic View* in March of that year, attributing the dropping of 'arguably the greatest winger ever seen' to the demise of the club, adding, 'I suggest the absence of Johnstone from subsequent line-ups as a contributory factor in our slump to mediocrity.' The editor replied to this, knowing full well the manager was constantly within earshot. 'The players are well aware that the manager's assessment is the one that counts. A top-form Johnstone would adorn any team. But Jimmy has been finding that form elusive, hence his absence.'

Views on him were now sharply divided. What the correspondents to the *Celtic View*, in all probability, did not realise, was that Stein was running out of patience with Jimmy, and their relationship was in a terminal state, for as Sean Fallon admits there was that other factor. 'It was Jimmy's lifestyle. It was catching up with him. He wasn't as fit as he should have been by that time. Remember he still had the heart of a lion, but too often he just couldn't match it with fitness.'

Other managers have had difficult tasks in dealing with the erratic behaviour of players. One thinks of Sir Matt Busby with George Best, Sir Alex Ferguson with Eric Cantona, and practically every manager Paul Gascoigne ever played under, all of those men often seen decorating the front pages of newspapers, as if it were a natural by-product of their talent. But these were problems of a different order, in a different culture, with men who were cosmopolitan wanderers accustomed to opening bottles of Bollinger in the backs of Rolls Royces, and being seen, particularly Best, with more than an overcoat draped around him. They were part of a 'scene,' of the two-way relationship between the *paparazzi* and their own rampant egos, and whether or not it was deliberate, they seemed to relish most of the attention, if not all.

Despite the fact that Jimmy did not escape the clutches of the media and did furnish the front pages of newspapers with some provocative headlines, he was not ego-driven. By and large he simply wanted to be amongst his own people and enjoy the tolerance they would show for his increasing liking, for what could politely be termed as a good night out with the lads. His friends knew he could get drunk too easily; that his constitution seemed too vulnerable to minimal amounts, and, although it was happening too frequently, it led, more often than not, to woozy affability and loud, melodic singing. Others who believe there are no variations of drunkenness were less tolerant and saw him as a nuisance. They were in the minority though. For his name and the fact that he always had a beguiling, inoffensive look about him was a protective factor.

One of his friends described it this way to me, 'He had the kind of face that nobody would refuse a 'jeely piece' to, if he knocked on your door.' As such, rarely were people offended when he was in full spate, in one of his binges, after he had stopped playing, offering the world the full value of vocal chords which could still rise above the clamour of bars. There was, of course, the Coatbridge nightclub incident which you would have to say was inevitable given the fact that somebody, somewhere was going to take umbrage to the carousing. But, under the influence of drink, as many others would vouch for, raucous braggart he was not. If anybody had taken a superstar ego into the Noggin Bar in Uddingston Main Street, Lanarkshire, or the Windmill Tavern, only a stone's throw from the house, which was a favourite howff of his after they had closed the

Noggin, they wouldn't have been served with so much as a can of Irn Bru.

So home, for him, was not just four walls and a family. It was, whether anybody would approve of it or not, the companionship of folk in pubs who knew and understood that he was a decent man, with not a whiff of pretension in his make-up, but who could detect booze with the unerring instinct of the homing pigeon. Stein also knew that only too well.

One night he suddenly appeared at the Johnstone home, with Sean Fallon, and shook Agnes to the core, as he demanded, bluntly, with no preamble, 'Where is he?' Agnes, sensing the menacing attitude of the manager, pleaded ignorance, although she guessed he could have been in any of several places. Then the great teetotaller and his assistant set-off in a pub crawl, of a different nature, trying to locate him, in various places in Viewpark and Uddingston. She could tell they were on the warpath; that something had triggered this off to make them so angry. Fortunately, for the sake of the wee man's health, she discovered later they had not found Jimmy. She was also aware that Stein knew all the places he drunk in, and that he had even made a phone call to the Noggin Bar one night and simply snapped at the barman, without questioning him about Jimmy's whereabouts, 'This is Jock Stein! Tell that wee man to get out of there right now!' And then slammed the phone down. The barman did as he was told, bewildered as to how Stein had been aware of Jimmy's presence. Let us just say, of his raids into Lanarkshire, and attempted confrontations with the wee man, that those who knew him would swear the Celtic manager seemed to possess the power of extra-sensory perception.

Players would be astonished at how much he could tell them about what they had been doing outside the park. If they were transgressing in some shape or form, as some inevitably did, they would do so looking over their shoulders, even if they knew he was on another continent. Sometimes you imagined Stein was aware of what they were saying in the Kremlin at any given moment. So, inevitably, he was hearing whispers about what the wee man was up to, from time to time, in his occasional nocturnal wanderings. There also existed a spy network which maintained surprising vigilance when it came to scrutinising players' behaviour away from Celtic Park. That of course was serviced by those supporters who had the welfare of the club at heart. Stein summarised this for me, long after he had left Celtic. He told me that one morning he had received a phone call from a man who had informed him that he had seen Jimmy Johnstone being carried out of a pub in Cambuslang, at six o'clock in the morning, and that as a season ticket holder at Celtic Park he was entitled to better behaviour than that from one of his most influential players.

Stein knew that many false trails can be laid by people, but somehow he felt that there was a ring of truth to what he had heard. He waited for his star winger to come in for training. At about ten minutes to ten that morning in he came and, according to Stein's description, was ashen-faced and fragile looking. The manager said nothing to him, but pulled two of the quickest and sharpest players in the club aside, Willie Wallace and Bobby Lennox, and told them they would be doing their work in threes, and since he felt that Jimmy had been slipping in form lately they had to work him hard, which they duly did. At one point during the training he saw the wee man at the far end of the pitch having a quick vomit, then proceeding again, at a fair rate of knots, as soon as he had wiped his mouth clean. He shirked not one exercise. He ran Wallace and Lennox into the ground, finished every routine, played like a demon in the bounce game, then walked smartly back to the dressing-room. 'What could I say?' Stein said to me. 'He had done all his work. I knew what he was getting up to, but if he was performing for me, then he wasn't letting me down. He came in on time, did everything that was asked of him, so, honestly, what could I say? I just had to let it go that time.'

'That time...' is the key phrase there. There were other times in which he was much less tolerant. Stein was to expand on that eventually when he told Rodger Baillie, of the *Sunday Mirror*, at the end of that season, 'I once said that no player during my time as Celtic manager has caused me more trouble. I do not withdraw that remark. There were many occasions when I leaned over backwards to help him, and yet at times we seemed to move from one crisis to the next with him.'

You have to wonder, not about the accuracy of the statement, but as to whether this was a rare of admission of defeat by one of the greatest managers in the history of the game. Jimmy was far from being too old to play: he could still do things others could not approach, though now admittedly on rarer occasions; but it was still there, still just below the surface. Would that lurking presence not have served Celtic for at least another season? Here you have to take into account the fact that the manager himself was a different man. He was no longer the crusading Stein of the 1960s. For all the incredible stamina and energy he had displayed in creating a new era for the club, it had taken its toll. Jock Stein, in 1975, was far from a spent force, of course, but when you talked to him in those days, even before his serious car crash, you could tell that the vitality, the visible aggression when you touched him the wrong way, was diminishing. He had probably reached the stage where he could not relish fighting a battle on two fronts, winning titles and holding the world at bay from learning of the misadventures of his now erratic genius. Enough was enough.

Observers were beginning to sniff something in the air. When Jimmy ran out to play in the last league game of the season, against St. Johnstone at Muirton Park, Perth on April 26th 1975, it seemed to have no significance, beyond the fact that he would have been trying to consolidate his place for the Scottish Cup final against Airdrie the following week, as Celtic were about to finish an ignominious league season in third place behind Rangers and Hibernian. In fact it was the last time he played in an official Celtic match.

They lost 2-1, and both Jimmy, substituted by Harry Hood, and Dixie Deans, substituted by Bobby Lennox, looked strictly off the pace, prompting journalist John Mann to make the shrewd observation, in the *Scottish Daily Express*, that neither Jimmy nor Dixie had strengthened their chances of a cup-final selection. He then added, more presciently, 'There is obviously a major re-building job ahead at Celtic Park.' In fact, the re-building had been going on for some time. But Mann's intention was to indicate that nobody seemed likely to be immune from reconstruction, not even a name as renowned as Jimmy Johnstone.

When he was not selected for the Scottish Cup final against Airdrie, on May 3rd, the following week, the chat around town was that his future with the club was now hanging by a thread, despite the fact that Stein had made this announcement. 'Jimmy Johnstone was not considered because he has not trained this week. He took a knock last week at Perth and this has ruled him out.'

I can recall at the time that this was greeted in the media with some scepticism, as if there were some other reason, given some of the stories about misbehaviour in the past, or that the manager knew precisely what selection would stand the best chance of winning the cup, and that he simply had no use now for the wee man. On the evening of Celtic's triumph in the final against Airdrie, we had cameras installed in the *New Orleans* restaurant in Rutherglen, run by Stein's friend Tony Queen, the bookmaker and Pat Harkins, Kenny Dalglish's father-in-law. It was there, just as we prepared to broadcast our Saturday evening *Sportscene* programme from that venue, Billy McNeill told us of his retirement from football. Something seemed to register that more was to follow, and the chatter about Jimmy's immediate future intensified.

The only wings that he seemed to be on now was that of the performer waiting for his cue to make an entry for a grand finale. If anybody now doubts the prevailing assumptions about his future, that were being aired at the time, then reading what Hugh Taylor of the *Daily Record* wrote of the Glasgow Cup final at Hampden Park, seven days after the Celtic 3-1 Scottish Cup final victory over Airdrie, gives you a true reflection of the thinking. On the morning of that game Taylor had written, in sentimental vein, that Celtic were 'possibly saying farewell to the Old Guard;' namely Brogan and Johnstone, of whom he wrote, 'I'm betting the wee winger, one of my favourite players – and the favourite of anyone who likes entertaining players – could be on at some time.' Taylor was accurately setting the kind of scene which many in the media were anticipating: the last hurrah.

This competition had not been played since 1971, but was being resurrected as part of the celebrations of Glasgow's 800th anniversary as a burgh. Rangers were the opponents and it gave Celtic the opportunity to win a fourth cup in the space of nine months. Jimmy had scored with a winning penalty in the post-extra time shoot-out in the Drybrough Cup final in August 1974. 70,000 were to turn up to watch a game played in weather reminiscent of the Scottish Cup final in which Jimmy had made his Hampden debut in 1963, and similar to the Ibrox weather of 1967 when he had scored his two memorable goals to secure the title. It poured unrelentingly throughout.

One can only hope Taylor had not put heavy money on his bet that Jimmy would play some part, for he was quite wrong. Jimmy sat on the bench throughout. Many of us could never understand why he was not used as a substitute in a game against Rangers, of all clubs, that ended 2-2, and which, given the treacherous surface, his sure-footedness, as he had proved before, could have swung a positive result, forestalling the two clubs being made joint holders of the trophy. And, let me repeat, Jock Stein never took even this sort of Old Firm match lightly. As he must have known by then, that he was to release Jimmy four weeks later, it is all the more surprising that he did not allow him to be seen by his admirers for the last time, if only for a few minutes, even though none of them would have known the significance of the gesture at the time. We had already noted Stein failing to pick Jimmy for that Scottish Cup final in 1965, and of how pragmatism informed Stein more than sentimentality.

You cannot argue against the success which that attitude produced. But although we are looking at this through the benefit of hindsight, it does leave a slightly uncomfortable feeling that in Jimmy's final official appearance in a Celtic squad, even though he did not play, he allowed the wee man, who had once held the ball aloft in the Bernabeu on that famous evening, as the Madrilenos rose in acclamation to him, to slip out of sight and into the history books as an 'unused sub.'

Four weeks later Jimmy felt as if his entrails had been gouged out when Celtic told him that they did not want him any longer. He did not hear of this firstly from Jock Stein. Sean Fallon vividly recalls the reason for that. 'To be honest Jock and I couldn't face up to it. Whatever passed between them through the years, Jock loved and respected the wee man, and he just couldn't bring himself to tell him he was finished at Celtic Park. We knew it would hurt Jimmy very badly. We honestly couldn't face up to it. It was chairman Desmond White who told him. I do know that Jimmy just broke down and wept. The tears were rolling down his face.' He was devastated. Bobby Lennox still realises what it meant to be rent asunder from the place they loved.

'Jimmy and I, from the same generation, actually believed we could play for Celtic until we were ninety. It was a daft kind of thought I suppose. But the idea of having to leave Celtic never passed through our minds. It was just impossible. So we thought.' Of course Stein and Fallon did meet with him, after Desmond White had broken the decision to him. All they encountered was a sad and disbelieving wee man.

Even for many years after that, every time John Clark drove Jimmy to Celtic Park, that same agonising day of departure cropped up. 'He kept repeating himself, over and over again. "It was awful when they told me I wasn't needed. I couldn't believe it. Especially when you've been a hero to so many people. It really hurt." That wasn't just once. Every time we came near Celtic Park, he would start on that, over and over again.' In terms of the way it was announced to him, Clark makes it clear that Stein had made an exception of Jimmy. 'Normally when Jock released a player, like myself, he would have Sean beside him and he would talk very reasonably about how it would benefit you to leave. It was all to soften the blow.'

Clearly the manager had felt that nothing could soften the blow for Jimmy. Stein did issue a clarifying statement to the *Celtic View*, about that departure, in the *'Summer Magazine 1975*,' 'Of late the wee man has not been fulfilling our expectations. The vital spark was not there. I believe Jimmy has climbed all the mountains possible with Celtic. He needs new challenges to inspire him.' So, one of the great productive relationships in the history of the game had come to an end.

Their twin involvements with Celtic are so intertwined that it has been one of the main contentions in this book, that although it is a chronicle of the life of an amazing footballing artist, it was Stein who sculpted his ultimate shape out of the raw material. Willie Henderson, whose colleagues were at the receiving end of some of Jimmy's greatest performances, makes the point cogently. 'Jimmy became a serious threat to us ... eventually. Before Jock Stein came he was a different man. He had tons of skill but after Jock came that was utilised in a much more professional fashion. It was with Stein that we began to fear the wee man.'

Of course his time in first team football, before Stein came, was limited. But Willie Henderson is not overstating the case. Although we are right to regard Jimmy as a 'natural,' it is not as if it was simply inherited genes that turned his jinks and twists into weapons of mass destruction in the professional game. He had to develop them. I have stressed throughout the enormous effort he put into building his physique and honing his skills with a ball, from a lobby in the house to a school playground, to the public parks, to the riverside paths, to the training ground, hour after hour, day after day, until you might understand his abilities were the product of perspiration as much as inspiration. So the word 'natural' ought not to be interpreted as suggesting he simply turned up, put on a pair of boots and instinct took care of the rest.

He certainly made it seem like that, of course, when you are told by the likes of John Clark that sometimes he wasn't quite sure who they were about to play on a specific day, and yet would run out and steal the show. He could do that because of the years of preparation, even before he knew what specifically lay in store for him in the game. Two months before his death in a late-night conversation with Willie Henderson, when they were looking back at some of the highlights of their careers, Jimmy turned to Ian Henderson, and whispered, 'You see, son, I had to work hard at what I could do. I had to work hard just to make my own luck in the game.'

Although there is an element of self-deprecation in that statement, it nevertheless underscores the point that factors other than natural ability colluded to make him what he was, and Stein was perhaps the most important of all. Admittedly, at times, the manager, in trying to control him, must have felt like a frustrated man trying to guddle a fish in a burn, and having it continually slip through his fingers. On others, you felt that he had calculated with great precision exactly what he would get out of the wee man. Stein's occasional thunderous denunciations of him, mixed with his frequent paternal huggings, was not empty exhibitionism, but part of his life-support strategy. Few managers had Stein's insights into human nature. He could read Jimmy like a book. And in employing all kinds of devices to keep the wee man alert to his responsibilities Stein kept him much longer at the highest level of the game than any other man could have. Frankly, he was the kind of 'faither' Jimmy badly needed. Stein's wife Jean, who normally kept strictly in the background, nevertheless admitted once, 'Jimmy was unquestionably his favourite son, because despite all the rows, Jock thought that there wasn't a bigger talent in the game than the wee man.'

Of course he could have entertained under any manager, but it is tempting to say that on the plinth of any statue erected to honour the wee man's achievements, should be inscribed, 'Jimmy Johnstone. The Stein Version.' So the rest of Jimmy's professional life, after leaving Celtic, seemed like a man searching for his lost tribe and, above all, for the spiritual leader who had led the club out of the wilderness.

After breaking the news to the family on that day of departure, he headed for his own pub. He had taken a blow to the solar plexus and was resorting to the best painkiller he could think of. Once there, he drank like his existence depended on it. He had reached a watershed in his personal life, and like the time he had pushed out the rowing-boat at Largs, he was minus a couple of capable rowlocks and quite unsure where the tide would take him. A year later in May 1976, Celtic, as had been promised, granted him and Bobby Lennox a testimonial match at Celtic Park, at which they both looked inspired by the tumultuous reception of the 50,000 crowd.

At the end of the game he hurled his boots into the famous 'Jungle,' being, after all, for the fans in there, 'The King of the Jungle.' But nothing could ease the sense of alienation from the club that had hugged him to its bosom for so long; driving him increasingly to alcohol. Part of his problem were the very folk who adored him and who wanted to show their appreciation of his services to Celtic by swamping him with hospitality. Although he had now been released, he was still being feted around the whole of the British Isles and in Ireland during which, by his own admission, he sometimes would not know where he would wake up in any given morning. It was a problem which intensified when he did something he never dreamed he would do. He turned his back on Scotland.

Summer 2005

*They tried the snake venom. It had been recommended to Agnes and Jimmy by an acquaintance who had claimed it had curative properties. The very phrase snake venom seems to take us back to those pioneering days of the American West, where there were plenty snakes, but few pharmacies. Men in covered wagons would sell snake-based potions to the unenlightened on the basis that something as horrid as that had to do you some good. But what was it doing in Lanarkshire in the 21*st *century?*

Because Jimmy was dying, and increasingly the reality of that was closing in on him. There was no way he was going to turn his back on friends who were straining their minds to come up with solutions. Somebody had put it into his head that he didn't really have Motor Neurone Disease but a curable condition which mimicked the symptoms of the scourge. It is a view that did not come from any medical authority, but in the persistence of its recommendation Jimmy went after it. This could have fallen within Willie Haughey's estimation of the 'witch doctor' category.

But Agnes had no inclination to discourage him from trying any remedy. She injected him faithfully with the stuff for over a year, three times a day. 'What could I do? I didn't really believe it was doing him any good, but I didn't have the heart to argue with him about it. I think he got a bit of a lift out of it every time I injected him. In fact, sometimes when I did it, he used to joke "Hey, that was sore. Are you trying to get back at me for all the trouble I caused you?" And it was costing us a fortune too.' Ian Henderson does admit that he seemed to respond positively to those injections. 'I can tell you that when Jimmy was given the task of putting small pegs into holes to test his motor skills or lack of them, he found it extremely difficult, if not impossible. After these injections, I swear he could do that test much more easily. That's all I would say.' Perhaps, at best, he was receiving a psychological boost.

Clearly, temporary euphoria ought never to be idly dismissed during a terminal illness. But it was on this pursuance of another treatment of such that brought Henderson's first disagreement with Jimmy. 'There was somebody who kept insisting to Agnes and Jimmy that if he went to Bermuda to get similar treatment then it would be of great benefit. Jimmy was enthusiastic about that. But for the first time in our association during his illness I put the foot down and said it would be a waste of time. It was a hard thing to do, because in a way it was as if we were throwing in the towel which, of course, we were not. And we were running out of funds to do these sorts of things and Jimmy and Agnes simply did not want to be seen to be begging. It was hard enough on her with all the physical lifting and laying of Jimmy from the start of it all, without having to worry about money.' They did eventually travel south to Kent along with 'Tiger' Tim Stevens of Radio Clyde who suffers from Multiple Sclerosis.

They had been informed of the effectiveness of a serum derived from goats. To dangle that prospect in front of a person, sound in mind and body, might appear as something of a joke. But the mindset of the ailing is of a different kind, as has to be emphasised again. They both pursued this eagerly and received injections of this potion, but there is no evidence that it produced any positive effect on the body, other than that psychological boost which would be similar to the surge of adrenalin that you can experience, on the back of expectancy.

Agnes treated this with a philosophical calmness. She did not expect miracles, although she continually prayed for one. Henderson paid her continual compliments for how, *uncomplainingly, she took on the laborious tasks she had to endure to cater for his very basic needs. She had been well trained before Jimmy's illness. Agnes has a brother who had required special attention since birth. Consequently she had spent a lifetime dealing, enthusiastically, it has to be said, with every aspect of those intimate personal, and daily, interventions that were required to help him, and which many of us would find difficult to thole.*

So no one ever heard her mutter a plea for assistance, no matter how onerous this was. Ironically, this meant that few people were aware of the sheer drudgery involved, and the physical effort in coping with matters which might make the average person queasy, to say the least. But all that was turned around in one day when, left alone with his father, his son James was confronted with his mother's daily task, and was shaken to the core by what confronted him. His father needed to relieve himself, but James, unaccustomed to this, and taken completely by surprise, had to act. It changed his whole conception of what this illness could mean to others. It is not something he would ever forget. They were sitting chatting when suddenly the call of nature came. James admits he panicked. He simply didn't know what to do. He found himself being acutely embarrassed.

'He was in a terrible mess, because we had waited too long. I had to carry him through to the bathroom and clean him. I had to use a mop to do it. You know the worse thing was the look on his face. I think the whole thing was demeaning for him. Here was his own son doing to him what he used to do for me when I was a kid, wipe him clean. Our roles had been reversed. All right, I admit I was sickened by the mess, but the worse thing was just thinking of what was going through his mind. You have to believe that the indignity of it all affected him badly.'

What it did though was alert James, and through him, to others, that this disease was not just about seeking cures or palliatives, it was about the menial tasks that had to be carried out just to maintain a decent level of existence. It was about the sacrifice others have to make to alleviate the acute discomforts. James was now a good companion to his father though, and like many sons of famous men, life had not been easy for him. What was it like growing up as the off-spring of one of the great players of any generation? 'The truth? Murder!' Expanding on that, he tells a not unfamiliar tale. 'Everybody thought I was going to be another Jimmy Johnstone. I played on the right-hand side. I was a decent enough player but I wasn't in the same planet as my da. When I would play for the local team, grown men would shout at me "You're not as good as your dad," and that was me playing for the Under-10s. It was horrible. I'm talking about schoolteachers shouting at me as well. "You're coming off," they would shout just because they were expecting me to do the same as my da'. So my name was actually a handicap. If I had just been left alone I might have developed into a reasonable player, but all that attention put me off, even though my da spent a lot of time coaching me.'

Their relationship, despite the trials and tribulations of James being an accidental casualty of his father's fame, matured during the illness. They were now mates. 'I remember the day Celtic blew the league at Fir Park against Motherwell in May 2005. I wasn't at the game but I heard the score when I was in the Asda car park. I went in and bought a bottle of Mateus Rose and decided I would go back and share it with him because I knew how he would be feeling about the result. It was lucky for us both that my mother wasn't in. So we decided to drown our sorrows, and I was feeding him half-pint tumblers of the stuff, through a straw, before she returned, for this was all against her rules. But the pair of us just felt so dejected. I heard her coming in the door and I quickly got up and left. I knew what I would be in for. When I got home I had a telephone call from her and she was calling me all the names of the day. "I come back here and I find your da' sitting here singing. I had to give him a half of whisky just to keep him quiet!" You know, I just laughed at the very idea of how miserable he was when I went in, on the back of that result, and how I managed to get him singing!'

Then something extremely radical, and controversial, took over Jimmy's mind completely.

FOURTEEN
The Fightback

Life had been hollow for him since leaving Celtic. He had tried, oh how he had tried, to look as if he had the same enthusiasm for the game. He had gone firstly to the USA, lured by the thought of sun and poolside in California, when he signed on for San Jose Earthquakes in June1975 after having turned down the New York Cosmos: the latter club claimed that Jimmy had let them down after promising to join them, and more than hinted that he had played one club against another to get the terms he wanted. He tried to persuade his great pal Bobby Lennox to join him, and in a late call to Jock Stein, to advise him what he had signed up for, he inadvertently and mistakenly mentioned that Lennox would be joining him. Stein pounced on Lennox.

'I got a call from the boss and I have never had such a telling-off from him in my life. He tore into me and told me it would be a waste of my time going to a place like the States. That I had better to offer. I felt then for what Jimmy had let himself in for,' said Lennox. The wee man would have been happier as a hot dog salesman, rather than trying to convince people he was enjoying his experience of attempting to attract crowds in a country in which soccer sat as comfortably as lacrosse would in Viewpark. The money was good, but the atmosphere was phoney. Agnes and he simply could not settle. She was particularly homesick. He was duly feted over there, all the same, but there was only one memory he really cherished. It was in New York when he was playing against the Cosmos. Somebody patted him on the back on the field during the game and whispered a sincere compliment into his ear about the way he had been playing. When he turned round he was looking into the face of the great Pele. That did a lot for his morale, but was not enough to persuade him to stay on in the holiday-camp environment of American soccer, which he took barely any time to realise was not for him. He left after making ten appearances and failing to score a goal.

Then a former Celtic player, Jimmy Sirrel, heard of Jimmy's availability and coaxed him to join him. Sirrel prided himself in having been called a 'tracksuit' manager, and had been appointed at Sheffield United at the age of 53 to rescue them from the bottom of the league to which they had sunk after only two months into the season. Jimmy had an admission to make about that. 'To be honest, I didn't know anything about Sheffield United. But my lawyer told me that Jimmy Sirrel had been a Celtic player, so that helped things. Also financially it was a very good offer ... I was well satisfied.' In November 1975 Jimmy made his debut for that club, three days after signing at the age of 31.

Aiden McGeady's father, John, signed for United as a teenager around the same time, and was in awe of the wee man. He testified to a Celtic fanzine in March 2006, that Jimmy was extremely popular amongst the players. But he added, 'Looking back now, however, there was a sadness about him. Understandable, of course. He never performed at anywhere near the same level that he did for Celtic. He missed Bobby Lennox. He missed Celtic.'

In fairness to United it is difficult to see anywhere Jimmy could have settled with peace of mind, other than, say, the other United in Manchester, although even that is dubious. When the body is incapable any longer of providing the sorts of dizzying performances to which admirers are accustomed, and to which he had always aspired, then inevitably frustration sets in. He simply couldn't hack it any longer.

The gas was on a low peep and he just couldn't turn it up. What he could do now, on an epic level, was drink. This was no longer the merry over-indulgence of his earlier days, but the escape mechanism which fools the addict into thinking oblivion is the answer to all life's problems. It became widely known that he ensconced himself, daily or nightly, in a local bar called 'The Bridge Inn' near to the home he had set up with Agnes and the children. He needed a sympathetic mate to perhaps ease him back off this calamitous descent. There was nobody of that calibre about. It is not that he didn't get on with his colleagues, as Jimmy would have been popular in any company. But when he expressed himself about the spirit in the dressing room, in *Flashing Blade,* a United fanzine in October 1995, it was not exactly with great enthusiasm.

'A lot of them were mercenaries,' he said. 'Don't get me wrong, they were all good lads and I got on well with them, but they all seemed just to be after making a few quid, then getting away. I wasn't used to this – I'd played at Celtic with passion, at Sheffield it was a merry-go-round. They'd sit in the dressing-room talking about who was after them, there was no loyalty ... I'd no idea of a football club like this.'

So there was no real bonding, and we have already seen in the past that kinship was something which encouraged the best from him. After his first four games there he was dropped. And then a change, which now seems so sacrilegious, took place. He relinquished the No 7 shirt for the No 8. This truly was symbolic of the fact that the Rolls Royce had now given way to the pony and cart. The air of unreality of him playing in that city in the first place, with a No 8 on his back, and being so far off the pace that the city's local newspaper produced a photograph of him, later reproduced in a fanzine, in which the caption read, facetiously, 'Here we see Jimmy, *unusually,* in the thick of the action,' should have inspired one of his admirers north of the border to perform a rescue act like Young Lochinvar, to swoop down from over the border and save him from that living hell. The fact is that he was on his own now, and little gave him satisfaction other than resorting to the bar stool. Memories of that spell are few.

But he cannot forget the two games that did carry meaning for him and told that same fanzine, 'I ran riot against Spurs. Against Fulham they'd all come to see Bestie, but it was my show that day. I got the same reaction from the fans as I did for Celtic and I loved it.' He had obviously been aroused by the illustrious names of Rodney Marsh, Bobby Moore and George Best, with Fulham at the time, thus underlining the fact that he could still perform if the stimulus was the right one. He was at the wrong club, at the wrong time, as they plummeted towards the foot of the league again. As he admitted years later, he was cheating on the club, in the sense that he was never fully fit because, apart from the heavy drinking, he had lost the impulse to train as hard as he used to.

After scoring his last professional goal in the higher levels of football in United's 3-2 defeat at Charlton, Jimmy was freed in June 1977, after having played only 11 games in the first team, and scoring only two goals. It is tempting to say that the least said about the rest of his time in football, the better. Nothing seemed to make sense. Not even his brief, season-ticket boosting, three games for Dundee in a short spell later that year. Tommy Gemmell's charitable signing of him for that club he now managed, floundered on the fact that Jimmy was housed in the hotel Tommy owned in Errol, just outside Dundee. On one infamous occasion the wee man and Gordon Strachan got so intoxicated after an all-day drinking session that they did not have the common sense to make themselves scarce, but went back to the same hotel in Errol, where they were confronted by an enraged manager.

The situation could be summarised in the following response, when Tommy Gemmell demanded of Strachan, 'Where do you think you are going?' To which he received the reply, 'Where am I going? I don't even know where I am!' Believing him to be the inspiration of the drink-fest, Gemmell gave up Jimmy in despair. At least this relieved the wee man of the dilemma of perhaps having to play against Celtic, the prospect of which he could not stomach. Gemmell had tried to put him on the straight and narrow. Others had tried. More would try. Too many were missing the point though. This was no longer a social frailty. This was a disease: this was now something he carried with him in brief, inconsequential and ultimately sad interludes thereafter, at Shelbourne in Dublin, Elgin City in the Highland League (where he admitted that the brevity of the stay there was partly due to 'a few flirtations with alcohol,' as he put it himself) and then back to his nursery-team Blantyre Celtic, as player-coach in junior football for a short, aimless, eight-week period. It was there, where he had started professionally, almost missing his debut as a teenager, and wrecking the future career of a full back, that he ended it all.

It was not his absolute disappearance from public view though. In June 1993 he took part in another special game at Celtic Park. The famous 'Jungle,' one of the most renowned terracing areas in British football, was about to be converted into an all-seated stand. The Scottish Cup final was held at the ground that season and it pained many that it would be Rangers who would play the last game in front of that area held sacred by the Celtic support. So Willie Haughey thought up a 'Blow The Blues Away,' game in which the Lisbon Lions would take on the veterans from Manchester United's European Cup-winning side of 1968. This was to be played only three days after the Scottish Cup final of May 29th 1993.

At the age of 48, Jimmy commanded attention again: slower of course, but still fuelled by the same spirit and armed with the same pirouetting intentions. He brought the house down, almost literally.

Before then he had made another return of a different nature. He had always hoped that he could work at Celtic Park as a coach. Why wouldn't the greatest winger of his generation not be avidly sought after, to pass on his skills to others? Davie Hay, as the Celtic manager, in the mid 1980s, saw the potential of that and brought him in to coach the under-16s. It did not end well. The outspoken Jimmy did not like some of the methods of coach Frank Connor, and certainly had nothing good to say about the chief scout John Kelman, who once dared to criticise the Lisbon Lion, and Jimmy's best friend, Bobby Lennox, behind his back, making Jimmy so angry he admits he would have punched him had they not been standing in the front entrance of Celtic Park. He also felt Connor was stifling the natural flair of players and was always bawling out young men, whom he felt were scared to express themselves as individuals as a result, and went so far as to say, after being promoted for a short spell to assisting with the reserve side, that these attitudes would set the club back for several years. There are some who felt that belief was not wide of the mark.

But Agnes was heartened, for the family's sake, by the fact that he had tried to consolidate himself in business again, when he sold his financially-failing pub *The Double J*, raised some useful cash from that, and through the assistance of lawyer and Celtic director James Farrell, invested in property in the South Side of Glasgow. Tragically, that failed, principally because in the development of the flats they were to discover, after their reconstruction, that they did not conform to the changing fire regulations. They lost a great deal in the venture. The money was running out. But there were many around him who would not allow him to flounder.

Frank Lafferty, the building contractor, leapt at the opportunity to employ him, and, during the three subsequent years, he drove lorries for the firm around the country, beginning to appreciate this new feeling of stability after all the uncertainties of life, and the lack of cash coming into the house. Although, sitting behind the wheel of the lorry he had to duck the occasional obvious remark made to him, as he himself once quoted, 'What are you doin' here, wee man? You should have been a millionaire by now.'

They would watch him coming out of the cabin, picking up a pick and shovel to help dig ditches as well. If his life's scenario had been written by someone else, of course, he might well have been a millionaire. But life, as he himself was now discovering, is largely in your own hands, and although he would often express regrets, to myself occasionally, and to many of his friends, of how he had squandered so much, it did not thwart his ambitions. What helped in part to keep his feet on the ground at that stage was his blossoming friendship with his great rival Willie Henderson. The former Rangers player and Jimmy enjoyed some evenings out together and, since Henderson had had severe drinking problems himself, there existed a kindred spirit which made for a natural blend. That apart, they simply liked each other.

They were wee, they were talented, they were humorous, and they were popular with the differing factions. As Henderson relates, it started with a photograph. 'The day Jimmy was picked to replace me in the Scotland side against Wales in 1964 because I was injured, the *Daily Record* asked if Jimmy could come to my house in Hamilton for a photograph of the pair of us. No problem. That was the first time we ever sat down together and got to know each other. It was an easy relationship. We respected each other.'

With their playing days over Jimmy and Willie paired up for chats at clubs and appeared on television and radio frequently, and, as both were blessed with a sense of humour they drew the crowds. Willie summed up their friendly rivalry with tongue in cheek. 'The only time we played together in a Scotland side, it was against Wales, at Ninian Park, Cardiff in 1966. Jimmy was on the right wing, I was on the left. But there was only one ball!'

Alongside those occasional outings, Jimmy was alive with ideas of how to make it on his own. The entrepreneurial bug bit him after leaving Lafferty's. There was barely a week passed when he was not pursuing a business idea. On one occasion he asked to see me, with a farmer friend of his, in the hope that I would invest in an open-cast mining project he had in mind. The money he was talking about would have turned you to a pillar of salt, and as I could barely afford to invest in a petunia patch at that stage I heard no more about it and, as I understand, not a clod was ever turned over on that farm. Some time after that he approached me with the possibility of making a video of himself and his playing days, which I would have been delighted to do. But, again, he was underestimating the cost of buying footage from the television companies, and it never got off the ground. But he was trying, desperately trying, to make something of his life.

The recipient of many of his ideas was businessman Willie Haughey. 'It was one of the treasures of my life to meet Jimmy after having seen him from afar for so long,' Haughey said. 'For all the faults he may have had, he brightened up my life completely. And he used to come to me with all sorts of ideas that he thought would make him 'millions.' He would bring folk along with him and I would sit and listen to their plans. He would peddle the idea of something like, for example, luminous paint that was about to take the world by storm. And then there would be a new herbal remedy he would want to market, or a new diet that he had discovered that would catch on with the public. Idea after idea poured out of him, but at the same time a lot of folk were just using him and sending him off on wild-goose chases that would make no business sense.'

This was recognised by John Reid, the present Celtic chairman, who as Jimmy's constituency MP in Lanarkshire, at one time, was visited regularly by the wee man, who had in mind a series of possible ventures. 'I got to know him personally over the years as his MP and the schemes he brought to me were really those suggested by other people. You see, he had an honesty and a naivety about him where people, from time to time, would try to misuse him because of his name. He would always tell me that he had met this bloke who had this plan to make thousands. Nothing ever happened.'

Willie Haughey attempted to put a halt to all of this. 'I got to the stage that to stop him pursuing all these lines I decided to employ him going round the pubs selling things for me. For the wee man simply did not want hand outs. He wanted to work for a living. But as you know he had a big problem.'

Agnes summarised that problem in four simple words, 'It was the drink.'

The plaintive resonance of that statement carries with it the sadness of those who loved this man and yet felt helpless as, for long periods, he seemed under the sway of the genie of the bottle which produced in him a recklessness which was rarely malevolent, but was nevertheless, loud, raucous, embarrassing, and as Willie Haughey recognised, if people had reacted the wrong way to it, could have got him into serious trouble. This was not just pushing the self-destruct button. It was crippling to others, especially to family. They would bear the indignities with a stoicism which families with alcoholism in their midst would readily recognise.

It is something of a tragedy that three of the greatest wingers of all time – Jimmy, George Best, and the Brazilian Garrincha – all fell victim to the inducements of the bottle. George Best's son, Calum, never shirked from admitting this. 'When I was 15 years old I had to carry him home from the pub and I knew then that something wasn't right.' James Johnstone recalls many nights of anxiety. 'I used to fear the sound of a taxi arriving late at night. I would run up the stairs and lock my door.' This was not because of any fear of abuse, it should be strongly asserted, but because he became embarrassed to see a man he worshipped reeling noisily about the house, night after night.

Garrincha, of the deformed spine, with a right leg that bent inwards, and a left which bent out, and was 6 centimetres shorter, and who eventually was to die of cirrhosis of the liver, drove a car into a lorry one night, totally drunk, killing his mother-in-law. All three were marvellous entertainers, which makes you wonder if leaving the engulfing adoration of the multitudes, the spotlight being turned off, created a dangerous vacuum within them, like a kind of pre-cancerous condition needing to be treated before it grew malignant. But then how could anybody spot that, until it was too late, given the social acquiescence to the drunk in any society, as typified by Frank Sinatra's *Rat Pack* credo when he declared, whimsically, 'I feel sorry for the people who don't drink. They wake up in the morning and that's the best they'll feel all day.' Perhaps even worse than that, being a celebrity drinker seemed to some people to be worthy of being awarded an accolade. For when Hollywood actor/director Robert Duval came to Scotland to make his disastrous film *A Shot At Glory*, he invited Jimmy and Jim Baxter to portray themselves, as drunks in a pub. He got short shrift. Baxter summed up the feelings of them both when he stated, 'Ah, can drink enough on my ain without a camera lookin' at me.'

Willie Haughey, who would have sold his soul to save Jimmy, believed eventually in shock treatment. 'I tolerated a lot of what I thought was erratic behaviour when he was under the influence and I knew he was drinking at all hours. When he came in one Monday morning at half past eight and I offered him a cup of tea, all he wanted to know was if I had any champagne. He would not believe I had no alcohol in my boardroom. Any man who is doing that at that time of the morning has a big problem. He had a towel wrapped round what looked like a large picture frame he was carrying. He suddenly unwrapped it and rammed something down on the table. And there was this beautiful picture frame, and inside it was a display of all the medals he had ever won in his professional life. "Buy them off me, big man. I need a few quid," he said to me. It was one of the saddest moments of my life seeing this genius at this stage in his life, befuddled by drink. To me it looked as if he had been drinking all weekend. He looked desperate and said he owed people money and he needed to sort them out.

'I said I would pay off his debt for him, but I wasn't going to give him money directly. I would buy them for Celtic, and that's where they are now, at the park. I paid off his debt. But then I was forced into giving him a warning. I had had enough. I told him that when he was sober you could see he practised all the proper values in life. He was an example to everybody. But when he wasn't, he was a disgrace. So I decided to shame him. I told him I would catch up with him the next time he was drunk, and I would make a video of him, and then I when I got him sober again I would show him the video, which I am sure would have given him the shock of his life. I believe that sunk in. I think that warning helped him off the booze.'

It may have kick-started some kind of response, but as any alcoholic will tell you, nothing much registers with them until, from somewhere within, there comes the desire to change themselves. Nobody can do anything for them until that realisation hits. Suddenly Jimmy started the fightback. He began to go to AA meetings. Once that was established he travelled all over Scotland to their meetings in the hope of helping others. He was out five times a week at the peak of his endeavours. He turned his back on the bars, and instead faced up to people who shared his problem, and through banding together and finding communal strength could control the condition. They were crowded meetings in Lanarkshire, involving people from their teens upwards, thus underlining the seriousness of the alcohol problem in the vicinity.

He met and talked to others, and did not hide the fact from anyone that he was a sufferer, and would go out of his way to go home with some of them, to encourage and inspire, simply by being there. There was nothing sophisticated about it. It was simple companionship of the suffering. He now could tell the difference between the two choices he had in life. People noticed the change of mood: his family more than most. Agnes was happier than she had been for a long time. The grandchildren were coming around more. The close unit they had once been before was taking shape again. And the interventions he made to help people was most dramatically revealed when he saved a man's life.

In July 2001 Ian Henderson was returning to Scotland from Belfast on the Stena Line Ferry. He had just lost everything else that mattered in his life: his business, his houses in Belfast and Tannochside, his long-term relationship, his self-respect. The combination was toxic. The business and personal disaster, which he had suffered, left him, on that Monday evening in July, with three choices churning through his mind. 'Do I pick up a drink after 17 years abstinence? Do I go overboard knowing I couldn't swim? Or do I phone a friend? The friend I phoned was Jimmy. I remember exactly what he said, "Get your arse over here and I'll sort you out." That was on the Monday night.' After that call Henderson, boosted by Jimmy's immediate intervention, contacted his daughter who eagerly offered him accommodation, realising that with the wee man's help life was going to change for her father. Henderson was now seeing an entirely different side to Jimmy.

'On the Tuesday Jimmy took me to my first Alcoholics Anonymous meeting. And for the next month he never left my side. I would never be here now if it hadn't been for Jimmy. He knew that any excuse would send me back to the bottle again, and since it had ruined my earlier life, that it would finish me this time. What I didn't know, and he didn't really know either, was that he was in the early stages of Motor Neurone Disease, and was beginning to show symptoms. Nothing could have stopped him from helping me through this though. That is the kind of man he was.'

What Henderson was encountering was a man with a mission. To the people he was trying to rescue from self-inflicted misery, he was now, in the mid and late 1990s, no longer Jimmy Johnstone, Lisbon Lion: he would quite simply state at the meetings, 'My name is Jimmy, and I'm an alcoholic.' His inspirational enthusiasm at these meetings, the same which he had brought to the field in his hey-day, was part of the most humanly fruitful periods since he had left Celtic. He had always been generous with his cash, irresponsibly so at times. Now it was generosity of spirit that he was showing. Even the old urge to watch football was coming back, but in truth, as Agnes admits, it was what came out of the box in the corner now. But most importantly he was training again. People saw him out and about, in much better healthier shape.

Even the local parish priest noticed that, when he told John Coakley, one of Jimmy's friends, one day, 'Jimmy must be off the booze now. He was in at 10 o'clock Mass in his tracksuit.' He was indeed back to form; in the local park doing his press-ups and with long runs, down by that most sylvan part of the Clyde: Bothwell on one side, Blantyre the other. It was like old times.

Then he felt those damned pins and needles running up and down his arms.

Winter 2005

The two words which had begun to dominate his life over the previous couple of years were 'stem cells.' They obsessed him. They certainly were obsessing the media. Indeed, the constant barrage of news about treatments, and the ethical issues which arose from scientific advance compelled this ill man to take heed. Was there a way out of the impasse of the scourge? Was the path to a future cure associated with stem cell research? When he was able, he would have books or newspapers held up to him to study, or else Ian Henderson would sit and read to him all the current news about this form of research. He certainly had dismissed from his mind any thoughts of a short-cut, an end to it all.

One day, when an item appeared on television about someone travelling to Switzerland to use the agency of Dignitas for an assisted suicide, he snapped at Agnes, 'Get that off! I don't want to see anything of that.' His Catholicism was deeply felt, and there is little doubt that he would wish to adhere to the teachings of the church and was fully aware that it had a firm ethical position in the matter of embryonic stem cell research. But he was also, like many of us, quite unsure how to grasp the complexities of the technical nature of the research and admitted to his family and friends that if anything was going to save his life then he would pursue it even though it may raise moral issues. He certainly would berate the Bush administration in the USA, to anybody who would listen, for their objection to any research.

He simply wanted to know what the possibilities were of a cure, through potential stem cell treatment, even though he had that ethical problem to face up to. Then he learned of an alternative, a possible way of overcoming that dilemma. He heard of the research being carried out by Professor Ian Wilmut, at the Roslin Institute near Edinburgh, more popularly known for cloning, and producing 'Dolly The Sheep.'

Professor Wilmut was now engaged in pursuing the idea of developing adult stem cells from skin, not embryos. There was a man Jimmy knew whom he felt might be able to advise him on this, his constituency MP Dr John Reid, whose affection for Jimmy and the club itself was an open secret. He was unlikely to turn a deaf ear to his idol. The man who was to become Celtic chairman will never forget this period. 'By the time of his illness, I had become very friendly with Jimmy through his visits to me as his MP, with all the ideas he wanted to pursue over the years. Then came another one he wanted me to follow. I was not only a friend but by a stroke of luck, his pal had just become Secretary of State for Health, in June 2003. I am sitting in my office one day when my private secretary comes through and tells me there is a constituent on the phone, a Mr Johnstone. At first I was puzzled as to whom it was, and then I was told it was a Mr Jimmy Johnstone. "Put him through!"

'The first comment was this, "John, are you following this stem cell argument?" This was to be the first of a series of calls he made. On this occasion it was to be reassured that I would not interfere to stop stem cell research. I did assure him that I wouldn't go down the same route as George Bush. I wasn't going to ban it, appreciated its importance and that I knew he was concerned about the ethical problems. He then initiated another series of calls in which he wanted to discuss the latest scientific research which was going down another route all together. Now when you are Health Secretary and you have a million and a half NHS employees, a million and a half employees in the social welfare section, the great arguments going on about foundation hospitals and laws being passed through Parliament, you don't really have much time to get into a particular piece of scientific

research about a particular problem. Except that this Health Secretary did. And the one we pursued, with Jimmy's prompting, was the one which would overcome the objections of his church, where instead of embryonic research, it was possible to do this with adult skin cells instead.

'This was a plea from a suffering human being, and a pal, who was desperately seeking answers. So, how could I not respond positively? I knew that he and Ian Henderson had studied this extensively, much more than myself. Therefore, I then asked my officials to look into all of this, to find out if there was something we could encourage in this new direction. For there was apparently a solution to his dilemma. So we went off down the line of seeing how we could develop adult stem cell research for the maximum benefit of people but with the minimum of ethical objections and to which the government could look upon benignly. All this came about because he was probably the only constituent, anywhere in the land, who had a direct line to a Secretary of State.'

It was no mean achievement to get a government moving on a difficult issue, compared to when he was fully fit, and could not get a single business initiative off the ground, including luminous paint. In pursuit of all this, he did visit the Roslin Institute and met with Professor Wilmut, whose aim now was therapeutic cloning, and who took skin samples from him. Then, with a film unit in tow, Jimmy made a day trip to Milan to see a Dr Letizia Mazzini who was pursuing the possibility of environmental causes of the disease. Jimmy had thought there was a possibility that playing amongst the sludge of the Clyde and its tributaries when he was a boy might have had some link to the Motor Neurone problem.

She was also investigating the puzzling problem of why four Italian footballers had developed Motor Neurone Disease, examining whether a footballers' syndrome existed in this area for some inexplicable reason. She was also involved in stem cell research. And into his house one day came one of the most distinguished researchers and clinicians, Professor Chris Shaw from King's College in London, who was greeted with the customary, 'How's it going, big man?' Shaw had talked to Jimmy over the phone and had become fascinated by him, and took the trouble to come all the way up to Lanarkshire, impressed as he was by the irresistible optimism. Shaw was deeply into stem cell research and seeking genetic relevance within the disease. He was also looking at cells from skin to progress a particular avenue. He examined Jimmy thoroughly, took some skin samples, and his very presence seemed to settle the wee man into thinking that things were really happening, and that he was going to come through this.

But a caveat to all of this is introduced by Dr Belinda Cupid of the Motor Neurone Disease Association. She tries to convey the complexity of Jimmy's quest. 'Imagine the old fashioned telephone engineering boxes you used to see at the end of the road. If you walked past when an engineer was working on them all you would see would be a mass of wires, each connected to its own individual space in the grid. If a mischievous toddler came along and pulled out some of the wires, it would be a pretty difficult task to re-connect them all in the right order to the right phone line. The scale of the task of re-connecting the neurones in people affected by MND is of a similar proportion and complexity. This is one of the reasons why researchers do not believe it will be possible to use stem cells to re-wire the nervous system.'

Would knowledge of that, at the time, have ended the stem cell pursuit for him? Not according to John Reid. 'It didn't matter what medical science had said to him, that there was no cure, he was not for accepting that.' This whole new pursuit, in fact, enlivened him spiritually. And a degree of optimism began to creep into his body. But was it going anywhere near arresting his decline? Those close to him realised this was certainly not so, but that Jimmy was so engrossed in the longer-term benefits for others, that being alive at that very moment in time, to further the cause of research, was like long-term personal survival itself. As he engaged in all of this it brought home to Agnes one of the cruellest aspects, that his mind was as sharp as it ever had been, even though the body was slowly failing. One was out of sync with the other. 'It was horrible to know that he could think as fast as anybody, just as everything else was slowing down. It was difficult to understand.'

But another issue sidetracked him which caused a split between himself, the Southern General Hospital, and Dr Roddy Macdonald, who had been solicitous throughout but also strictly orthodox in his advice on medical matters. He and the professors decided that they had to reject a plea from Jimmy to have a special drug administered to him. When the news of this broke, the newspaper headlines made medical science seem heartless, mean, indifferent, callous. But was it? It was now the early months of 2006.

FIFTEEN

'Good Night, Sweet Prince'

When he and Ian Henderson first heard of the drug Copaxone it seemed to offer distinct possibilities as it had been used to treat Multiple Sclerosis. Reports suggested that it had been applied with positive results to Motor Neurone victims. They pursued this vigorously. Would it work for him? Meanwhile, as they did so, the world was still knocking at Jimmy's door. It had knocked constantly since the onset of the illness. His voice was beginning to weaken markedly by now, but although he would talk mostly in whispers to his visitors, there was never any doubt about the clarity of his thoughts. It had just been as well that two years previously, in 2004, he had put that singing voice on disc to remind us of what the old days had been like when he could sing all night.

Jim Kerr of *Simple Minds* had desperately wanted to make a recording with Jimmy singing *'Dirty Old Town.'* But when the wee man agreed to go to a recording studio he thought it was only to listen to a new song that Kerr had written for him. He had not prepared for it. But there was a complication. In the days before this meeting Jimmy had succumbed to the old weakness again. He went on a bender. Nobody had the heart to stop him because it was clear he relished it and given the circumstances it was difficult for Agnes to stop him. Brutally put, it was just too late for lecturing and moralising on that subject. He would be taken out to the local clubs, and, overwhelmed by generosity, he succumbed. The bender lasted five days, she reckoned. By the time of the recording date Jimmy had the 'shakes,' all this on top of the disease slowly corroding his system.

Agnes worked frantically to shower and prepare him. Indeed, she showered him several times to steady him. This might seem a drastic portrayal of a man who had fought successfully against alcohol, and had defeated it for such a long spell. But everything has to be set against the physical state he was in, and the deeper, inner frustration he must have felt about his condition, despite projecting the public impression that he could handle it emotionally. In short, who wouldn't want a drink, after enduring what he had to, and living with the Grim Reaper as a close neighbour?

Nobody knew the state he had been in when Jeff Healey and Jim Kerr arrived to take him to the studio where to his utter astonishment he was asked to sing. 'You'll need to give me a brandy,' he demanded. Henderson replied, 'The quicker you get this done, the quicker you'll get your brandy!' To which the wee man said to Jim Kerr, 'Haw, sir, I hope you can sing.' He then did it in one take. The rendition is now there for posterity. It had been a long trail from that summer on the Channel Islands when he had beaten Vince Hill to the podium, in those singing contests. And he had sung at my own 50th birthday party, his voice still as fresh as when he had serenaded us by poolside on the Mediterranean. On the Jim Kerr recording we hear a more mature voice, slightly redolent of the passing of time and the hardships endured, but a triumph nevertheless. Since that recording day the visits to see him, by so many others, had increased, almost as if in ratio to his obvious decline.

On the whole, those who visited him even at this advanced stage met a bright and lucid Jimmy. There was a memorable day in 2005, when John Reid, by then Secretary of State for Defence, visited the Johnstone household when Jimmy was visibly weakening. It was not his only visit, of course, but on this occasion the neighbours were mightily impressed as the Metropolitan Special Branch had closed off both ends of this modest Lanarkshire avenue in the normal precautionary manner for a minister of that rank. It was the first time that John Reid had seen his formidable guardians insisting on coming into a house to be photographed with anybody. But this was Jimmy, still a star in their minds.

Special Branch, we assume, are not normally celebrity hunters, unless of course, wearing wires on occasion. The spooks had no wires, just cameras this time. Such visits certainly bolstered Jimmy as he was now largely supine in the special chair and looking increasingly helpless, his head looking as if, at any moment, it would flop off his body. The Defence Secretary and his officials experienced this astonishing contrast between the limp figure and the vivacious mind and tongue. The voice was weakening certainly. John Reid was impressed with all the gadgets that had been installed in the house which were operating effectively – his chair, his phone, his special toilet – but of course nothing could halt the inexorable advance of the disease. His legs by that stage were becoming simply appendages, losing the strength that was his saving grace in the earlier stages. And his neck seemed to be losing the strength and elasticity to keep it solidly erect, when needed.

In October 2004 he had gone to The Jimmy Johnstone Tribute Night in a Glasgow hotel but could barely keep his head up, and both Agnes and Ian Henderson were disappointed that he was filmed in this fragile condition. His head was beginning to tilt to one side, almost as if it would flop on to his shoulder. This upper-torso weakness seemed to intensify the look of finality.

Then he received a message to make a visit to the Southern and General Hospital in Glasgow, and for some reason he interpreted that to mean they had positive news for him. He built up his hopes. Bertie Auld decided to drive him there and found the experience so profoundly upsetting that to this day he cannot speak about it without struggling to maintain self-control. 'I think the reason he was built up about this visit is because he really did believe that he was going to beat this disease and that because there had been so much talk about stem cell treatment, which he was desperate for, that something might have changed to his benefit. He said to me, "I think the professor is going to tell me that I'm going to get this treatment."

'Driving over there he was so cheery and hopeful about this visit. When we were struggling along the corridor in the hospital you could see he was trying to burst out of his skin, to get back to what he used to be. You could see that in his eyes. But then we saw Professor Bone coming towards us, and after he had welcomed us, he told Jimmy that he was going to see another specialist that day, because, as he put it, time moves on, and at the stage he was at, this man could help him out. You know when I heard that, and thought about Jimmy's expectancy about this visit, I found myself shuddering. I could sense something. We went in and I stood behind Jimmy sitting in the seat, as he began to talk football to the other professor who sat there with a pad and pencil. After the football talk, the professor opened the pad and told Jimmy that he was at a stage when he was going to need more help, because the condition had gone a stage further. To be honest, I don't think it was really penetrating through to Jimmy.

'I know if it had been me I wouldn't have taken it in either. For although the consultant never said how long he had left, he was really telling him he was finished, that there was nothing more they could do other than make sure Agnes was given more assistance around the house. Meaning that things were going to get worse. I was standing behind the wee man and I tell you these words hit me like I was being bulldozed. It was the implication of what he was saying that I found so powerful. And I just thought Jimmy was shutting his mind to this. He was blanking it. We then got back in the car and honestly it was the longest drive of my life. I was sitting beside this great wee man who really had just been told his life was about over. I was in a kind of trance. I couldn't tell you which way we drove back. For the first question he asked me as we got out of the gates of the hospital was, "What did you make of that?" What could I say? I've never felt so helpless. The only thing I could think of was to tell him that I hadn't really heard what had been said. I couldn't bring myself to say what would have been clear to anybody. You know we had been an hour with that man and I don't think Jimmy took any of it in. There was I sitting beside somebody who really had been told that it was all up. I felt numb and I couldn't answer his questions honestly.'

On the return there was little sign that Jimmy had been greatly distressed by that meeting, which underlines Bertie Auld's point that the wee man had put the shutters up against the very idea of a cruel conclusion. What did help, at that time, was that he was getting incredible moral and financial support from the outside world. Ian Henderson and his associate John Clifford, who had done enormous work for Jimmy, had organised that, previously mentioned, Jimmy Johnstone Tribute Dinner night for him at a hotel in Glasgow which raised £80,000 after all the subsequent events had been completed. Then in 2005 Jeff Healey had come up with the astonishing idea of purchasing a specially-made, limited edition Faberge egg to be auctioned for charity. At the eventual dinner to back this initiative, Willie Haughey bought the egg in auction for £47,000. He then passed it on to the prominent Rangers supporter James Mortimer in recognition of his efforts in raising money for Motor Neurone research. 19 eggs were made in total and one was gifted to Jimmy who decided to raffle it. 'Nae fat cats,' he warned Ian Henderson, hoping that this would be picked up by an ordinary punter. Much of the money raised went to aid the Johnstone household in a trust fund and some to Motor Neurone research.

Peter Lawwell, the Chief Executive of Celtic and long an admirer of Jimmy as a fan, involved the club in raising money for research, saying, 'He had given me personally so much entertainment that I leapt at this enthusiastically to give as much support as possible. I had been there at most of his triumphs including the famous Red Star game. So this was a privilege.' Thus, apart from money for research, Celtic were to spend £60,000 on the erection of the wee man's statue, in front of the stadium, which was unveiled in December 2008.

These efforts by everybody as he slowly declined, and could now barely move, was all inspirational for the family who were, nevertheless, becoming slowly aware of a change, a significant change, which disturbed them. In late 2005 his legs began to weaken. This had always been his strongest function during the illness. The running had long since ceased, but he had developed the minimal power to enable him to tap out phone numbers. Even that was getting beyond him. Earlier they had purchased a tiny static cycle for him to exercise, but that was now too difficult. They had put a spring trigger in between his feet, so if nobody had been about he could manipulate this by touch, to raise or lower himself from the special chair he had been in for the past year. But even this was getting beyond him. His neck control was almost gone. Now he was worse than he had ever been, the sheath of immobility wrapping itself around him, invisible, merciless.

And as he weakened, a story broke in the tabloids about the feud he was engaged in with the Southern General Hospital. On Thursday March 9th 2006, *The Sun* printed the headline on the front page, 'Jinky Drugs Ban Agony.' *The Daily Record* article, the same day, was headed, 'Jinky Fury Over Drug Blow.' It was recording the fact that the medical authorities at the Southern and General Hospital had decided that the drug Copaxone was not going to be issued on a trial basis to Jimmy. Dr Roddy Macdonald, who had originally led Jimmy to his first consultations, had correctly diagnosed what his condition might be, and who was supportive throughout, nevertheless endorsed the hospital's decision not to administer the drug. Roddy was deeply sensitive to Jimmy's needs, and far from heartless. But there was a limit to what even he could accept.

'The decision about this drug was made by Professor Bone at the Southern General,' said Macdonald. 'He was the highest possible authority on this disease you could consult about that. He was fully aware that this drug had not been the subject of any formal scientific studies in its effect on Motor Neurone Disease. These claims about how it had been shown to have some effect with Motor Neurone were purely anecdotal. How could we apply something which, untested, could even have worsened Jimmy's condition? You cannot go on the basis of friends urging you to try something, anything. If you work on that principle then it puts even this drug into the junk medicine category along with snake venom.'

The medical view was shown later to have been correct in their assessment of its effect on the disease, that it was negative, had no effect on it, did not prolong life, and could, indeed, have been dangerous for someone at an advanced stage like Jimmy.

Which takes us back to the crucial dilemma about how much latitude do you allow a dying man to seek even the most bizarre promise of a cure, even though it could contain a life-threatening risk? A great deal, you might obviously think. His medical advisers obviously believed it was time to call a halt to promoting only the illusion of betterment by any drug. If that seems harsh to a reader of this, you can imagine how the family felt. However, doctors dealing with the end game in terminal cases are necessarily the purveyors of reality checks, which we have to assume demand professional detachment, or else they would be of no use to anybody. On this occasion Roddy Macdonald, who loved the wee man, had to fulfil that very role.

That same week, on Saturday March 11th Jimmy was bright and talkative, although the voice was now almost a whisper. His son

James admits that the last time he visited his father he had asked him how he was feeling. 'Fed up,' was all he whispered. James then confessed, 'I knew then it would be a mercy for him to be relieved of his suffering.'

But that night, although Agnes had managed to get him on his feet to take him to the toilet he collapsed in front of her, and she couldn't lift him back to his chair. That was the first time his legs had actually gone from under him as dramatically as that. She had to fetch a neighbour to help her get him back into his seat. However, she didn't sense anything untoward. On the Sunday morning he asked if he could be left in his upstairs bed longer than usual, where he liked to be at the weekends. As he lay there a thought passed through Agnes's mind as she watched him. 'I thought he had this funny colour, kind of purple, and I have never seen him look so much like his old mother. I had this scary kind of feeling, and you know I was glad when he woke up. But I couldn't get him out of bed that day. He even asked me to lie down beside him for company, which during the day was unusual.' She joked to Henderson afterwards, 'I was wondering what that wee man had in mind when he asked me to lie beside him today. It was odd.'

Willie Haughey and his wife came into see him later that Sunday night, as they were going off to Spain, and one of his friends, Tom McLaughlin, came in from the church to give him Holy Communion. Ian Henderson had never sat with him upstairs before, but he had to that night. He found Jimmy in good form, talking about the possibility of travelling to Rotterdam for stem cell information and possible therapy. Henderson listened patiently, but was now painfully realising that Jimmy was getting beyond travel, anywhere. When they both heard a car stopping outside the house, Jimmy, believing it was a visitor, whispered to him, 'I don't want to see anybody else, son.'

The voice was low. Then two phone calls came in. The first was from Denis Law. Henderson held the phone up for him. 'Jimmy could only talk in a whisper, but he was audible.' He then had a pleasant but short conversation with the man who had waved him farewell as he set out on that rowing-boat, all those years before, on the shore at Largs. At 11.20pm the phone went again. It was Willie Henderson making arrangements to come to see him the following day. 'Looking forward to see you, son,' Jimmy managed to whisper. What made Willie phone? He cannot explain it. 'I just had a funny feeling that I needed to talk to him. As simple as that,' Willie admits.

As Ian Henderson left the room Jimmy was able to whisper a message to him, 'Tell Ann I have found it out. The 'Ann' in question was a fellow Motor Neurone sufferer from Creetown, who could no longer speak, and to whom he had become attached through their common suffering over the years. He was recommending a clinic in Dublin to her for stem cell treatment. These were his last words to Ian Henderson.

It was snowing heavily outside. Because of that Bertie Auld had been unable to defeat the snowdrifts out by Larkhall, and could not travel to see him on the Sunday, something he still deeply regrets. Agnes was now left on her own, after all the visitations and telephone calls. She went upstairs and went to bed to lie beside him. She was mentally preparing for a change in the daily routine, for the following day professional helpers were to come to the house to assist her for the first time since his illness had started almost six years previously. She was in two minds about that. She would welcome the help, of course, since dealing with Jimmy was now even more arduous. But on the other hand she still felt the need to be actively close to him, not to become a kind of spectator.

These feelings were evident in the middle of the night, when she had to use the full power of her body to get him to the toilet. He settled again after complaining about the weight of the blanket on him. When she woke once more at about six o'clock she was surprised that he hadn't disturbed her again, as he did so frequently through any night. She rose and looked at him, and realised immediately that his long, valiant struggle had come to an end. At some time, during the dark hours, he had died. It was Monday morning March 13th 2006.

The Legacy

So the woman who had lifted and laid him, heaved him around the house, bathed him, cleansed him, spoon-fed him, injected him, sobered him up, joked with him, chastised him, answered his every call from his chair, was at that moment, feeling utterly desolate.

Agnes Johnstone, who had gone through super-human efforts at times, coping with a body ravaged by the disease, was now suffering a colossal sense of loss, watching the wee man lying there, looking as if he, at last, had attained contentment. Even though his condition had deteriorated she really had not been prepared for this. When she had recovered from the shock she thought back to the curious little signs of the previous day and wondered if they had been telling her something, warning her of the end. Not that it mattered any longer. But that thought irked her. She started to phone family and friends.

Those who had been close to him were inconsolable: Bertie Auld in particular, who still could not get through the snow to come down immediately. The rest of the Lisbon Lions were informed. Bobby Lennox, who had been like a twin brother to him throughout their parallel careers, keeps telling people how he had last seen him, a couple of days previously, and what had passed between them. 'I had said, "You think you've got problems, I've got to go in to hospital and get a pacemaker." He just said back to me, "So what do we call you now, bloody Gerry?" I went out laughing.'

That set the tone for many of his playing colleagues to reminisce about how they had sat for hours cracking jokes with him, and leaving the house with a spring in their step, as if they had been in group therapy. Shocked though they all were, the anecdotes came tumbling out of them, as they relived the joy of their relationships. Ian Henderson, who had closely guided him through his last five years, and mindful of how much the wee man had influenced his life and those of other alcoholics who had regarded Jimmy as a source of inspiration, took some time to absorb the news. His disbelief continued until he went to the house to see the wee man in repose. He was at the head of a long line of people who came to offer their sympathies, in the succeeding hours. Even Celtic supporters whom Agnes had never known were welcomed, in keeping with the 'open' house she had presided over since he had taken ill.

From all corners of the globe, following the public announcement that he had died, came a flood of tributes and condolences. Outside Celtic Park, supporters assembled in large numbers, quiet, respectful, saddened and, indeed, at that early stage, unsure how to express their feelings properly. Then the floral tributes began to arrive. Celtic supporters from around the land came to pay their respects with wreaths and scarves, which grew day by day, until it provided a green and white halo of reverence around the front of the stadium. Amongst them were a few which were red, white and blue. They did not seem in the least incongruous.

His funeral took place on St Patrick's Day Friday 17th March. It was the 44th anniversary of the day the old Celtic scout Jimmy Gribben had watched him play in the junior international in Northern Ireland, and then made his historic recommendation to Celtic to change him from provisional signing, into a fully-fledged player. The Requiem Mass for Jimmy was held in St John the Baptist Church, Uddingston with the principal celebrant being the Right Reverend Joseph Devine, the Bishop of Motherwell, whose homily touched upon the most salient factor of the wee man's public personality, 'I sensed a tidal wave of sorrow across the land when people began to be aware that he had died, a river of sadness. It was the kind of sadness that eclipsed Old Firm rivalries, indeed all manner of rivalries, as Jimmy was beloved of all supporters of the beautiful game.'

Billy McNeill spoke tenderly of the man he loved so much and ended his touching speech, with perhaps the words people had been waiting for. 'Wee man, you will never walk alone.'

Willie Haughey, who had given new impetus to Jimmy's latter life, with his all-embracing support, had co-ordinated the complicated funeral arrangements, given that so many people wished to be present in the church. Anybody of any credible status in British football was there. Sir Alex Ferguson, Martin O'Neill, Walter Smith, Denis Law, John Greig and Kenny Dalglish led the many football dignitaries, and sitting alongside them, the celebrity supporters like Rod Stewart, and the singer Jimmy adored, Frankie Miller, who, ravaged by ill-health, arrived in a wheelchair pushed by actor Ian Robertson. There was Willie Henderson making a remark to a reporter outside the church, which reflected the genial relationship that surmounted their Old Firm rivalry, 'He broke our hearts so many times ... and he also done me out of so many win bonuses.'

Most of the surviving Lisbon Lions were there. Some of that team helped carry the coffin from the church to the hearse. Thereafter in the six-mile journey from Uddingston to Celtic Park, the roadsides were crowded with thousands of people, many of whom, festooned in the club colours, clapped as the funeral cortege made its way from what used to be industrial Lanarkshire to the East End of Glasgow, almost as a paradigm of his professional career. Willie Haughey recalls that as they passed under the bridge at Mount Vernon on their way to London Road, he saw this big Rangers supporter standing to attention and saluting, as if in recognition of a passing president.

When they arrived at the stadium a crowd estimated at 20,000 had turned up. They had come from all over the country. Sheila Hamilton observed in the Glasgow *Evening Times*, 'Grannies, granddads, mums and dads, people in wheelchairs and on crutches, children who had bunked off school, people who had skipped work, toddlers, even babies in prams – all there to say farewell to Celtic's greatest ever player...' They were only too willing to pour out their feelings to reporters as if a family member had passed away.

For instance, labourer, John McGarrel, from Royston in Glasgow, told Hamilton, 'This is Scotland's JFK day.' Les Ross, an audiologist, who was there to help the deaf fans, was one of the few in the crowd who could have claimed to have kicked a ball with Jimmy in the twilight of his career with Blantyre Celtic, and told the reporter, 'I just remember Jimmy was an absolute gem. He was at the end of his career but wasn't aloof at all.' And added, as if those of us knowing his life story would have been at all surprised, 'But he was a joker too. He put itching powder down all the jock straps and we were all scratching.'

When the Johnstone family emerged to greet the supporters, the sound of *You'll Never Walk Alone'* swelled up from the crowd. The applause continued as, after brief stop, they then drove along roads back into Lanarkshire, still lined with thousands of the respectful public, some of them throwing Celtic scarves at the hearse, to Bothwell Park Cemetery. There, he was put to rest.

Jimmy's goodness was not 'interred with his bones' as Shakespeare alluded could be the fate of some. It survives. His protracted illness not only caused tremors of anxiety in many places around the world, but stimulated curiosity and then deep interest in this disease and was to lead to the promotion of practical programmes to fund research into this monstrous affliction. He raised its profile in an unprecedented manner. Famous people had contracted the disease in the past, but awareness in this country had been minimal. There was David Niven, Mao Tse Tung (who as wee Willie Henderson pointed out to me didn't make the famous Long March, 'He was carried, sir.') and the man portrayed by Gary Cooper on film, the famous baseball player Lou Gehrig: all victims. John Cushley, his colleague, who made his Celtic first-team debut the same night as Jimmy, was brought down by it. And on the night Jimmy played one of his most effective games ever in Europe, in the semi-final against Dukla Prague on April 12th 1967, a man died of Motor Neurone Disease in the Vale of Leven Hospital. His name, Sam English: the Rangers centre-forward involved in the tragic clash with the Celtic goalkeeper John Thomson in 1931. But it was Jimmy's name, linked with the disease, that gave it such a startling public profile.

Jim Simonette, the man who had worked so hard to ease the burden of daily living for Jimmy, in the house, was determined to keep his image as a player dynamically alive. He started a youth football team, midway through the illness, which Jimmy promoted and followed, when he was still fit enough, which eventually won every trophy it ever played for, and from which has emerged the Jimmy Johnstone Academy, open to boys and girls from all quarters, regardless of their background, and which will continue to flourish in Glasgow. There was also the 'Jinky Johnstone Trust' established by an ardent admirer, Rab McLuckie, which raised money for football strips, bearing the wee man's crest, to benefit all teams who practised a non-discriminatory policy of recruitment of kids and, as Jimmy put it, 'It's got to go to those who are skint!'

Over a hundred teams have so far benefitted by generous donations, including one of £10,000 by ex-Rangers player Arthur Numan, which underlines the enduring broad appeal of Jimmy. That is a practical project of loving continuity. The doctors who admired him for his self-belief also refer to him constantly. Those people in bondage to this disease, which offers, at this stage, little hope of survival, need nevertheless to know of how others try to cope. Consequently the wee man from Viewpark is talked about as the tenacious one, the one who refused to meekly succumb. For the average survival rate of Motor Neurone Disease in this country, after diagnosis, is fourteen months. Jimmy lasted almost six years.

You have to think back to what his colleagues thought of his powers of recovery, even after some of the binges he went on. He was still a voracious trainer, on any day, regardless. All that running and exercising in parks, and along the banks of the Clyde, from his teens right up to his late fifties, not only meant a durable physical condition, but also an awareness of tiny changes occurring in his body, which alerted him, and from which he had to seek advice. There is a stark contrast between a man conscious of his fitness, and the particular difficulty which suddenly arose doing press-ups in a park one day, to that of someone who, as one researcher puts it, 'Finds out the first symptoms when he discovers he can't lift his pint to his mouth any more.' There is little doubt, also, that his years of training and exercising had lent his mind that irreducible resolve to fight it.

Willie Haughey, in his final address to the congregation in the church in Uddingston, in a good-humoured address, which underlined the absence of deep depression among the congregation, and reflecting the more enduring mood of peace and contentment, which suffused the entire day, said, almost in the now so familiar mode of 'Jimmy being Jimmy…,' 'To all the people who lent Jimmy money, they have to remember an old Scottish saying, "When you die, your debt dies with you."'

He might have been addressing some vultures ready to pounce on the family, but perhaps was impishly reflecting on how Jimmy had tied himself into knots financially, because too readily he would put his hand in his pocket to help others, when he simply could not afford it, and consequently went to extraordinary lengths to try to pay them back, and almost always succeeded. But in all probability some debts were remaining. The latter part of his life consisted, too often, of trying to extricate himself from the fankles that his undisciplined, but good nature, had got him into.

Haughey was fully aware of that. His words were a reminder that the waywardness of part of Jimmy's life would never blot out the images for which he will be remembered: of those in the bleaching sun of Lisbon, when his reputation alone bewildered Inter Milan as they sought to shackle him but drove themselves, instead, into the ground in hopeless pursuit: of that pedestal in the Bernabeu, which he pinched from the great Di Stefano, and how a wee Lanarkshire man touched constellatory brilliance that night in front of an audience who fell in love with him: of those in the 'glaur' of Ibrox that day when his left foot sang sweeter than his own voice: of that evening of the haunting of Red Star Belgrade as he tried to exorcise his fear of flying: of him being hacked and punched and kicked in Buenos Aires and Montevideo, and coming back for more: of that of his bravery against the Atletico Madrid mountebanks: and of all those numerous cup finals, and the countless humdrum league matches when, if even for only a fleeting moment, he could produce something which would make even the most churlish actually feel that life was worth living after all. All these triumphs made up the unforgettable mantra, 'Jimmy, being Jimmy...'

But in truth, it was his last years which produced his greatest triumph. Tony Judt's words, in this book's frontispiece, chill you to the core. The famous historian died eventually on 6th August, 2010. Graphically they reveal the insidious nature of that kind of approaching death and of what Jimmy had to withstand. Sadly, there were too many who, although admiring him as a player, could never take him seriously as a man because of his capricious nature and his jousts with over-indulgence. He was aware of those views. So he could so easily have become, and perhaps have been entitled to be an embittered man, soured by the cruel trick that nature had played on him, mournful of his lot, bemoaning the lack of cure; cynical and mistrustful.

He was instead a shining paragon of optimism and spiky humour, cushioning the despair of those who had to tend to him. The triumph that must never be overlooked is the profound effect he had on those who witnessed his courage in the final years. None of us left that house during his illness without suddenly becoming highly conscious of the precious nature of our own mortality, of how every second of life counts for us in some way or other, and reappraising our attitude to death. He was the lender of an unvanquished spirit; we were the borrowers. So, leaving us thus in his debt, he did not pass his final breath on that wintry March morning as a tiny, withered, failed figure.

He died as a giant, undefeated.